T0235681

# Tiny Android Projects Using Kotlin

In today's fast-paced world, Android development is a rapidly evolving field that requires regular updates to keep up with the latest trends and technologies. *Tiny Android Projects Using Kotlin* is an excellent resource for developers who want to learn to build Android applications using the latest tools and frameworks.

**KEY FEATURES**

- Teaches building Android apps using Kotlin, XML, and Jetpack Compose
- Includes saving data on the device using the Room database library
- Teaches communication between an Android device and data on the internet using REST API
- Shows how to create different Android menu navigations using Jetpack Compose
- Introduces the most architectures used in Android Projects and implements MVVM

With Kotlin being the most preferred language for Android development, this book provides a practical, hands-on approach to learning the language and building high-quality Android apps using Kotlin, XML, and Jetpack Compose.

# Tiny Android Projects Using Kotlin

Denis Panjuta
Loveth Nwokike

CRC Press
Taylor & Francis Group
Boca Raton  London  New York

CRC Press is an imprint of the
Taylor & Francis Group, an **informa** business
A CHAPMAN & HALL BOOK

Designed cover image: Jafar Jabbarzadeh

First edition published 2024
by CRC Press
2385 NW Executive Center Drive, Suite 320, Boca Raton FL 33431

and by CRC Press
4 Park Square, Milton Park, Abingdon, Oxon, OX14 4RN

*CRC Press is an imprint of Taylor & Francis Group, LLC*

© 2024 Denis Panjuta and Loveth Nwokike

ISBN: 978-1-032-62251-4 (hbk)
ISBN: 978-1-032-60687-3 (pbk)
ISBN: 978-1-032-62253-8 (ebk)

DOI: 10.1201/9781032622538

Typeset in Minion
by SPi Technologies India Pvt Ltd (Straive)

Support material available at https://github.com/tutorialseu/tiny-kotlin-projects

# Contents

# Preface

In today's fast-paced world, Android development is a rapidly evolving field that requires regular updates to keep up with the latest trends and technologies. The *Tiny Android Projects Using Kotlin* book is an excellent resource for developers who want to learn to build Android applications using the latest tools and frameworks. With Kotlin being the most pre-ferred language for Android development, this book provides a practical, hands-on approach to learning the language and building high-quality Android applications.

This book comprises 12 chapters that provide a step-by-step guide to building practical Android applications using Kotlin, XML, and Jetpack Compose. Chapter 1 introduces the role of Kotlin and Android in today's software development world. They will gain insights into the advantages of using Kotlin over other programming languages for Android develop-ment and learn about the fundamental components of an Android app. Chapter 2 dives into application development using the common elements of XML and Android Activity. By the end, the reader will build their first Android application project for calculating the BMI of a person based on the height and weight factors. In Chapters 3 and 4, readers embark on their second project, a Quiz application. Through this project, users will learn about more XML elements creating more complex user interfaces. They will learn to move between Activity screens while applying logic on the UI elements. Chapter 5 is dedicated to introducing readers to frag-ments, a critical component of the Android user interface (UI) design. Through Chapter 5, readers will learn how to create reusable UI compo-nents while building their third project for an Android onboarding screen section. In Chapter 6, the reader will be building a weather app. This will introduce them to REST API, an important aspect of most applications that allows to connect it to a server on the internet. Here they will learn how to use the Retrofit library which is specially created for such purpose.

In Chapter 7, readers will discover how to leverage the Google Firebase platform, which offers a wide range of services for mobile and web application development. Through a hands-on project, readers will learn how to quickly integrate Firebase's authentication, media storage, and data storage services into a Tour Guide application. In Chapter 8, readers will take the Tour Guide application to the next level by incorporating an essential aspect of Android app development: project architecture. Specifically, readers will learn about the Model-View-ViewModel (MVVM) architecture and how to implement it in their Android projects. This knowledge will enable readers to build more robust, scalable, and maintainable applications.

In Chapter 9, readers will be introduced to one of the newest and most exciting developments in Android app development: Jetpack Compose. This reactive framework allows developers to create dynamic and responsive user interfaces using a declarative programming model with Kotlin rather than XML.

Throughout Chapter 9, readers will learn the fundamentals of Jetpack Compose and how to use it to build beautiful and responsive user interfaces. They will learn about the basic components while building a Tip Calculator app.

Chapter 10 takes Jetpack Compose to the next level. The reader will build a countdown timer application while getting familiar with more compose elements and features. Chapter 11 focuses on teaching the readers about local data storage on an Android device. Specifically, readers will learn how to utilize the Room database library to develop a functional wish list application. Through this project-based learning, readers will gain hands-on experience in designing and implementing an efficient data storage solution for their Android applications. In Chapter 12, readers will be introduced to Jetpack Compose Navigation. The final chapter of this book will focus on teaching the readers how to create dynamic menus and dialog screens using Navigation in Jetpack Compose. By the end of Chapter 12, they will have built a music application user interface including essential menus and popup screen.

By the end of this book, readers will have gained the knowledge and skills necessary to build practical, high-quality Android applications using Kotlin, XML, and Jetpack Compose. They will have learned about Android application architecture, user interface design, and data storage.

With this book's practical, project-based approach, readers will have a solid understanding of how to apply these concepts and techniques to real-world scenarios.

- **Target Audience:** This book is aimed at developers interested in learning how to build Android applications. It is assumed that readers have a basic understanding of the Kotlin programming language, but prior experience with other languages, such as Java and Swift, can be helpful. This book is suitable for developers looking to expand their skill set and create Android applications using Kotlin.

- **Key Features:** This book will provide readers with the knowledge to create Android applications using Kotlin, XML, and Jetpack Compose through a set of practical projects. These projects range from beginner to intermediate levels and cover essential topics such as creating user interfaces, implementing navigation, handling user input, and managing local and cloud data storage.

  Learning how to build Android applications is essential for developers looking to build mobile apps for one of the world's most popular operating systems. By following the project-based approach presented in this book, readers can acquire hands-on experience and build a solid foundation in Android app development, leading to greater career opportunities and potential for success in the mobile app market.

  Readers will learn by working on hands-on projects that provide practical experience with building Android apps. Each chapter focuses on a specific project, introducing new concepts and techniques along the way. Readers will build a variety of apps, including a Quiz app, a Tour guide app, and a Wish list, among others.

- **Tech List:** Android studio, Android, Kotlin, XML, Jetpack Compose, Retrofit, Google Firebase, MVVM architecture, Room database.

- **The Code Files:** You can access the sample code for the projects used in this book at https://github.com/tutorialseu/Tiny-Kotlin-Projects.

# About the Authors

**Denis Panjuta**'s journey from curiosity to mastery began in Russia, where he was born, and took shape in Germany, where he was raised. The youngest of three siblings, Denis's early exposure to computers at the age of 11 ignited a lifelong fascination. Despite challenges, such as struggling to learn Java at 17 with outdated resources, Denis's perseverance never wavered. By 23, with a fresh mindset and better materials, he mastered software development. His academic endeavors at the University of Applied Sciences in Konstanz, Germany, led him to combine his coding skills with a passion for teaching, culminating in an award-winning bachelor's thesis in coding tutorials and a career as a distinguished instructor in Android App Development and .NET Programming. Denis's belief in the multiplication of knowledge through sharing has been a guiding principle in his teaching approach. Beyond his professional life, he is an enthusiastic gamer, skater, and hiker, embodying an adventurous spirit always seeking new challenges. His recent venture into authorship aims to extend his reach to 10 million coding students, aspiring to improve the world with the software they develop, a testament to Denis Panjuta's inspirational role in coding education.

**Loveth Nwokike** is a software developer and a technical content creator with keen interest in mobile applications and proficiency in native Android development. She has worked on customer facing solutions serving millions of Android users. She has interests in developer communities and is continuously in participation as either a volunteer or an organizer. She is enthusiastic about new technologies and loves to explore latest advancement in the IT field. When she is not on a computer she can be at the gym, playing table tennis, or taking a walk.

# CHAPTER 1

# Introduction and Getting Started

## 1.1 INTRODUCTION TO KOTLIN

Kotlin is a programming language that the development community has rapidly adopted since it was announced as an officially supported language for Android development by Google at the annual Google I/O conference in May 2017. In addition, Google announced Android to be "Kotlin First" during the I/O event in 2019. One of the reasons it is preferred over Java is its ability to reduce the number of boilerplate codes by approximately 40%.

Kotlin is statically typed and runs on the JVM, making it fully interoperable with Java. This means that both languages can exist in the same project, making it easier to incorporate Kotlin into existing Java projects. Kotlin is an excellent choice for Android development because it reduces the amount of boilerplate code and is null safe, which mitigates the risk of null pointer exception, a common source of crashes in Android development. In addition, it comes with other great features, such as support for functional programming, extension functions, and properties.

One advantage of Kotlin is the ability to develop multiplatform mobile applications. This allows you to share some of your logic, like networking and data storage code between Android and iOS, while still implementing the user interfaces and some other platform-specific features natively. Unlike other mobile cross-platform frameworks, you do not need to introduce a new language into your codebase but rather extend it to support a

DOI: 10.1201/9781032622538-1

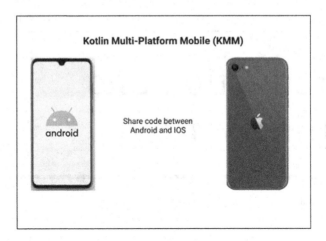

FIGURE 1.1   Kotlin can be used to share code between Android and IOS apps powered by Kotlin Multiplatform Mobile (KMM).

new platform. Figure 1.1 shows the mobile platforms with which Kotlin code can be easily shared.

Website applications, macOS, Windows, and Linux applications are included here. There are Kotlin Multiplatform (KMP) libraries you can use to write common code that can be shared by the platforms mentioned above. Moreover, Kotlin can also replace Java in writing the backend code—also called server-side. In short, Kotlin can work anywhere Java works! Figure 1.2 demonstrates the desktop platforms where Kotlin can be used for its app development.

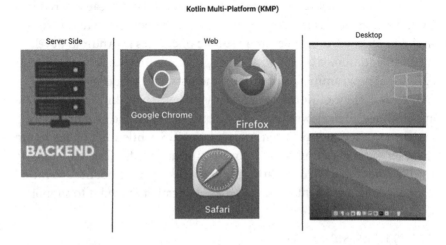

FIGURE 1.2   Kotlin apps can run on different platforms powered by KMP.

If you have an interest in data and already possess knowledge of Kotlin, you can explore the field of data science. Data science involves extracting valuable insights from data, and there are various software tools available for this purpose, such as Jupyter Notebook and Apache Zeppelin, which provide powerful capabilities for data visualization. Kotlin-Jupyter serves as the Kotlin Kernel, enabling seamless integration of Kotlin libraries with Jupyter Notebook.

One key aspect of Kotlin is its static typing. This means that we can explicitly declare the data types of variables in our program, as the type is known at compile time. The compilation process translates the Kotlin code into machine-readable instructions. For example:

```
val fruit: String = "orange"
```

Alternatively, Kotlin allows type inference, where the type can be deduced at compile time. In this case, you can omit specifying the type and provide a value that helps the compiler determine the appropriate type. This analysis is based on the program or expression's usage. For instance:

```
val fruit = "orange"
```

Kotlin is a versatile language that supports multiple programming paradigms, including object-oriented programming (OOP) and functional programming (FP). In OOP, the emphasis is on using objects to represent data and operations, promoting organized, efficient, and reusable code. Objects encapsulate properties, which are the behaviors or characteristics of the object that perform specific actions.

On the other hand, FP is a programming style that emphasizes using functions and function compositions to achieve desired outcomes. Kotlin facilitates functional programming through the use of higher-order functions, which can accept other functions as arguments. This declarative programming style focuses on specifying what the program should do rather than explicitly describing how it should be done.

## 1.2 THE BENEFITS OF KOTLIN

Kotlin is a robust and versatile programming language that offers numerous benefits over traditional languages like Java. One key advantage of Kotlin is its conciseness, making code more readable and maintainable.

It also supports functional programming, which can lead to more efficient code. In addition, Kotlin has better tooling support and can be used with various integrated development environment (IDE), making development more streamlined. Here are the benefits explained.

### 1.2.1 Kotlin's Code Is Concise

Kotlin is a concise programming language, meaning that it is designed to be easily readable and understandable. Programs written in Kotlin are usually shorter and easier to follow than those written in other languages. Although Java inspired Kotlin, you can write a code solution with the same output in both programming languages, and Kotlin code will be shorter and simplified. Take, for example, when you compare the main methods of both languages, which serve as an entry point into an application and, in this case, prints "hello world".

```
public class Hello {
    public static void main (String[]args){
        System.out.println("hello world!");
    }
}

    fun main (){
        println("hello world!")
    }
```

You can see the difference in length between the two and that Kotlin has fewer lines of code and is easier to read, which makes it preferable.

### 1.2.2 Kotlin Offers More Safety

Kotlin code also offers more safety, as it reduces the risk of null pointer errors, which are common in Java. With Kotlin, it's possible to specify a variable as null, and the safe call operator (?) can be used to avoid crashing the application.

### 1.2.3 Kotlin Multiplatform

As we mentioned earlier, while introducing Kotlin, you can share Kotlin code between different platforms, reducing the cost or need for more resources and development time for a product. Think of a product that requires software for its users. Ideally, it should support a wide variety of platforms and devices. But these platforms have specific languages dedicated to writing their software. Instead of hiring programmers with different language knowledge to make your software available on different platforms, Kotlin provides tools that allow you to write code once and send it to many devices.

### 1.2.4 Kotlin is Open Source

Finally, Kotlin is an open-source language, enabling developers to contribute to its development, improve its quality, and build a supportive community for all users.

## 1.3 ANDROID APPLICATION DEVELOPMENT WITH KOTLIN

Android app development has undergone a significant shift with the introduction of Kotlin in 2017. While Java was the go-to language for Android app development, Kotlin has become the official language for this purpose, resulting in a more streamlined and efficient development process. New language features like coroutine for asynchronous programming and Kotlin extension functions that provide idiomatic syntax to the Android APIs have been added to android development.

When developing Android apps with Kotlin—which will be the focus of this book—there are two approaches for creating the user interface (UI).

- Using XML code in a separate file and later connecting it to your Kotlin code. This is the same method Java has been using.

- Using Jetpack Compose, a toolkit that lets you create your UI entirely in Kotlin.

## 1.4 THE ANDROID OPERATING SYSTEM

Android is an operating system built primarily for mobile devices like phones and tablets. It has been around for 15 years and currently runs on mobiles and other devices like watches, smart glasses, home appliances, cars, cameras, smart TVs, and game consoles. Android is the most widely used smartphone platform, and according to TechJury, as of April 2021, Android still powers about 75% of all smartphones and tablets. It is open source and hence the emergence of many other devices using it as their operating system.

### 1.4.1 Android as Open Source

All tools and frameworks required for android development are well provided for by Google and its larger developer community. As a developer, you can modify the existing source code to build your application and decide to make it public or keep it for your app alone.

## 1.5 A FUNCTIONAL ANDROID APPLICATION

A fully functional application should include at least two of the following elements:

- User interface

- Interactivity

- Storage options

### 1.5.1 User Interface

This is what the user sees on the screen showing clear components or menus to serve as a point of interaction between the user and the application. In Android, there are two ways by which you can implement a user interface.

- Using XML

- Using Jetpack Compose

XML is an acronym for Extensible Markup Language and is used for designing the layout that makes up the interface of an android application. A layout is defined using a hierarchy of ViewGroup and Views. The "ViewGroup", also called the parent layout, is created to accept widgets as children. It defines how these children, the other components like Text and Buttons that make up the different parts of the interface, are positioned. Depending on the structure of the UI, a ViewGroup can also be a child of another ViewGroup. The following XML code shows the use of ConstraintLayout which is a type of ViewGroup.

```
<!-- A ConstraintLayout is a ViewGroup for positioning
     UI elements -->
<androidx.constraintlayout.widget.ConstraintLayout
  xmlns:android=http://schemas.android.com/apk/res/
  android
```

```
    xmlns:app="http://schemas.android.com/apk/res-auto"
    xmlns:tools="http://schemas.android.com/tools"
    android:layout_width="match_parent"
    android:layout_height="match_parent"
    tools:context=".MainActivity">

<!-- A TextView is used to display a Text -->
  <TextView.
    android:id="@+id/helloTv"
    android:layout_width="wrap_content"
    android:layout_height="wrap_content"
    android:text= "HelloWorld!"
    android:textColor="@color/black"
    app:layout_constraintBottom_toBottomOf= "parent"
    app:layout_constraintLeft_toLeftOf= "parent"
    app:layout_constraintRight_toRightOf= "parent"
    app:layout_constraintTop_toTopOf= "parent"/>

  <!-- A Button can be clicked to perform an action -->
  <Button.
      android:layout_width="wrap_content"
      android:layout_height="wrap_content"
      android:layout_marginTop="8dp"
      android:text= "SayHello"
      app:layout_constraintEnd_toEndOf= "parent"
      app:layout_constraintStart_toStartOf= "parent"
      app:layout_constraintTop_toBottomOf="@id/
      helloTv" />
  </androidx.constraintlayout.widget.ConstraintLayout>
```

Jetpack Compose is the emerging UI toolkit that enables user interfaces to be written in Kotlin. So far, this method has proven effective with its concise nature and difference when creating a similar interface using XML. With Jetpack Compose, you can build out UI components as Kotlin functions with the help of declarative APIs. You will experience the XML and compose styles in this book and decide which works best for you. The following code is for a compose function that displays a Text and a Button vertically side by side.

```
    @Composable
    fun Greeting() {
        Column(modifier = Modifier.fillMaxSize(),
            horizontalAlignment = Alignment.Center
             Horizontally,
```

```
                verticalArrangement = Arrangement.Center
    ) {
            Text(text = "Hello World!")
            Button(onClick = { }) {
                Text(text = "Say Hello")
            }
    }
}
```

Figure 1.3 shows the UI result of this compose function.

## 1.5.2 Interactivity

We have seen how UI elements are drawn on the screen but to get them showing on the device itself when the app is run you need to connect it to an Activity class. Every Android application includes one or more Activities. The Activity class is the entry point for every android application and

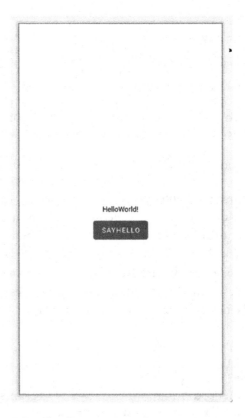

FIGURE 1.3   The UI Result of Listing 1.3 and 1.4.

can be written in Kotlin. When XML is used to create a user interface, its behavior and interaction will be controlled by its Activity. The code shown below is an Activity class that draws and XML user interface.

```
class MainActivity:AppCompatActivity() {
    override fun onCreate(savedInstanceState: Bundle?) {
        super.onCreate(savedInstanceState)
        setContentView(R.layout.activity_main)
    }
}
```

In Android app development using XML, you can link a layout to its corresponding Activity, turning it into a standalone screen with various functionalities added to its components. Using the Activity, you can also make the layout elements interactive and respond to user input. To add a layout file to an Activity, you can use the setContentView method. The method takes the layout name as a parameter, and "R" refers to the resource folder. The following code is an Activity that draws a compose user interface.

```
class MainActivity : ComponentActivity() {
    override fun onCreate(savedInstanceState: Bundle?) {
        super.onCreate(savedInstanceState)
        setContent {
            FirstComposeProjectTheme {

                Surface(
                    modifier = Modifier.fillMaxSize(),
                    color = MaterialTheme.colors.
                     background
                ) {
                    Greeting()
                }
            }
        }
    }
}
```

In the same way, Composable also requires an Activity as the entry point into its application. However, you can integrate an element's functionality directly within the Composable function without referencing an external ID or layout.

### 1.5.3 Storage Options

It is common practice for most applications to want to create, read, update, or delete data when being used. This is also known as CRUD management, where there is the need for data to be managed between the user, application, and storage entity. The Android system provides many options for saving your data on your device. This can be locally on the SD cards, directly on the device's internal memory, or online using cloud storage.

#### 1.5.3.1 Local Storage

There are several options for storing data locally on an Android device. The most common is using the built-in SQLite database for saving structured data. Other options include storing data using internal storage or external storage. Internal storage is a storage space built into the device and is limited in size. In contrast, external storage is a storage space external to the device, typically an SD card or a USB storage device. The local storage can be grouped into different categories, app-specific storage, preferences, and database as seen in Table 1.1.

- **App-specific storage:** This is for storing files that are meant for your application's use only, either within internal or external memory. For files that you don't want other apps to have access to, it's important to store them within directories in internal memory.

- **Preferences:** Sometimes, applications want to save small values that are of primitive types. You can use preferences to store them in the form of key-value pairs for a quick read and write. These APIs include shared preference, preference datastore, and proto data store.

- **Databases:** Android provides a library call Room which can be used to store private data on your device.

TABLE 1.1   Local Storage Options

| Storage Options | Type of Files | Storage Name |
| --- | --- | --- |
| App-specific storage | Files meant for your app use only | Internal and external storage |
| Preferences | Key-value pairs like String and Int | Shared preference, preference datastore |
| Database | Structured data like to-do list | Room Database, SQLDelight and more |

TABLE 1.2  Comparison between Online Storage Service Types

| A Backend Server | A Serverless Backend |
|---|---|
| Managed and maintained within the company | Managed and maintained by a third party |
| Data access limited to company | Third-party access to data |
| Higher cost of maintenance | Lower cost of maintenance |
| More control and visibility | Lacks control and visibility |

### 1.5.3.2 Online Storage

There are many options for saving data to an online database. The most common method is using a Representational State Transfer (REST) API, a web service that uses the HTTP protocol to receive and save data. Another option is using serverless databases, which allows you to begin development quickly without worrying about the server resources and setups because your chosen vendor will take care of it.

There are two ways by which Android data can be stored and managed online as compared in Table 1.2:

1. **A backend server:** This usually consists of a server, an application, and a database that provides data on request. it is usually managed and maintained within a product company and, therefore can be easily scaled to suit the needs of a particular application. It is mostly queried as a Restful API. Representational State Transfer (REST) is an architectural style that facilitates communication between web services using a restful approach. You need not worry about how this is created but about how much leverage networking in Android to manage the data provides in building your own application. This will be covered in detail in Chapter 5.

2. **A serverless backend:** Regardless of the name, this also runs on a server but is usually delegated to a third party. It means that instead of building most of its functionalities from scratch and hosting on your dedicated server like lots of personalized backend services, the third party provides the computing resources required to run a computer on demand and allows the developers to focus on their applications. Google Cloud with Firebase Services and Firebase Cloud Functions and Amazon Web Services with AWS Lambda are well known for providing these services.

We will build applications that utilize some of these online services within different chapters.

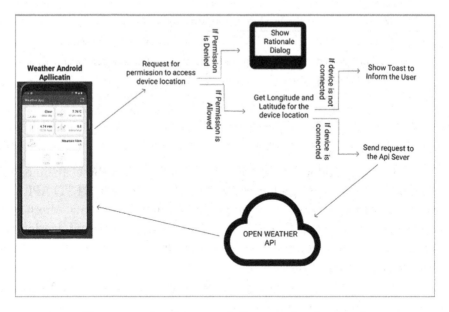

FIGURE 1.4   The process flow for a sample functional android application.

Figure 1.4 connects a weather app to a REST API to get weather information for a device location. The API is always up to date with the weather forecast for various locations around the globe within a short time. The stored data includes temperature, humidity, wind, and much more. You decide on what data your application requires and read them from the API to achieve the intended user interface and user experience.

With the help of the OPEN WEATHER API, in Figure 1.4, the application will send the current location's latitude and longitude to a web address to retrieve the current weather forecast and displays the detail on the screen. Each process required to achieve this flow will be explained in detail in Chapter 6.

## 1.6 CREATING YOUR FIRST ANDROID PROJECT

In the Appendix, you will find the download and installation instructions for the Android Studio IDE. Once the platform is set up, you are ready to write your first android application. Although there are numerous online and offline software for developing android apps, Android Studio is the preferred IDE as it has better support for essential tools, settings, and shortcuts to ensure an efficient development experience.

In Android Studio, various starter templates are available when starting a new project as seen in Figure 1.5.

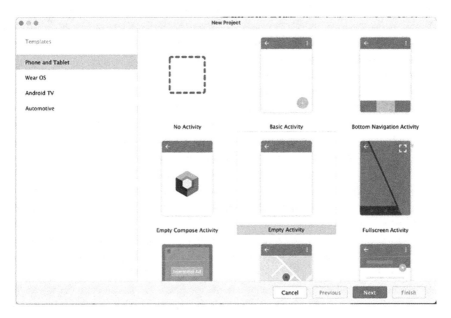

FIGURE 1.5   New project templates provided in Android Studio.

The template you choose depends on the intended user interface and experience you have in mind for your application. The available templates include default interfaces for the Drawer navigation menu, a menu commonly used for applications with a long list of actions and can be opened by swiping a finger from the left edge of the screen. Another is the Bottom navigation bar which displays a row of menus at the bottom of the screen, and many more important integrations for faster development. Using any of the templates requires you to fill in some information about the intended project as seen in Figure 1.6.

Here is a breakdown for each requirement.

- **Name**: This is where you enter the name of the app. This shows by default when the app is installed but can be changed later in the project.

- **Package name**: This provides the app with a unique identification which is most important when releasing the app to the public. The format is usually a domain name in reverse and should be specific to the app plus the name of the app, but for now, you can name it anything or use exactly what we have here.

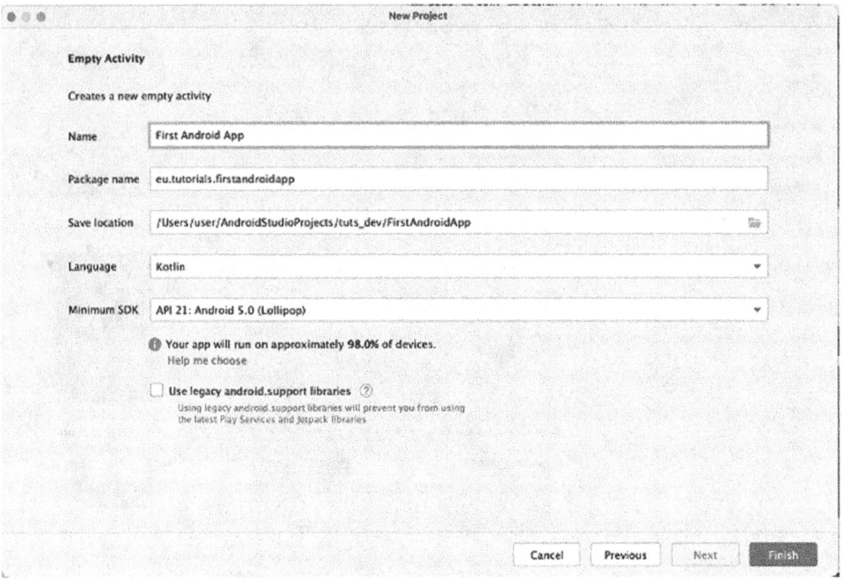

FIGURE 1.6   Project information required for every new project creation.

- **Save location**: This tells android studio where to save the app. You can choose any location on your computer by clicking the folder icon to the right.

- **Language**: This is the programming language you want to use for your application and has the option of Java or Kotlin. We will be using Kotlin throughout this book.

- **Minimum SDK** sets the minimum version of the android app you would like to support. You will support a certain percentage of android devices depending on your selected version. With API 21, you will support 98%.

Now click the Finish button. Depending on your internet connection, it will take some time to complete the process.

When the process is complete, you will see the screen shown in Figure 1.7.

There are three action menus to get yourself familiar with. The first is the green play button which allows you to run your application. When you click on this button and use an emulator as your testing device, it brings up the emulator and installs the application. If you do not have a testing device setup for your IDE, check out a step-by-step guide in the Appendix,

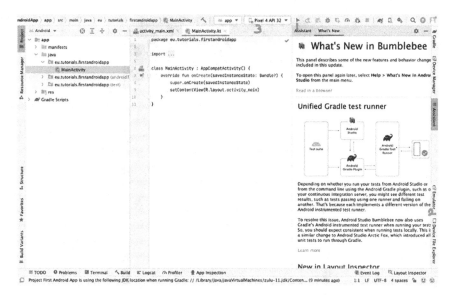

FIGURE 1.7    The first screen that you see after creating your first Android project.

which shows how to get an emulator up and running and, alternatively, get a real device ready for development.

The second menu is a quick action to show or hide the emulator. This is very useful, especially when you need the coding area to occupy a major part of the environment.

Assuming you have more than one emulator installed and have a real device connected, the third action is the dropdown listing all available testing devices, and you get to select which of them you want to run the application on.

Now click on the run button to launch your first Android application as shown in Figure 1.8.

## 1.7 THE COMPONENTS OF AN ANDROID APPLICATION

App components are the main building blocks of Android apps. Each component can serve as an entry point for the system or user to access your app. Some components depend on others, but each type serves a specific purpose and has its lifecycle that defines how each one is created and destroyed. All these components are defined in the application manifest file. The Android Manifest file is a required file for all Android applications. This file contains necessary metadata about each component and how they interact. This includes the package name, activity names, main activity, permissions, and other configurations. The Android operating system, therefore, uses it to determine how to launch the application. These components are described below.

FIGURE 1.8   Running your first Android application.

- **Activities:** As previously mentioned, the Activity is commonly an entry point into an Android application. It is a single focused thing that the user can do and provides a window for the UI to be placed. An application can have one or multiple activities, each representing a screen the app presents to the user. When an application has just one Activity, then there can be other windows like the Fragment or Composable that present other parts of its UI to the user.

  Activities are meant to be the presentation layer of your application. Your application's user interface is based on one or more extensions of the Activity class. By using fragments and views, activities determine the layout and presentation of their output and react to user actions.

Imagine your favorite application with different destination screens within it. There can be a registration screen, a login screen, and a home screen. These can be three separate Activities with a button click action leading to each other or one Activity with a Fragment.

- **Services:** Android services are long-running processes designed to perform specific tasks in the background. They can keep your app running without providing a Bound user service. A started service tells the system to keep running until it completes its work. An example is music playing in the background even when you are not interacting with the app. A bound service is running because another app (or the system) has requested to use it.

- **Broadcast Receiver:** A broadcast receiver is another well-defined entry within an app, allowing the system to deliver broadcasts even to apps that are not currently running. Many broadcasts are sent from the system. For example, a broadcast tells you that your screen has turned off, your battery is low, or a picture has been taken. Applications can also initiate broadcasts. For example, you can notify other applications that some data has been downloaded to your device.

- **Content Provider:** Content providers are used in managing and storing shared data. They are often used to save data that needs to be synced with other devices or shared with other applications. It contains a set of methods to store and retrieve data and make it accessible to applications on the device. Content providers are implemented as a subclass of the ContentProvider class and must implement a set of APIs that allow other apps to perform transactions.

- **Intent:** Android Intents are messaging objects used to communicate between three of the Android components mentioned above. It can launch activities, start services, or deliver broadcasts. It can also be used for data transfer between applications. In the case of activities and services, an intent defines the action to perform (display something, send something, etc.) and, among other things, the data to act on, which the launched component might need to know. For instance, you can specify a URL to be opened on a web page or start an Activity to get a result. Both cases are possible with an intent object which will be discussed in detail in Chapter 4 of this book.

Now that we have discovered the wide range of capabilities offered by the Kotlin programming language and its associated benefits and have gained some understanding of Android application components and their various use cases, Chapter 2 will guide you through building your initial application utilizing the elements and components explained in this chapter.

## 1.8 SUMMARY

- Kotlin is a general-purpose programming language allowing adopters to share codes between different platforms at the same time while reducing the cost of extra developers for each one.

- Kotlin is concise, safe, and interoperable, thereby supporting easy-to-read code, reducing common errors, and works well with languages like Java.

- Kotlin is multiparadigm in nature as it supports both object-oriented and functional styles of programming, allowing not only the use of classes and objects but at the same time enabling first-class functions.

- Kotlin is now the official language for Android apps development, it works well for backend applications, is adaptive to web apps, and with the help of Jetpack Compose also can be used for desktop applications.

- It is an open-source language allowing contributions from users, thereby increasing community support and improvement.

- An Android application requires two or more of the following, user interface, interactivity, and a storage option to be fully functional.

- Android studio is the official IDE for building android apps.

- Android studio has many templates to enable developers to create applications that use standard features and action menus quickly.

- Android applications consist of the following basic components, including activities, services, content providers, and broadcast receivers.

- An Activity serves as the entry point into your application.

- Services are background processes that perform work for an app, such as fetching data from a server.

- Content providers manage data that is shared between app components.

- Broadcast receivers respond to system-wide events, such as incoming phone calls or text messages.

# CHAPTER 2

# Basic XML Widgets in Android

## 2.1 BMI CALCULATOR OVERVIEW

Body Mass Index (BMI) is a tool that can help individuals assess the healthiness of their weight and determine whether they need to gain, lose, or maintain weight. Calculating BMI involves dividing an individual's weight by the square of their height, and a BMI calculator can make this process quick and easy. In fact, it is possible to develop an application that allows users to input their accurate height and weight values and obtain their BMI with just the click of a button. However, several additional factors should be considered when using BMI to assess overall health, and this chapter will provide the information regarding the factors relevant to the one we will build. Figure 2.1 explains the application's interaction process.

As shown in Figure 2.1, the application will receive input for the user's height and weight. Upon clicking the "Calculate" button, the app will compute the user's BMI result based on the entered input and display it in the TextField. However, before performing the calculation and displaying the result, the app will verify that the input entered is an integer and provide an appropriate message if it is not. With this flow in mind, we will begin with creating the user interface for the app, as seen in Figure 2.2.

DOI: 10.1201/9781032622538-2

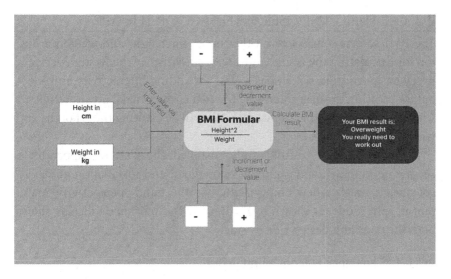

FIGURE 2.1    The BMI application user interaction flow.

FIGURE 2.2    Final BMI application.

## 2.2 CREATING THE USER INTERFACE OF THE APP

The BMI screen consists of a title, inputs for height and weight, a button for calculating the result, and a widget to display the Result overview. Every basic Android screen has a class for adding interactivity and a layout for creating the user interface. The two entities make up an Activity, a single focused thing the user can do. We will be creating the UI of the app within a layout.

If you do not have Android Studio installed, check out the Appendix to see the development environment's download and installation guide. To get started, create a new Empty Activity project and open activity_main. xml in split mode, as shown in Figure 2.3. The split mode display shows both the code and design side by side.

### 2.2.1 Understanding ConstraintLayout

A new Empty Activity project generates a default XML layout with a ViewGroup and a View. A ViewGroup is a category of Android widgets that can contain other views. It can also be called a parent view or the root view. ConstraintLayout is one of the ViewGroup available in Android and has become the recommended one for every layout, which is why the IDE provides it as default for every Activity you create. ConstraintLayout is a powerful and flexible layout manager for Android development, which allows developers to create complex and dynamic user interfaces.

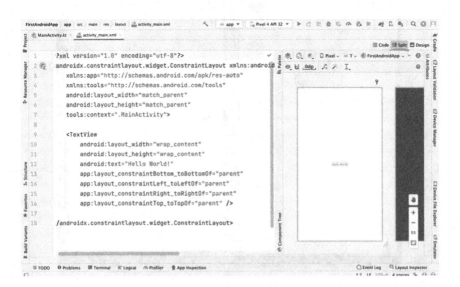

FIGURE 2.3   The activity_main.xml split view.

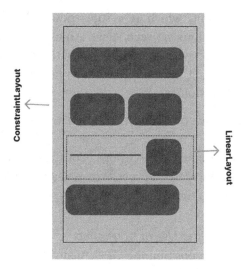

FIGURE 2.4   Nested ViewGroup with a LinearLayout inside a ConstraintLayout.

It provides much flexibility, allowing for constraints between different UI elements, which means that the layout can adapt to different screen sizes and orientations. This feature makes it an excellent choice for building responsive applications that adjust to various screen sizes, from small mobile devices to large tablets. One of the most significant benefits of ConstraintLayout is that it helps to reduce the nesting of ViewGroups. By using constraints to specify the position of each UI element, it can help developers create flatter and more efficient view hierarchies.

A flat view hierarchy is one with only one ViewGroup in a layout. This approach can improve the application's performance because it takes time to draw a ViewGroup before drawing the views. A layout containing child ViewGroups can significantly lower the app's user interface rendering time, particularly in more complex applications. This is less noticeable in simple, small apps. As depicted in Figure 2.4, a nested ViewGroup has a parent layout inside another.

The most used ViewGroups in Android include:

- LinearLayout, which positions views either horizontally or vertically side by side.

- RelativeLayout, which positions views relative to each other and relative to the parent.

- FrameLayout, which stacks views on top of each other.

- CoordinatorLayout, which is a super-powered FrameLayout and allows for animations between views. An example is the WhatsApp group profile page, where scrolling within the page smoothly transitions from showing the complete profile header to displaying only brief info on the toolbar.

- TableLayout, which positions its children into rows and columns.

For all the abovementioned ViewGroups, ConstraintLayout can be used as a replacement to increase app performance and achieve a flat layout hierarchy, mainly when there is a need for a nested ViewGroup.

### 2.2.1.1 Understanding the Use of Constraints

Constraints are used to position the UI elements relative to each other or the parent. To achieve this, we can use constraints to specify the position of each UI element. Each constraint represents a relationship between a UI element and its parent or sibling views. There are four types of constraints: top, bottom, start, and end.

The top constraint is used to specify the distance between the top edge of the UI element and the top edge of its parent or sibling view. The bottom constraint is used to specify the distance between the bottom edge of the UI element and the bottom edge of its parent or sibling view. The left constraint is used to specify the distance between the left edge of the UI element and the left edge of its parent or sibling view. The right constraint is used to specify the distance between the right edge of the UI element and the right edge of its parent or sibling view.

In addition to these four basic constraints, ConstraintLayout also supports other types of constraints, such as baseline constraints, which are used to align the text baseline of two UI elements, and bias constraints, which are used to position a UI element between two views.

### 2.2.1.2 Adding the App Title

We will use the first UI element of the BMI calculator app to create our first constraint. This is the screen title that displays text to the user in the form of a label on the Android screen. A TextView can be used to achieve this and is one of the basic UI elements that is often used during Android app development. The TextView is aligned at the center of the screen horizontally and must be constrained to the start and the end of the parent layout with compulsory height and width attributes that every View within a layout requires. The following code shows the placement of the TextView within its layout.

```
<androidx.constraintlayout.widget.ConstraintLayout
    xmlns:android="http://schemas.android.com/apk/res/
      android"
    xmlns:app="http://schemas.android.com/apk/
      res-auto"
    xmlns:tools="http://schemas.android.com/tools"
    android:layout_width="match_parent"
    android:layout_height="match_parent"
    android:padding="16dp"
    tools:context=".MainActivity">

    <TextView
        android:id="@+id/titleTv"
        android:layout_width="match_parent"
        android:layout_height="wrap_content"
        android:gravity="center"
        android:text="BMI Calculator"
        android:textColor="@color/black"
        android:textSize="32sp"
        android:textStyle="bold"
        app:layout_constraintTop_toTopOf="parent" />

</androidx.constraintlayout.widget.ConstraintLayout>
```

When using a ConstraintLayout as the root View, each child must have an identifier (id) that surrounding Views can be constrained against. Identifiers are usually important when you reference a view within its layout Activity. With ConstraintLayout it is different and necessary even if the value of some of the Views won't change. The android: id attribute is used for setting identifiers to a View. In the next section, you will see why the id is important and how other views are constrained using it.

The android:layout_width is used to set the width of a widget, and android:layout_height is used to set the widget's height. You can use a specific dimension as the value for this height and width attribute or use any of the available constants, such as the match_parent, to make the View take the size of the ViewGroup and wrap_content to make it take up the space according to its content. Any aspect of the view's height or width that does not have a value set to match_parent must have its constraint set. Otherwise, the view will jump to the top of the screen at runtime. You will also see the error indication by the IDE in this effect as shown in Figure 2.5.

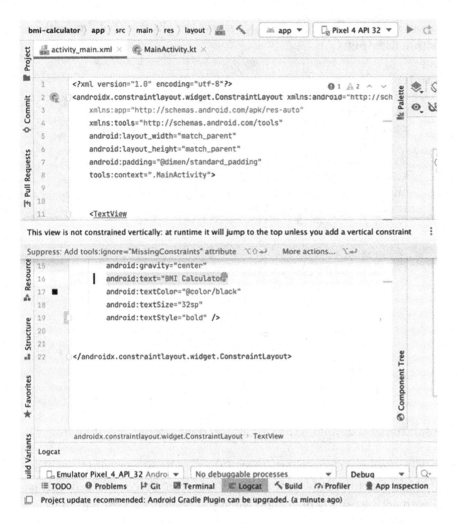

FIGURE 2.5   Error when height is set to wrap_content with no constraint.

Since the title view's height is set to wrap_content, a top constraint is added to position it at the top of the screen. In addition to the common attributes mentioned above, other attributes are required to give a TextView the desired styling. One is the android:textColor for changing the color of the text. Another is the android:textStyle for setting the type-face for the text. Of course, there is the android:text for setting the text to be displayed on the view.

In the ConstraintLayout tag, we have added a padding of 16dp. Padding in XML creates space between its content and the actual view itself. All the

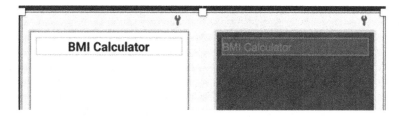

FIGURE 2.6 The final design view with the app title.

children in the layout will be 16dp away from the screen. Figure 2.6 shows the resulting display of the app title.

### 2.2.1.3 Adding the Height Widgets

Moving on with the other parts of the calculator UI, we require an input field to accept a height from the application user. Android EditText is the basic widget for accepting inputs from a user. It can be customized and used in different ways for accepting only numbers, passwords, email addresses, etc. It has two subclasses with additional styling to improve your user interface and experience. These include TextInputEditText and AppCompatEditText. Three of them differ in that they have access to additional attributes. We will use TextInputEditText because it has a hint property and easy styling that achieves the desired UI. It has its layout called the TextInputLayout to show a floating hint when the hint is hidden while the user inputs text. It also adds a nice border around the input field by adding a style attribute that is not easily available with just EditText. Figures 2.7 and 2.8 shows the two input fields before and after a user begins typing.

For the height section of the app, there are several key widgets that play a role in the user interface. First, we have a TextView widget, which serves as a label or hint, providing information about the expected input in the field.

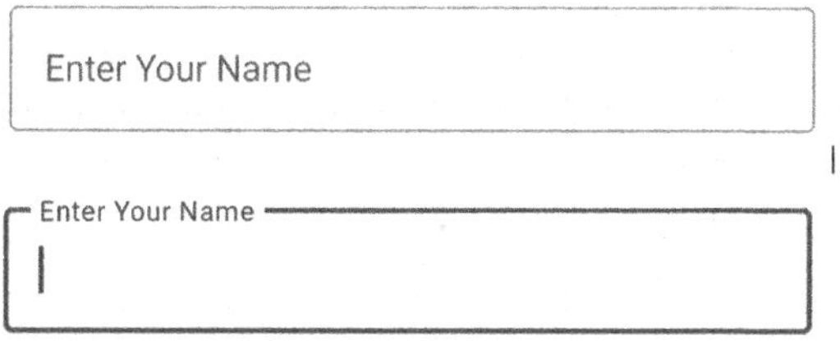

Enter Your Name

Enter Your Name

FIGURE 2.7 TextInputEditText before and when a user starts typing.

FIGURE 2.8   EditText before and when a user starts typing.

Next, the actual input field is represented by a TextInputEditText widget, and its layout is managed by a TextInputLayout widget.

In addition to these widgets, there are two buttons that allow the user to quickly increment or decrement the value in the input field. Each widget is assigned a unique ID, which not only helps establish constraints within the ConstraintLayout but also allows easy referencing from the Activity for implementing interactive functionality.

The positioning of these widgets is achieved using constraints within the ConstraintLayout. For example, the label is positioned directly below the title by setting the constraint app:layout_constraintTop_toBottomOf= "@id/titleTv" and to the start of the height input field with the constraint app:layout_constraintEnd_toStartOf="@id/heightIL". To create some spacing between the height label and the title, an android:layout_marginTop of 16dp is applied.

Below the label, we have the positive button, which is responsible for increasing the height value. It is constrained with its start aligned to the start of the parent and its end aligned to the start of the height input field.

Within the TextInputEditText, which is a child of the TextInputLayout, the input field itself is positioned just below its corresponding label. Its constraints are set with the start aligned to the end of the plus button, the top aligned to the top of the plus button, the bottom aligned to the bottom of the plus button, and the end aligned to the end of the minus button. The TextInputEditText is sized to match its parent input layout, with height and width set to match_parent.

Lastly, the minus button is constrained with its end aligned to the end of the parent, its start aligned to the end of the input field, and its top aligned to the bottom of the height label. This ensures proper positioning and interaction between the different elements of the height section within the app's user interface.

```xml
<TextView
    android:id="@+id/heightLabel"
    android:layout_width="wrap_content"
    android:layout_height="wrap_content"
    android:layout_marginTop="16dp "
    android:gravity="center"
    android:text="Your Height in metres"
    android:textColor="@color/black"
    app:layout_constraintStart_toStartOf="@id/
     heightIL"
    app:layout_constraintTop_toBottomOf="@id/titleTv" />

<Button
    android:id="@+id/heightPlusBtn"
    android:layout_width="50dp"
    android:layout_height="wrap_content"
    android:layout_marginTop="16dp "
    android:layout_marginEnd="16dp"
    android:text="+"
    app:layout_constraintEnd_toStartOf="@id/heightIL"
    app:layout_constraintStart_toStartOf="parent"
    app:layout_constraintTop_toBottomOf="@id/height
     Label" />

<com.google.android.material.textfield.TextInputLayout
    android:id="@+id/heightIL"

style="@style/Widget.MaterialComponents.TextInput
 Layout.OutlinedBox"
    android:layout_width="0dp"
    android:layout_height="60dp"
    app:layout_constraintBottom_toBottomOf="@id/
     heightPlusBtn"
    app:layout_constraintEnd_toStartOf="@id/
     heightMinusBtn"
    app:layout_constraintStart_toEndOf="@id/
     heightPlusBtn"
    app:layout_constraintTop_toBottomOf="@id/
     heightLabel"
    app:layout_constraintTop_toTopOf="@id/
     heightPlusBtn">

    <com.google.android.material.textfield.TextInput
      EditText
        android:id="@+id/heightEt"
        android:layout_width="match_parent"
        android:layout_height="match_parent" />
```

```
</com.google.android.material.textfield.TextInput
   Layout>

<Button
    android:id="@+id/heightMinusBtn"
    android:layout_width="@dimen/btn_height"
    android:layout_height="wrap_content"
    android:layout_marginStart="16dp"
    android:layout_marginTop="16dp"
    android:text="-"
    app:layout_constraintEnd_toEndOf="parent"
    app:layout_constraintStart_toEndOf="@id/heightIL"
    app:layout_constraintTop_toBottomOf="@id/height
     Label" />
```

Figure 2.9 shows the resulting UI for this code snippet.

## 2.2.2 Adding the Weight Widgets

The weight elements will be set up similarly to the height widgets. It also requires a label or a hint attribute that signifies how the value to be entered will be used. Now you can see the importance of hints. Two similar widgets like Width and height TextInputEditText can only be distinguished by the user using labels. The weight widgets are positioned below the height input layout and just like the height widgets, you start by setting the top

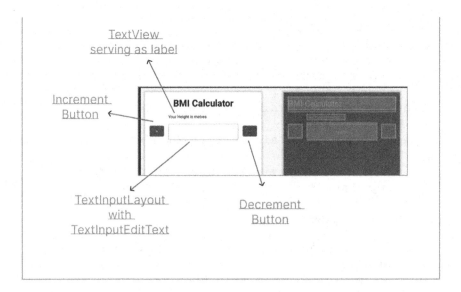

FIGURE 2.9    The height widgets.

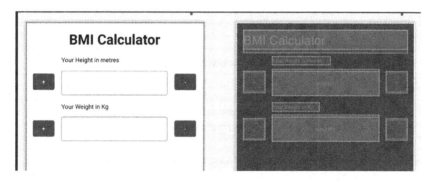

FIGURE 2.10   The UI with weight widgets added.

constraint below the height input layout and set the start constraint to the start of the weight input layout. Figure 2.10 is the final UI after the weight widgets are added.

```
<!--
```
**@+id is used to set an ID for each widget to be used for referencing it**
```
app:layout_constraintStart_toStartOf and
        app:layout_constraintTop_toBottomOf
```
**adds a constraint to position the app title to the left side of the screen and top of the screen**
```
-->

<TextView
        android:id="@+id/weightLabel"
        android:layout_width="wrap_content"
        android:layout_height="wrap_content"
        android:layout_marginTop="16dp"
        android:gravity="center"
        android:text="Your Weight in Kg"
        android:textColor="@color/black"
        app:layout_constraintStart_toStartOf="@id/
          weightIL"
        app:layout_constraintTop_toBottomOf="@id/
          heightIL" />

<! -
```

**The increment button is added with constraints to the left of the input field.**

**The style attribute adds a theme to the input field with an appealing UI than the default EditText**

```xml
-->

    <Button
        android:id="@+id/weightPlusBtn"
        android:layout_width="50dp"
        android:layout_height="wrap_content"
        android:layout_marginTop="16dp"
        android:layout_marginEnd="16dp"
        android:text="+"
        app:layout_constraintEnd_toStartOf="@id/
          weightIL"
        app:layout_constraintStart_toStartOf="parent"
        app:layout_constraintTop_toBottomOf="@id/
          weightLabel" />

    <com.google.android.material.textfield.TextInput
      Layout
        android:id="@+id/weightIL"
      style="@style/Widget.MaterialComponents.TextInput
      Layout.OutlinedBox"
        android:layout_width="0dp"
        android:layout_height="60dp"
        android:layout_marginTop="8dp"
        app:layout_constraintEnd_toStartOf="@id/
          weightMinusBtn"
        app:layout_constraintStart_toEndOf="@id/
          weightPlusBtn"
        app:layout_constraintTop_toBottomOf="@id/
          weightLabel">

        <com.google.android.material.textfield.Text
          InputEditText
            android:id="@+id/weightEt"
            android:layout_width="match_parent"
            android:layout_height="match_parent" />
    </com.google.android.material.textfield.
      TextInputLayout>


    <Button
        android:id="@+id/weightMinusBtn"
        android:layout_width="50dp"
        android:layout_height="wrap_content"
        android:layout_marginStart="16dp"
        android:layout_marginTop="16dp"
```

```
android:text="-"
app:layout_constraintEnd_toEndOf="parent"
app:layout_constraintStart_toEndOf="@id/
  weightIL"
app:layout_constraintTop_toBottomOf="@id/
  weightLabel" />
```

### 2.2.3 The Result View and the Calculate Button

The result view will display the BMI value and the category the value belongs to. A TextView is the best widget for the task and will be positioned directly below the "Calculate" button. Below the Weight input field, the calculate button is positioned to the center horizontally with constraint start set to the start of the parent and constraint end set to the parent's end. The result TextView is positioned below the calculate button where the BMI information will be displayed.

```
<TextView
    android:id="@+id/resultTv"
    android:layout_width="match_parent"
    android:layout_height="wrap_content"
    android:gravity="center"
    android:padding="16dp"
    android:textColor="@color/black"
    android:textStyle="bold"
    app:layout_constraintTop_toBottomOf="@id/
      calculateBtn" />

<com.google.android.material.button.MaterialButton
    android:id="@+id/calculateBtn"
    android:layout_width="wrap_content"
    android:layout_height="wrap_content"
    android:layout_marginTop="16dp"
    android:text="Calculate"
    app:layout_constraintBottom_toTopOf="@id/resultTv"
    app:layout_constraintEnd_toEndOf="parent"
    app:layout_constraintStart_toStartOf="parent"
    app:layout_constraintTop_toBottomOf="@id/weightIL"
    />
```

## 2.3 THE ACTIVITY AND VIEWBINDING

Every element required by the app is now added to the user interface. You can run the application now to see how they all align with each other as seen in Figure 2.11. If you don't see a run button, check the preface for a quick

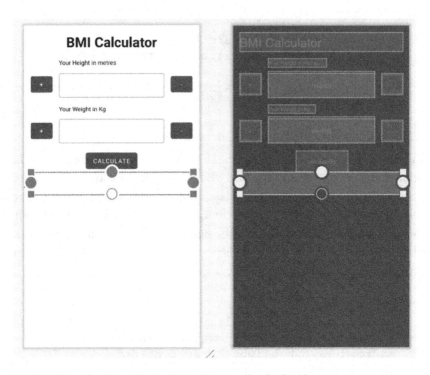

FIGURE 2.11   The UI with result TextView and calculate button.

instruction on how to setup a testing device for your Android Studio, which also activates the run button. When the app is running, you click on any of the buttons nothing happens. This is because no functionality has been added to the app. You have only designed the UI. The widgets must be linked to an Activity to make our app functional. Every layout requires an Activity to make a complete screen. If you have run the application, you can only see something on the screen because the layout is connected to an Activity by default.

There is a layout for each user interface, and for each layout, there is an Activity. To add interactivity to our application's user interface, we will look at the MainActivity to which the layout is connected. If you don't have the MainActivity open already, you can find it within the app folder as shown in Figure 2.12.

An Android Activity provides the window in which an app draws its UI. It also provides a screen where the user can interact to do something. In the MainActivity, the layout is connected to it using setContentView() within the onCreate method. Once the Activity is created, this method ensures the UI is also drawn.

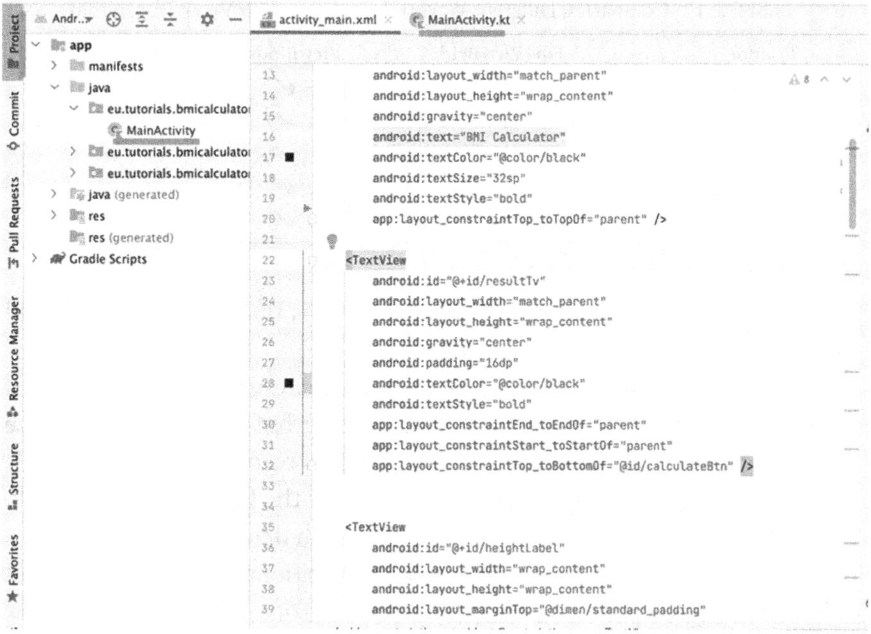

FIGURE 2.12   The location where you can find the MainActivity file.

```kotlin
class MainActivity : AppCompatActivity() {
    override fun onCreate(savedInstanceState:
    Bundle?) {
        super.onCreate(savedInstanceState)
        setContentView(R.layout.activity_main)
    }
}
```

## 2.3.1 Referencing Layout Views with ViewBinding in an Activity

To make an Activity interactive, the views in its layout must be referenced by their IDs. This allows for the addition of specific functionality or actions to each widget. Android provides three methods for achieving this: findViewById, ViewBinding, and DataBinding.

The findViewById method is the traditional way of referencing views and has been used since the inception of Android. However, one drawback is that it can return null if the referenced view is unavailable at the time of access.

DataBinding is an approach that generates a class for the layout of a particular Activity. It also allows you to bind data directly in your XML

TABLE 2.1   Comparing Different Ways of Interacting with Views in Android

| Feature | FindViewById | ViewBinding | DataBinding |
|---|---|---|---|
| Null safety | ✘ | ✔ | ✔ |
| Ease of use | ✘ | ✔ | ✘ |
| Type safety | ✘ | ✔ | ✔ |
| Faster compilation | ✔ | ✔ | ✘ |
| Elegance | ✘ | ✔ | ✘ |

with little to no Kotlin code. Its disadvantage is that it lowers your build speed due to annotation processing.

ViewBinding was introduced as a replacement for the now-deprecated Kotlin synthetics API. It is like DataBinding but has no performance issues and faster build times. This approach is recommended by Google and is suitable for most scenarios. Throughout the first part of this book, we will be using and discussing ViewBinding in detail.

Each one has its pros and cons as mentioned in Table 2.1, but ViewBinding has proven to be suitable with reasons such as shorter syntax and better performance. Now the first step to using ViewBinding is to enable it in build.gradle file. This file contains some of the configurations required by your project or application. You can add them when needed, and you will see more of them as we progress. You can find this within the Gradle Scripts section as shown in Figure 2.13.

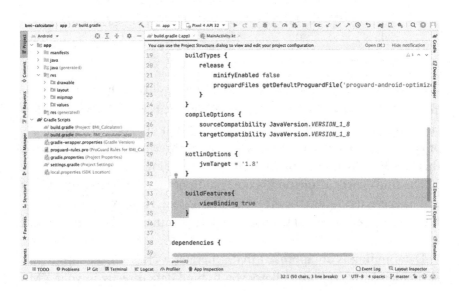

FIGURE 2.13   Enabling ViewBinding in build.gradle.

Then add the below code to your build.gradle as shown in Figure 2.13

```
buildFeatures{
  viewBinding true
}
```

Then click on sync now to reflect the changes

Enabling ViewBinding generates a binding class for each layout file that exists in that module. An instance of the binding class contains direct references to all views with IDs in the corresponding layout. For activitiy_main.xml, you have ActivityMainBinding, notice the naming style, which is the layout name, starting with upper case and ending with the word Binding. In MainActivity.kt you can connect the binding class to the content by creating a variable for the binding layout. ActivityMainBinding.inflate(layoutInflater) inflates activity_main.xml. Every layout within a project with ViewBinding included has a binding file created using the layout's name plus binding. After creating a variable for the inflater, within the onCreate method, the setContentView parameter will be replaced using the binding class rather than the layout file so that the binding variable gets connected with the MainActivity.

```
class MainActivity : AppCompatActivity() {
    private val binding by lazy{
        ActivityMainBinding.inflate(layoutInflater)
    }
    override fun onCreate(savedInstanceState: Bundle?) {
        super.onCreate(savedInstanceState)
        setContentView(binding.root)

    }
}
```

## 2.4 CONNECTING EACH INPUT FIELD WITH THE INCREMENT AND DECREMENT BUTTONS

To ensure that each input field for both the height and the width is always in sync when getting the value from a user, we will connect the operations of both the input and their buttons. The first step is to create variables for each of the values. We will do this within the Activity's onCreate method, starting with the height. The onCreate method is called immediately after the Android system creates an Activity. It is the initialization point for any startup logic. For example, the setContentView that creates the Activity's UI is called in the onCreate to ensure the UI is drawn and ready for use.

To begin the implementation, we must create a global variable for each value. For all respective values to be correct and remain the same at every entry, including the increment and decrement, you use the same variable to hold the related resulting value for each calculation.

```
private var heightValue: Double = 0.0
private var weightValue: Double = 0.0
private var bmi: Double = 0.0
```

Just below the binding variable add the height, weight, and BMI variables with a default value of 0.0 which becomes its value at the start of the application.

### 2.4.1 Getting the Value from Height Value

The "heightValue" variable will keep track of all height inputs, including the increment and decrement operations. In the onCreate method, a click listener is set to the buttons separately, and for each one, the value from the input field is retrieved and assigned to the heightValue. We also do the same for the height minus button. Set a click listener to it and within the block, check that the input field is not empty, get its value, and assign it to heightValue.

This way, the heightValue is always correct regardless of which widget it is altered from. It's important not to leave the heightValue empty during the calculation hence the check before it is finally assigned.

```
// Reference the height input field and assign it to a variable
val heightEt = binding.heightEt

/*
set a click listener to the height increment button that when clicked increases
the value in the input field by 1
*/
binding.heightPlusBtn.setOnClickListener {
    if (heightEt.text.toString().isNotEmpty()) {
        heightValue = heightEt.text.toString().
          toDouble()
    }
    heightValue++
    heightEt.setText(heightValue.toString())
}
```

```
/*
set a click listener on the height decrement button that when clicked decreases
the value in the input field by 1
*/
binding.heightMinusBtn.setOnClickListener {
    if (heightEt.text.toString().isNotEmpty()) {
        heightValue = heightEt.text.toString().
          toDouble()
    }
    heightValue--
    heightEt.setText(heightValue.toString())
}
```

## 2.4.2 Getting the Weight Value

As we did with the height input field, we will connect the weight input field, and its buttons to be in sync will be recorded using the "weightValue" variable. Within the onCreate method, the onClickListener will be set to the weight increment button to listen for a click event. When the button is clicked, and the input field is not empty, get the value in it and set it to "weightValue" and then increase the "weightValue" by one and set it back to the input field.

We do the same for the weight decrement button and set onClickListener to it. The onClick implementation checks to see if the weight input field is not empty, gets the value, assigns it to "weightValue", and then decreases the value by one and sets it back to the input field.

Below is what the code looks like.

```
val weightEt = binding.weightEt

binding.weightPlusBtn.setOnClickListener {
    if (weightEt.text.toString().isNotEmpty()){
        weightValue = weightEt.text.toString().
          toDouble()
    }
    weightValue++
    weightEt.setText(weightValue.toString())
}
binding.weightMinusBtn.setOnClickListener {
    if (weightEt.text.toString().isNotEmpty()){
        weightValue = weightEt.text.toString().
          toDouble()
    }
    weightValue--
    weightEt.setText(weightValue.toString())
}
```

TABLE 2.2    The Different BMI Values and Their Category

| BMI Value | Category |
|---|---|
| <18.5 | Underweight |
| 18.5 to 24.9 | Normal |
| 25 to 29.9 | Overweight |
| 30 and above | Obese class |

## 2.5 CALCULATE THE BMI RESULT

Now that we can effectively collect the height and weight from the user, we will create a function to calculate the BMI result. First, you need to understand how the BMI value is categorized.

From Table 2.2, if the BMI value is less than 18.5, the person is underweight and needs to eat more. Between 18.5 and 24.9 indicates the person is normal and is in a good shape and 25.0 and 29.9 indicates the person is overweight and really needs to work out and from 30 upwards indicates the person is in the obese class and in a dangerous condition. Let's look at the code solution

```kotlin
private fun displayBMIResult(bmi: Float) {

    var bmiLabel = ""
    var bmiDescription =   ""

    when {
                bmi < 18.5 -> {
                    bmiLabel = "You are underweight"
                    bmiDescription = "You should take
                        better care of yourself! Eat
                        more!"
                }
                bmi in 18.5..24.9 -> {
                    bmiLabel = "Normal"
                    bmiDescription = "Congratulations!
                     You are in a good shape!"
                }
                bmi in 25.0..29.9 -> {
                    bmiLabel = "Overweight"
            bmiDescription = "You really need to
            take care of yourself! Workout maybe!"
                }
                bmi >= 30.0 -> {
                    bmiLabel = "Obese Class"
```

```
                    bmiDescription = "You might be in
                    a dangerous condition! Act now!"
          }
      }
  val bmiValue = BigDecimal(bmi.toDouble())

  // A This is used to access a String's value from the
  // Activity class.

  binding.resultTv.text = resources.getString(R.string.
  bmi_result,bmiValue,bmiLabel,bmiDescription)
}
```

In the above code, a function called displayBMIResult with a parameter of type Float is created. Within this function block, declare bmiLabel and bmiDescription to hold the result category and description, respectively. Use a when statement to check if the BMI value is less than 18.5 and assign the underweight label and description to bmiLabel or bmiDescription, respectively.

If the value is from 18.5 to 24.9, then assign the normal label and description; if the value is from 25 to 29.9, assign the overweight label and description. And if the value is 30 and above, assign the obese class label and description. After the when statement, we set the result, label, and description to the result TextView. You will notice that we use the resources API to call the getString method rather than hardcoding it directly.

## 2.5.1 The String Resource File

Android string resource provide optional text styles and Android text formatting. You need to set the combination of texts that form the display of the result view. The proper way to do this is with a strings file. An alternative is to hard code it directly into the Activity, which makes it difficult to access and maintain across different languages and cultures. This is made easier with a string resource file. In Android Studio, layouts are in the res folder, but this folder also contains additional files and static content used in your code, such as strings, images, and colors.

When looking at the final output in the results view as seen in Figure 2.14, you will see additional text in addition to the BMI results, labels, and details. To combine them properly, open the string resource file as seen in Figure 2.15.

Within the file we create a new string tag:

```
<string name="bmi _ result">Your BMI result is %.f
  \n%s \n%s</string>
```

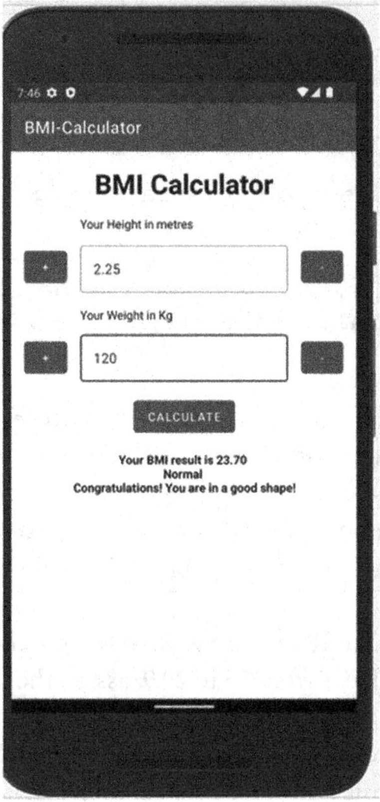

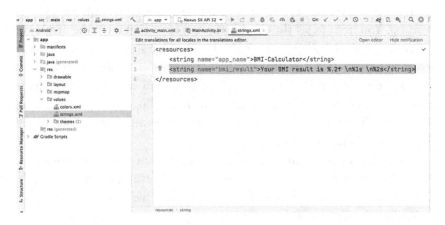

FIGURE 2.14    Final application output.

FIGURE 2.15    The strings.xml file.

This tag has a name bmi_result which will be used to reference it from any Activity and then the content of the string which includes some place-holders. To break down this content, first we have the prefix text to show that it is your BMI result. This is followed by the first placeholder %.f which will accept the BMI result that is a double which is also a floating-point number. The reason for f at the end is that the % sign indicates the beginning of a format.

The second placeholder is %s which will accept the BMI label. You will also notice a preceding character \n that is called a new line and will move the label to a new line. The "s" stands for string. It is the same for the third placeholder which will be for the description.

So, this is how we came about the resources set to the BMI result text view and the parameters of the getString.

## 2.6 THE CALCULATE BUTTON

When the calculate button is clicked, the displayBmiResult method should be called. Having created the function already, using the onCreate method, you will reference the calculate button using ViewBinding and set onClickListener to it.

```
override fun onCreate(savedInstanceState: Bundle?) {
        super.onCreate(savedInstanceState)
        setContentView(binding.root)
        binding.calculateBtn.setOnClickListener {
            val height = heightEt.text.toString().
              toDouble()
            val weight = weightEt.text.toString().
              toDouble()
            bmi =(weight/height.times(height))
            Toast.makeText(this,"$bmi",Toast.
              LENGTH_LONG).show()
            displayBMIResult(bmi)
        }
    }
```

At the end of the onCreate method, add the above code. Here is what is going on within the onClickListener; You get the value entered by the user from both height input and weight input to perform the calculation. Because the value from the input field is a type of editable using which calculation cannot be performed upon, we change its type to double.

Since editable cannot be converted to double directly, it is first converted to String and then to double. The BMI formula is:

$$BMI = \frac{Weight}{Height^2}$$

BMI is calculated using weight divided by the square of height. Next, we call the displayBMIResult method and pass in the BMI value. This method will then check the BMI value against the conditions within its functionalities and display the result. Now run the app and input your weight in kg and height in meters to test the application.

### 2.6.1 Testing and Running the App

When you run the app, you should enter the values for height in meters and weight in kilograms. You can also test the increment and decrement buttons for both values and then use the calculate button to return and display the BMI result. The expected result can be found as shown in Figure 2.14.

Before wrapping up this chapter, it's crucial to understand how to identify errors when running your applications at this point. This will be helpful for the rest of the project we will develop in the coming chapters.

## 2.7 ERRORS AND THE LOGCAT WINDOW

During the execution of an application, various errors or issues can occur, which may cause the application to crash, terminate suddenly, or even run without producing the expected outcome. The Logcat window in Android Studio provides a comprehensive record of system messages and log messages generated by the Android system and the application. By reviewing the log messages in the Logcat window as seen in Figure 2.16, developers can identify the cause of the issues and debug the application accordingly.

When you run an Android project, at the bottom of the IDE, you can click the Logcat tab to pull up its window.

This window has filters and search functionality, making it easy to find and diagnose errors in your app quickly. You can filter log messages by level, app process, or tag or search for specific messages by keyword. If you have different devices mounted, you can choose the specific one you are testing on.

By reviewing the log messages in the Logcat window, you can identify the source of an error and take the necessary steps to correct it. You can

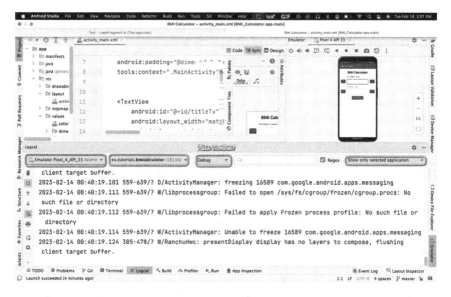

FIGURE 2.16    The Logcat Window.

filter specific information by log levels when the application displays many messages. There are six common ones which include. error, assert, debug, info, verbose, and warn. Below are their usages.

- **Verbose**: Verbose is the lowest log level and provides the most detailed information. Verbose logs provide general system behavior and operations and can sometimes be overwhelming and not specific.

- **Debug**: Debug logs provide information that can help you understand what the system is doing and can be used to identify issues with your app. Debug logs are more concise than verbose logs and are typically used for debugging problems during development.

- **Error**: Error logs indicate a critical problem that prevents the normal operation of your app. Error logs provide detailed information about the problem, including the source of the error, the type of error, and a stack trace of the error.

- **Info**: Info logs provide information about the normal operation of your app, such as the start and end of a process or the status of a task. Info logs are used to keep track of important events in your app.

FIGURE 2.17    The different filtering options in the Logcat window.

- **Warning**: Warning logs indicate a potential problem that could affect the normal operation of your app. For example, a warning log might be generated when an unexpected error occurs or a resource is not found.

Although these logs, by default, have processes that trigger them, especially verbose and error, you can also create them within your program for debugging purposes using the Log class. To see the different levels, click on the dropdown selection, as shown in Figure 2.17.

With this knowledge, you can quickly find out what is wrong with your application going forward to enable you to search for solutions online or ask specific questions if the answer is difficult to get on Google or stack overflows. As we continue to Chapter 3, in which we will be learning about more UI features and functionality developing a quiz app, this will be a very beneficial approach to figuring out errors that may occur.

## 2.8 SUMMARY

- XML is the format used for creating the layout views for Android user interfaces.

- ViewGroups like ConstraintLayout in Android serve as the parent layout for child views.

- We can use TextInputEditText to accept user input.

- We can use TextView to set a text like a title or a label.

- Every XML layout requires an Activity to function.

- To reference a layout in its Activity, we can use one of findViewById, ViewBinding, or DataBinding.

- The string resource file provides optional styling for strings in Android.

- You can use placeholders in string resource files to temporarily fill a space for the value that changes at runtime.

- Click Listeners can be set on views to trigger an action, especially on buttons.

- The Logcat window in Android displays log messages generated by the Android system and the application that can help you in monitoring errors within your application.

# CHAPTER 3

# More on Android XML Views

*Project 2 – Quiz App: Part 1*

## 3.1 THE QUIZ APP OVERVIEW

If you have ever interacted with any question-and-answer application, be it a questionnaire, aptitude test, trivia, or game. You will be already familiar with the kind of application we will be creating in this chapter. The app will have three screens: a welcome screen, a questions screen, and a result screen. When the app is run for the first time, the welcome screen is displayed, and the user enters their name. If no name is entered and the "Start Button" is clicked, an error is displayed using the "Toast" interface. Once the user enters a name and clicks the "Start Button", the "Question Screen" is displayed with the first question out of ten. Each question will comprise the country flag, four options showing country names, and a submit button.

To answer each question, a user can click on a chosen name as the name of the country to which the flag belongs. They can change their answer by selecting a different one which will automatically deselect the previous one until the "Submit Button" is clicked. When the "Submit Button" is clicked, the system checks if the selected option is the correct answer and sets its background to green. If the selected option is wrong, the background is then set to a red color, and the correct answer is set to a green

DOI: 10.1201/9781032622538-3

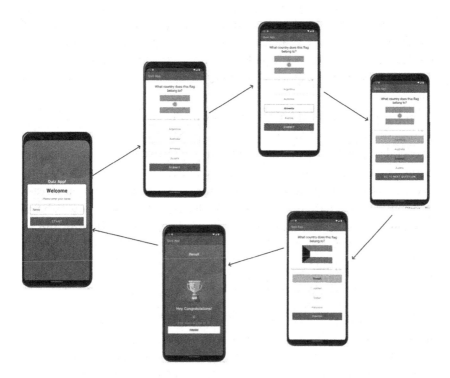

FIGURE 3.1   The app user flow.

color. As soon as the "Submit Button" is clicked, the button changes from "Submit" to "Go to the next question", which, when clicked, takes the user to the next question.

For the last question, when the "Submit Button" is clicked because there is no other question, the button changes to "Finish" rather than "Go to the next question". Clicking the Finish button takes the user to the "Result screen" to see the total number of correct answers, including the name entered at the beginning in the "Welcome screen".

Finally, we have a "Finish Button" on the "Result screen" that takes the user back to the "Welcome screen" to start the quiz afresh. We will begin by creating the UI for the "Welcome screen". Figure 3.1 demonstrates the screen user flow of this application.

## 3.2  CREATING THE WELCOME SCREEN

The welcome screen will consist of six widgets, including three TextFields, a MaterialCardView, a TextInputEditText, and a Button. It has a nice background achieved with an image's help. This image will be imported into the project and set as a value to the android: background attribute of the ConstraintLayout. There will be three TextFields to show the screen title "Quiz App!", the subtitle "Welcome", and the username label "Please enter your name".

Taking a closer look at the area with a white background, you will notice the rounded corners. A CardView can be used to quickly achieve them due to several features it provides which include a border, elevation, and corner radius. This widget is used to create a card-like interface in an easy-to-digest format. To be able to accept a username from a user, you already know what widgets are suitable—the TextInputEditText widget which will be wrapped by a TextInputLayout. Lastly, we have the Start button and we will use the AppCompatButton rather than the regular Button widget. To get started developing this application, you can create a new Empty Activity project, so we begin from scratch.

### 3.2.1 Adding Images to Your Project in Android Studio

Images are a very important part of Android development as they make the user interface look attractive and convey a specific message to the user. Now let's see how to import an image into Android Studio and prepare it for use in a project.

First, you need to identify the images you need for your application, and in this case, it is the background image for the "Welcome screen", the flags for each question, and the background image for the "Results screen". The next step is to click on "Resource Manager" at the left side of your Android Studio and click on the plus icon as shown in Figure 3.2.

Select "Import Drawables" from the pop-up options to see your computer files and choose the images needed for the project.

Figure 3.3 has all the images selected at once, including the background image, the country flags, and the trophy image. Click the Next button and then import to complete the process. You will find the images listed within Drawable as shown in Figure 3.4. You can find the resources from the project's GitHub page following this link https://github.com/tutorialseu/TheQuizApp.

### 3.2.2 Designing the Welcome Screen

This will be the first time we use an image in a project. The MainActivity will be the welcome screen, which is connected to the activity_main.

FIGURE 3.2    Android Studio resource manager.

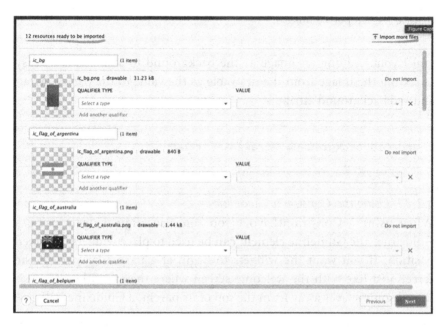

FIGURE 3.3    Selected images.

FIGURE 3.4 Imported images.

xml layout. Adding an image as the background to a screen is as easy as setting the image from the drawable as the value to the parent layout android:background attribute.

```
android:background="@drawable/ic_bg"
```

### 3.2.2.1 Using the Constraint Guideline

When using a ConstraintLayout you can also align widgets using a Guideline. The Guideline element can be used to place widgets in a fixed position. If you want the widgets to begin at a particular part of the screen just like with the welcome screen where the app title gets positioned some spaces away from the top of its parent, a Guideline will give you a better result for all screen sizes than a margin. There are two types of Guideline elements, horizontal and vertical. Guidelines can be placed on the left, right, top, or bottom of a layout. Using the orientation attribute, you can set a Guideline vertically using the horizontal value and horizontally using the vertical value. And to decide at what point on the screen the Guideline starts, you can use the attribute app:layout_constraintGuide_begin and assign an integer value to it. After you have set a Guideline you can begin positioning Views relative to it using the constraint attribute.

```
<!-- Sets a Vertical constraint guideline to place the
  layout views
 100 points from the top of the screen -->
    <androidx.constraintlayout.widget.Guideline
        android:id="@+id/guideline"
        app:layout_constraintTop_toTopOf="parent"
        android:orientation="horizontal"
        android:layout_width="wrap_content"
        app:layout_constraintGuide_begin="100pt"

  android:layout_height="wrap_content"/>

    <!-- Set the top constraint of this Text tag to
      be positioned below the guideline. The text
      displayed will be taken from the "quiz_app"
      string resource. -->
    <TextView
        app:layout_constraintTop_toBottomOf="@+id/
         guideline"
        android:id="@+id/tvAppName"
        android:layout_width="match_parent"
        android:layout_height="wrap_content"
        android:layout_marginBottom="30dp"
        android:gravity="center"
        android:text="@string/quiz_app"
        android:textColor="@color/white"
        android:textSize="25sp"
        android:textStyle="bold" />
```

The "TextView" for the app name is the first widget positioned at the bottom of the "Guideline" as you will see in Figure 3.5.

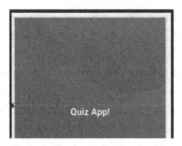

FIGURE 3.5   The app name below the guideline.

The guideline is only visible on the design editor, the user doesn't see it when the app is run on the device. We can continue placing other widgets below the App Name starting with the MaterialCardView.

### 3.2.2.2 How to Use the MaterialCardView

Using the MaterialCardView provides two important features on the Welcome interface, an elevation for the white background area and rounded corner edges as shown in Figure 3.6. It generally helps to give an interface a rich look and feel and can only display views on top of each other. To position views within a CardView beside each other, you will need any of the ViewGroups or the Views will be stacked on top of each other.

```
<!-- android:elevation: Sets the elevation of the card
view, giving it a shadow effect. - app:cardCornerRadius:
Specifies the corner radius of the card view, creating
rounded corners. -->

    <com.google.android.material.card.MaterialCardView
            app:layout_constraintTop_toBottomOf="@id/
             tvAppName"
            android:layout_width="match_parent"
            android:layout_height="wrap_content"
            android:layout_marginStart="20dp"
            android:layout_marginEnd="20dp"
            android:background="@color/white"
            android:elevation="5dp"
            app:cardCornerRadius="8dp"
    >

        </com.google.android.material.card.Material
        CardView>
```

FIGURE 3.6    MaterialCardView with and without elevation.

FIGURE 3.7    Hint for the input field.

The elevation attribute present in the MaterialCardView gives the area a surrounding depth shadow that beautifies the UI while the cardCorner-Radious adds a rounded corner to the edges. Figure 3.7 shows its visual representation.

### 3.2.2.3 Using Linear Layout as a Parent for Child Views

Positioning more than one element directly within the CardView is impossible due to how it is created to only stack views on top of each other which does not fit what the result of the welcome screen looks like. There are three widgets positioned vertically below each other and we will need a different ViewGroup to align them as it is.

Guess what ViewGroup will be suitable to achieve this? In Chapter 1, we mentioned that LinearLayout allows views to be aligned in a single direction either vertically or horizontally. The white background part of the welcome screen shows the elements positioned in a vertical direction which requires the vertical orientation.

```xml
<!-- Set the orientation of the LinearLayout to
  vertical -->
<LinearLayout
            android:layout_width="match_parent"
            android:layout_height="wrap_content"
            android:layout_margin="16dp"
            android:orientation="vertical"
    >

            <TextView
                android:id="@+id/tvTitle"
                android:layout_width="match_parent"
                android:layout_height="wrap_content"
                android:gravity="center"
                android:text="@string/welcome"
                android:textColor="#363A43"
                android:textSize="30sp"
                android:textStyle="bold" />

            <TextView
                android:id="@+id/tvDescription"
                android:layout_width="match_parent"
                android:layout_height="wrap_content"
                android:layout_marginTop="16dp"
                android:gravity="center"
                android:text="@string/name_label"
                android:textColor="#7A8089"
                android:textSize="16sp" />
```

```
<!-- Apply the Material Components style "Outlined
  Box" to the TextInputLayout
which adds a Box around it
  -->

              <com.google.android.material.text
                field.TextInputLayout
                  android:id="@+id/tilName"
style="@style/Widget.MaterialComponents.TextInput
  Layout.OutlinedBox"
                  android:layout_width="match_parent"
                  android:layout_height="wrap_content"
                  android:layout_marginTop="20dp">

                  <androidx.appcompat.widget.App
                    CompatEditText
                      android:id="@+id/etName"
                      android:layout_width="match_
                        parent"
                      android:layout_height="wrap_
                        content"
                      android:imeOptions="actionGo"
                      android:hint="@string/
                        name_hint"
                      android:inputType="textCap
                        Words"
                      android:textColor="#363A43"
                      android:textColorHint=
                        "#7A8089" />
              </com.google.android.material.text
                field.TextInputLayout>

              <Button
                  android:id="@+id/btnStart"
                  android:layout_width="match_
                    parent"
                  android:layout_height="wrap_
                    content"
                  android:layout_marginTop="16dp"
                  android:background="@color/
                    purple_200"
                  android:text="@string/start"
```

```
android:textColor="@android:color/
    white"
android:textSize="18sp" />
</LinearLayout>
```

With the widgets aligned vertically on the final look of the welcome screen, the layout orientation is set to vertical. The android: orientation attribute is used with LinearLayout to set the views' direction. If you want its children to be aligned horizontally then you can simply change the orientation value from vertical to horizontal. The first two children of the layout area are the subtitle and input label. The first TextView is set to "Welcome" while the second is set to "Please enter your name" to explain to the user what the input field below expects.

Although we have a Label for the input field, you can also notice a text within the input field on the design view of the layout as shown in Figure 3.7.

This text is called a hint. This is also another way to tell a user what is expected within the field. The AppCompatEditText of the TextInput Layout contains a hint attribute with the value "Name". As soon as a user starts typing the hint disappears and if there is no text in the field the hint is displayed. There is also the start button that takes a user to the next screen after they have entered a name. This next screen is the Quiz Questions for which we will now create the UI.

## 3.3 PREPARING THE QUIZ QUESTIONS ACTIVITY

The user navigates into the Questions Activity from the welcome screen with the first question displayed. Each one shows a country flag with four options to choose the correct country bearing the displayed flag. The options view is a TextView and then a Button to submit each question and move to the next.

The first step to creating this screen is to create a new Empty Activity Project.

Click on file > New > Activity > Empty Activity and enter Quiz QuestionsActivity as the Activity Name.

As usual a layout file is automatically created for you. We will start by updating the activity_quiz_questions layout file with child views to match the expected UI. The first widget is a TextView that displays the question, followed by an ImageView to show a country flag. Figure 3.8

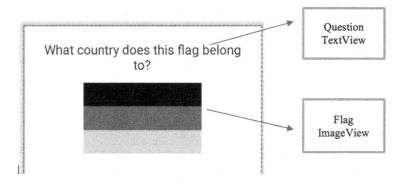

FIGURE 3.8    Question TextView and flag ImagView.

shows the display of the two elements. There are new attributes for the Question TextView Tag: android: gravity and tools: text. With the android: layout_height attribute set to wrap_content, android:gravity = "center" will always align the question to the center horizontally. For the tools:text value, this will only show on the editor during design and not when the app is run. Like other XML attributes such as app and android namespace, the tools namespace has various attributes, all design-time features that do not affect the runtime behavior. Looking at the ImageView, there is also a tools attribute, src. The tools attribute has different xml properties. This is used to only show the content in the development environment and not at runtime. The general idea of the tools attribute is to help the developer visualize what the interface will look like when the data to be displayed is set programmatically through the Activity class.

```
<!-- tools:text only sets a value on a TextView within
   the IDE and not at runtime   -->
<TextView
       app:layout_constraintTop_toTopOf="parent"
       android:id="@+id/tvQuestion"
       android:layout_width="match_parent"
       android:layout_height="wrap_content"
       android:layout_margin="10dp"
       android:gravity="center"
       android:textColor="#363A43"
       android:textSize="22sp"
       tools:text="What country does this flag belong
         to?" />
```

```
<!-- tools:src only sets a value on a View within
  the IDE -->
    <ImageView
      app:layout_constraintTop_toBottomOf="@+id/
        tvQuestion"
      android:id="@+id/ivFlag"
      android:layout_width="wrap_content"
      app:layout_constraintStart_
        toStartOf="parent"
      app:layout_constraintEnd_toEndOf="parent"
      android:layout_height="wrap_content"
      android:layout_marginTop="16dp"
      android:contentDescription="image"
      tools:src="@drawable/ic_flag_of_germany"   />
```

### 3.3.1 ProgressBar and Question Number TextView

To display a set of ten questions on a single screen, we will programmatically show each question individually, starting from the first question and progressing to the last. To track the user's progress, we will utilize a ProgressBar and a question number TextView. In Android, a ProgressBar View visually represents the completion of a task, providing the user with an indication of the remaining progress.

To arrange the ProgressBar and question number TextView side by side, we will employ a LinearLayout with a horizontal orientation. This allows us to align the two elements next to each other on the screen.

```
<LinearLayout
        app:layout_constraintTop_toBottomOf="@
          id/ivFlag"
        android:id="@+id/llProgressDetails"
        android:layout_width="match_parent"
        android:layout_height="wrap_content"
        android:layout_marginTop="16dp"
        android:gravity="center_vertical"
        android:orientation="horizontal">

  <!-- The style attribute changes the progress style from the default circular
to horizontal
      -->
                <ProgressBar
                  android:id="@+id/progressBar"
                  style="?android:attr/progressBar
                    StyleHorizontal"
```

```
android:layout_width="0dp"
android:layout_height="wrap_
    content"
android:layout_weight="1"
android:indeterminate="false"
android:max="10"
android:minHeight="50dp"
android:progress="0" />

<TextView
    android:id="@+id/tv_progress"
    android:layout_width="wrap_
        content"
    android:layout_height="wrap_
        content"
    android:gravity="center"
    android:padding="15dp"
    android:textColorHint="#7A8089"
    android:textSize="14sp"
    tools:text="0/10" />
</LinearLayout>
```

In the above code, the LinearLayout's android:orientation attribute is set to horizontal with a 16dp top margin that adds a space between it and the ImageView. There are two common types of ProgressBar: circular and horizontal. The circular ProgressBar is the default style, while in the code above you can see a style added to the ProgressBar. This attribute ensures that the horizontal ProgressBar is displayed rather than the default circular style. Notice the android:layout_width is set to 0dp. This will make the view take all remaining space available to it after the TextView has been placed. Figure 3.9 shows the final look of the Progress section interface.

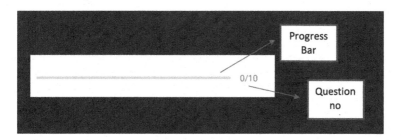

FIGURE 3.9   The Progress user interface.

### 3.3.2 Creating and Using Drawable in Android

Before we can add the widgets for the option views, we need to talk about drawables that will be used for different states the options will be in.

An Android drawable is a resource for customizing Views within a layout or an Activity. They are created or placed in the res folder and set as a background for a widget when needed. The option views will need four different drawable.

- One to be used as the default state of the TextView.

- Another to be used when an option is selected.

- The third with a green color to be set on the correct answer.

- The fourth one with red color is to be set when the wrong answer is selected.

Starting with the default state drawable, open the res folder which can be accessed from the location as seen in Figure 3.10, right click on the Drawable folder, select New, and click on the Drawable Resource File.

On the screen for entering resource details, input "default_option_border_bg" as the File name. Modify the Root element to "shape" while leaving the other fields unchanged, then click "OK". Take note of the change we made to the root element, switching it from "selector" to "shape".

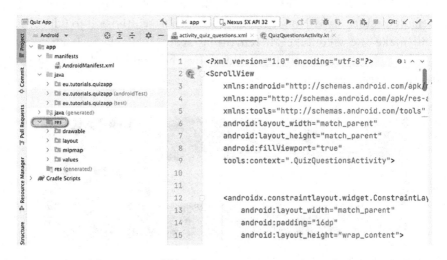

FIGURE 3.10   The resource folder location.

The root element acts like a ViewGroup in a layout but has a distinct purpose. It specifies the type of drawable that can be created and its designated usage. Here is a list of root elements and their use cases.

- **<layer-list></layer-list>**: This is used when creating layer drawable objects that manage an array of other drawable.

- **<selector></selector>**: This is used to define a Statelist drawable object that uses several images to define the same graphic object depending on the object's state. For example, a button can exist in one of several states like pressed, focused, and default.

- **<level-list></level-list>**: A layer list is a drawable resource that can define multiple layers and layers of drawable.

- **<transition></transition>**: This can be used to create a transition drawable that can crossfade between two drawable resources. An example can be an on and off switch mode.

- **</shape>**: Using the shape root element, you can create a drawable of different shapes like rectangles, ovals, or line rings. The drawable can be used as a background with widgets and the shape scales to the size of its container.

Each of the three optional view states will be created using the shape root element. In the default_option_border_bg drawable you have created, replace the shape tag with the following.

```
<shape xmlns:android="http://schemas.android.com/
   apk/res/android"
     android:shape="rectangle">
```

**<!-- The stroke tag modifies the edges of a drawable with the solid tag affecting its body and the corners tag affecting the edges with a 5dp radius**
```
   -->
     <stroke
         android:width="1dp"
         android:color="#E8E8E8" />

     <solid android:color="@android:color/white" />

     <corners android:radius="8dp" />
</shape>
```

FIGURE 3.11   Default option drawable.

The shape tag is the root element with the android: shape set to a rectangle. Within the body of this shape, we have used a stroke tag and set its width to 1dp and color set to "#E8E8E8". The stroke tag is used to modify the surrounding body and the width attribute will increase the border size and color. For changing the background color of a shape drawable, you can use the solid tag and to implement a rounded corner, you use the corners tag with android: radius set to your desired DP. Figure 3.11 shows the final look of the default drawable.

The next drawable is the selected option. Create a new shape drawable resource file and name it "selected_option_border_bg" and replace the shape tag with the following code

```
<shape xmlns:android="http://schemas.android.com/apk/
    res/android"
    android:shape="rectangle">

    <stroke
        android:width="1dp"
        android:color="@color/purple_200" />

    <solid android:color="@android:color/white" />

    <corners android:radius="8dp" />
</shape>
```

FIGURE 3.12  The selected option drawable.

Like the default drawable, the selected drawable looks the same with a difference in the stroke color. Like the string resource file, there is also a color file that allows you to define all colors in the same place. This way the colors are reusable and organized. In the above code, we have used a color available in the color resource file rather than a hard-coded one. To find the color file, go to res > values > colors.

Figure 3.12 shows the result of the selected drawable, it should have a purple border.

### 3.3.3 A Mini Exercise on Drawable

In addition to the two drawable already created, there are two more to create the correct and wrong options. Figure 3.13 shows the final look of the two drawables. Following the steps in creating the first two, you can

FIGURE 3.13  Correct option and wrong option drawables.

complete the others. You should name them "correct_option_border" and "wrong_option_border", respectively. Pay special attention to the solid color of both drawable to achieve the expected result.

## 3.4 ADDING THE OPTIONS VIEW

Buttons are not the only widgets in Android Views that can be clicked. Almost any view can become clickable by using the setOnClickListener method, as it is accessible to all views. In our case, we will be using TextViews to display the options and make them clickable by calling this method. Before doing so, we need to add the elements to the layout file, assigning each one an ID for future reference, and setting a default background drawable to be displayed when a question is initially shown. Below is the XML code snippet for the options views, which should be added below the LinearLayout tag for the progress view in the layout file.

```
<TextView
    app:layout_constraintTop_toBottomOf="@id/
    llProgressDetails"
        android:id="@+id/tvOptionOne"
        android:layout_width="match_parent"
        android:layout_height="wrap_content"
        android:layout_margin="10dp"
        android:background="@drawable/default_
        option_border_bg"
        android:gravity="center"
        android:padding="15dp"
        android:textColor="#7A8089"
        android:textSize="18sp"
        tools:text="Apple" />

<TextView
    app:layout_constraintTop_toBottomOf="@
        id/tvOptionOne"
        android:id="@+id/tvOptionTwo"
        android:layout_width="match_parent"
        android:layout_height="wrap_content"
        android:layout_marginStart="10dp"
        android:layout_marginTop="10dp"
        android:layout_marginEnd="10dp"
        android:layout_marginBottom="10dp"
        android:background="@drawable/
        default_option_border_bg"
        android:gravity="center"
        android:padding="15dp"
```

```
        android:textColor="#7A8089"
        android:textSize="18sp"
        tools:text="Google" />

    <TextView
        app:layout_constraintTop_toBottomOf="@
            id/tvOptionTwo"
        android:id="@+id/tvOptionThree"
        android:layout_width="match_parent"
        android:layout_height="wrap_content"
        android:layout_marginStart="10dp"
        android:layout_marginTop="10dp"
        android:layout_marginEnd="10dp"
        android:layout_marginBottom="10dp"
        android:background="@drawable/
            default_option_border_bg"
        android:gravity="center"
        android:padding="15dp"
        android:textColor="#7A8089"
        android:textSize="18sp"
        tools:text="Android Inc." />

    <TextView
        app:layout_constraintTop_toBottomOf="@
            id/tvOptionThree"
        android:id="@+id/tvOptionFour"
        android:layout_width="match_parent"
        android:layout_height="wrap_content"
        android:layout_marginStart="10dp"
        android:layout_marginTop="10dp"
        android:layout_marginEnd="10dp"
        android:layout_marginBottom="10dp"
        android:background="@drawable/
            default_option_border_bg"
        android:gravity="center"
        android:padding="15dp"
        android:textColor="#7A8089"
        android:textSize="18sp"
        tools:text="Nokia" />
```

Figure 3.14 shows the UI result of the above code. Here is a little exercise for you, looking at each of the TextView the android:textColor has the same color code repeated four times. Extract the code into the color resource file or manually create a color name for the code in the color resource file and replace the value of the textColor for each of the TextView to use the color name you have created.

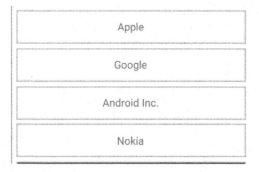

FIGURE 3.14   The Quiz Options TextView.

In Chapter 2, we talked about the string resource file and how crucial it is that you must add this file. A similar process can be used for the color values as they both are kept within the resource file

Below is what each text color value will look like.

```
android:textColor="@color/option_text_color"
```

The final widget to be added to the layout of the questions is a submit button. This button will serve three purposes,

- A submit button after a user has selected an option.

- A continue button to display the next question.

- A finish button to display the result screen.

How can one button be alternated between three tasks at the same time? You will find out soon later in this chapter.

```
<Button
     app:layout_constraintTop_toBottomOf="@id/tvOption
        Four"
     android:id="@+id/btnSubmit"
     android:layout_width="match_parent"
     android:layout_height="wrap_content"
```

```
android:layout_margin="10dp"
android:background="@color/purple_200"
android:text="SUBMIT"
android:textColor="@android:color/white"
android:textSize="18sp"
android:textStyle="bold" />
```

## 3.5 THE RESULT UI

We have gotten to the final screen for this application. Congratulations on getting to this stage, you have learned a lot and is close to completing your second android application. You will create the Result Activity as seen in Figure 3.15, where we will show the score at the end of the quiz. This will

FIGURE 3.15   The final look for the Question UI.

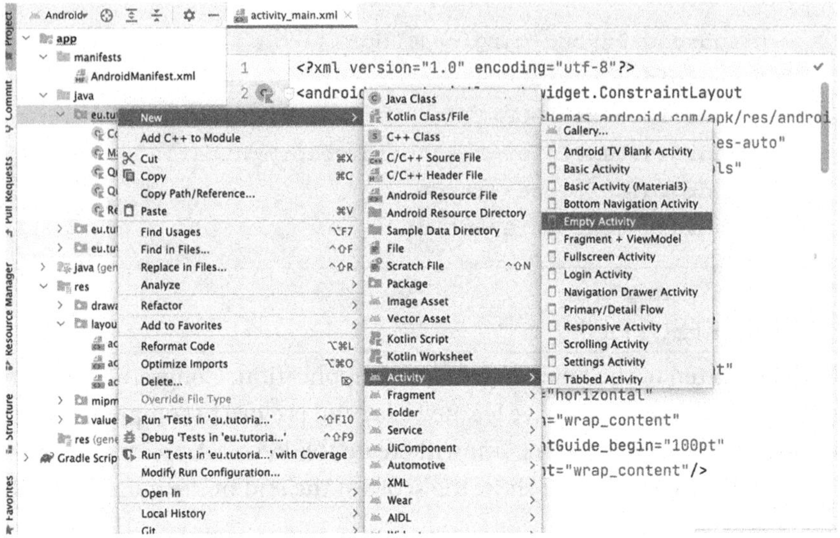

FIGURE 3.16    Creating a new empty activity.

include a message, the user's name entered in the welcome screen, and the total correct answers from the quiz. In addition, there will also be a background image and a trophy image to make the interface look great.

To create this Activity, right click on the project package name and select New>Activity>Empty Activity. Then enter the Activity name and click the Finish button. Figure 3.16 shows these steps to creating a new Activity.

Within the layout of the Result Activity, you will replace the file content with the below code to complete the UI we have mentioned in Section 3.5. You will find that images are part of the code which you should have imported in Section 3.2.1

```
<androidx.constraintlayout.widget.ConstraintLayout
  xmlns:android="http://schemas.android.com/apk/res/
    android"
  xmlns:app="http://schemas.android.com/apk/res-auto"
  xmlns:tools="http://schemas.android.com/tools"
  android:layout_width="match_parent"
  android:layout_height="match_parent"
  android:background="@drawable/ic_bg"
```

```xml
android:padding="20dp"
tools:context=".ResultActivity">

<TextView
  app:layout_constraintTop_toTopOf="parent"
  android:id="@+id/tvResult"
  app:layout_constraintStart_toStartOf="parent"
  app:layout_constraintEnd_toEndOf="parent"
  android:layout_width="wrap_content"
  android:layout_height="wrap_content"
  android:layout_marginTop="25dp"
  android:text="Result"
  android:textColor="@android:color/white"
  android:textSize="25sp"
  android:textStyle="bold" />

<ImageView
  app:layout_constraintTop_toBottomOf="@id/tvResult"
  android:id="@+id/ivTrophy"
  app:layout_constraintStart_toStartOf="parent"
  app:layout_constraintEnd_toEndOf="parent"
  android:layout_width="wrap_content"
  android:layout_height="wrap_content"
  android:contentDescription="trophy"
  android:src="@drawable/ic_trophy" />

<TextView
  app:layout_constraintTop_toBottomOf="@id/ivTrophy"
  android:id="@+id/tvCongratulations"
  app:layout_constraintStart_toStartOf="parent"
  app:layout_constraintEnd_toEndOf="parent"
  android:layout_width="wrap_content"
  android:layout_height="wrap_content"
  android:layout_marginTop="16dp"
  android:text="Hey, Congratulations!"
  android:textColor="@android:color/white"
  android:textSize="25sp"
  android:textStyle="bold"/>
```

```xml
    <TextView
      app:layout_constraintTop_toBottomOf="@id/
        tvCongratulations"
      android:id="@+id/tvName"
      app:layout_constraintStart_toStartOf="parent"
      app:layout_constraintEnd_toEndOf="parent"
      android:layout_width="wrap_content"
      android:layout_height="wrap_content"
      android:layout_marginTop="25dp"
      android:textColor="@android:color/white"
      android:textSize="22sp"
      android:textStyle="bold"
      tools:text="Username" />

    <TextView
      app:layout_constraintTop_toBottomOf="@id/tvName"
      android:id="@+id/tvScore"
      app:layout_constraintStart_toStartOf="parent"
      app:layout_constraintEnd_toEndOf="parent"
      android:layout_width="wrap_content"
      android:layout_height="wrap_content"
      android:layout_marginTop="10dp"
      android:textColor="@android:color/
      secondary_text_dark"
      android:textSize="20sp"
      tools:text="Your Score is 9 out of 10" />

    <androidx.appcompat.widget.AppCompatButton
      app:layout_constraintTop_toBottomOf="@id/tvScore"
      android:id="@+id/btnFinish"
      android:layout_width="match_parent"
      android:layout_height="wrap_content"
      android:layout_marginTop="10dp"
      android:background="@android:color/white"
      android:text="FINISH"
      android:textColor="@color/purple_200"
      android:textSize="18sp"
      android:textStyle="bold" />

</androidx.constraintlayout.widget.ConstraintLayout>
```

FIGURE 3.17  The result screen user interface.

To set the background image, we used the android: background attribute to set the drawable image of your choice as its value as discussed while creating the welcome screen. Other views are constrained to each other with the title TextView placed at the top of the parent, the ImageView displaying the Trophy placed below the title, the congratulatory text placed below the image, the TextView for the total score placed below the congratulatory message, and finally a button to exit the ResultActivity and take the user back to the welcome screen to start again. Figure 3.17 shows the final UI for this screen.

### 3.5.1 Testing the Application

Because no functionality has been added to the Activities, there is nothing to be tested. You can still build and run the app to ensure that the codes are free of errors up until this stage. Also, check each layout design view and confirm that the interfaces look as expected for the three screens.

We will continue with this application in Chapter 4, where we will add implementations to make it functional. Before that, let's look at some other resources that need to be centralized and defined within the value folder.

### 3.5.2 Dimens and Colors Value

As we did for the String resource in Chapter 2, there are also dimension and color values. In Android, dimensions are used to define sizes and distances for various UI elements such as views, layouts, and text. These are usually specified in either density-independent pixels (dp), scale-independent pixels (sp), or points (pt). Pixels (px) are the smallest unit of measurement and are based on the physical pixel density of the screen. Density-independent pixels (dp) are based on the physical density of the screen and are defined relative to a baseline density of 160 dots per inch (dpi). Scale-independent pixels (sp) are like dp but are specifically used for defining text size. They consider the user's preferred text size settings and scale accordingly. It is recommended to use dp for defining sizes and distances for UI elements and sp for defining text size. Using these units helps ensure that your application looks consistent across different screen sizes and densities.

The margins and paddings in the layout are hard-coded and have repetitions. We will extract one for each duplicated value and then replace the other duplicates. To do this, click on any of the values within the file, and a yellow bulb will appear on the right as seen in Figure 3.18. Click on this bulb and an option to extract the value will be displayed. Clicking on it will then show a pop-up to enter the value name.

Make sure to check both value boxes, as seen in Figure 3.19 and then click okay. A dimens folder will be created in the values folder with the files and value names added.

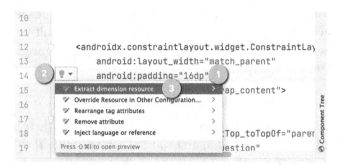

FIGURE 3.18  Extracting a dimension resource.

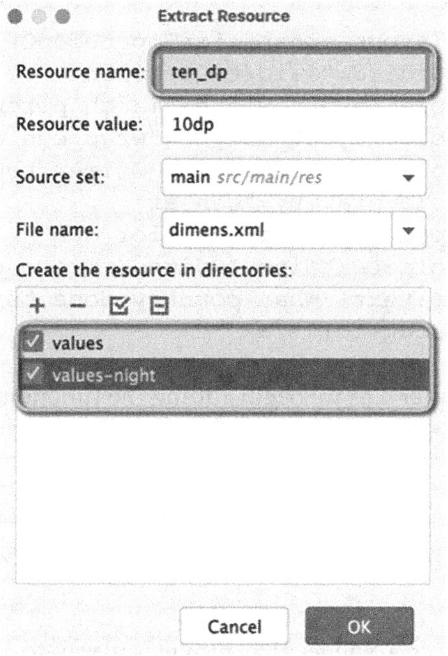

FIGURE 3.19    Enter the value name and check off the two boxes.

You should extract the rest of the dimensions and hard-coded colors and replace the hard-coded values with the respective dimension names. The dimens file should contain the various name as seen in Figure 3.20. Here is the question TextView containing the extracted resources.

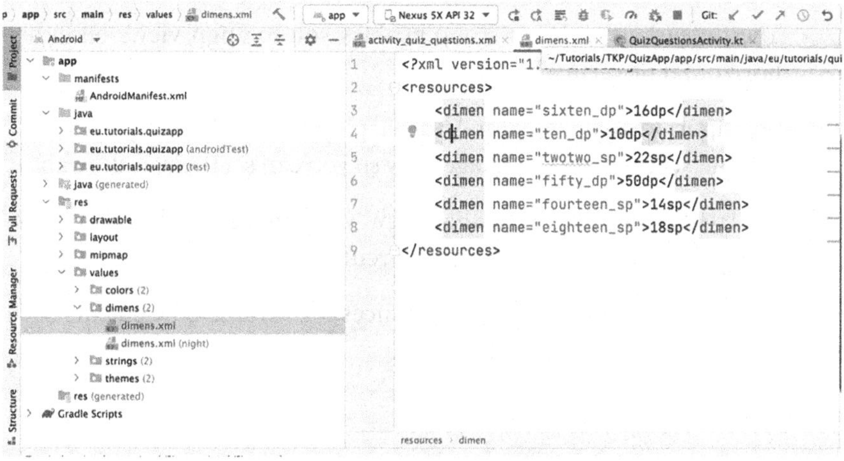

FIGURE 3.20    The values created within the dimens file.

```
<TextView
    app:layout_constraintTop_toTopOf="parent"
    android:id="@+id/tvQuestion"
    android:layout_width="match_parent"
    android:layout_height="wrap_content"
    android:layout_margin="@dimen/ten_dp"
    android:gravity="center"
    android:textColor="@color/ash"
    android:textSize="@dimen/twotwo_sp"
    tools:text="What country does this flag
        belong to?" />
```

See you in Chapter 4 as we begin adding the functionalities for the UIs we have created here.

## 3.6 SUMMARY

- The constraint Guideline helps you place the widget in a fixed position.

- A CardView is a widget that provides a way to show information on Android in a card-like manner with easy modifications to the borders.

- A Drawable resource file can be used to customize the background of both Views and ViewGroup.

- Creating drawables requires root tags like shapes, layerlists, selectors, transitions, and more.

- The LinearLayout ViewGroup enables you to align views on either horizontal or vertical sides.

- To import images into your Android project, you can use the resource tab and set them on the image view so you can set them as drawables.

- With the Android ProgressBar View, you can display the completion of a task to your user, either as a circular or horizontal view.

- Dimensions define sizes and distances for various UI elements such as views, layouts, and text.

# CHAPTER 4

# Intents in Android

## *Project 2 – Quiz App – Part 2*

## 4.1 INTRODUCTION TO INTENTS

Before now, you used the default Intent category while launching the application's entry point. This is with the help of an Intent filter which is an expression of the app's manifest file that specifies the type of Intent a component would like to receive. Every Android application has an Android Manifest added by default when creating a new project. This file is essential in determining some features your application can provide. It contains information about the applications component, which are an Android application's building blocks, including Activity, Services, Broadcast Receivers, and Content Providers. To make the application aware of these components before they are used, they must be registered within the manifest file, or an error will occur.

With the intent filter, you can mention the Activity you want to be launched first at the start of your application. This is done by setting the launcher category as a value to the android: name attribute for the intent filter. In the same way, you can declare an Activity as the launcher Activity; you can also make it available to an implicit intent (we will discuss this in detail shortly). Let us look at the current state of the manifest in the Quiz project.

DOI: 10.1201/9781032622538-4

```xml
<?xml version="1.0" encoding="utf-8"?>
<manifest xmlns:android="http://schemas.android.
  com/apk/res/android"
    package="eu.tutorials.quizapp">

    <application
        android:allowBackup="true"
        android:icon="@mipmap/ic_launcher"
        android:label="@string/app_name"
        android:roundIcon="@mipmap/ic_launcher_
          round"
        android:supportsRtl="true"
        android:theme="@style/Theme.QuizApp">
        <activity
            android:name=".ResultActivity"
            android:exported="false" />
        <activity
            android:name=".QuizQuestionsActivity"
            android:exported="false" />
        <activity
            android:name=".MainActivity"
            android:exported="true"
            android:theme="@style/NoActionBar">
```

**<!-- The intent filter is used to declare the MainActivity as the launcher Activity using the android:name attribute .**
-->

```xml
            <intent-filter>
                <action android:name="android. Intent.
                  action.MAIN" />

                <category android:name="android.
                  Intent.category.LAUNCHER" />
            </intent-filter>
        </activity>
    </application>

</manifest>
```

In the file above, you will see the three Activities we created in Chapter 3 automatically registered within the manifest file and the MainActivity set as the launcher Activity. If you want to launch a different Activity first, you can move the intent filter into the desired Activity tag within the manifest file. Generally, intents are used to start an Android component, and there are two types of intents, explicit and implicit.

### 4.1.1 Implicit Intent

An implicit intent is a type that does not name a specific component to be started but specifies an action and provides some data to perform the action. For example, within your application, you can have a button to open a link to a website. There can be different browser applications available on your device that can open this—the kind of intent you will set up for this is an implicit intent specifying the action and the link to the website. Here is an example code.

```
val intent = Intent()
intent.action = Intent.ACTION_VIEW
intent.addCategory(Intent.CATEGORY_BROWSABLE)
intent.data = Uri.parse("http://www.google.com")
startActivity(intent)
```

The code indicates that the action is to view content, with a category set to browsable and then the data set to a URL before the Activity is started. When you click on a button to initiate the above code, all browser applications will pop up for you to pick from. Another example is when you are using an app that includes a share button; various apps on your device have made their Activities available to receive specific implicit actions with the help of an intent filter in the following way.

```
<!-- The "send" action value within the intent
    filter enables the activity to receive implicit
    intents within the app's messaging category. The
    "mimeType" is used to specify the type of files
    that can be shared. -->

<intent-filter>
            <action android:name="android.
              Intent.action.SEND" />
            <category android:name="android.
              Intent.category.APP_MESSAGING"/>
            <data android:mimeType="audio/*" />
            <data android:mimeType="image/*" />
            <data android:mimeType="video/*" />
        </intent-filter>
```

When you add an intent filter with a send action with an APP_ MESSAGING category and a certain mime type to an Activity within your application and an action to share such file is initiated on a device with your application installed, it will be listed as a launch suggestion. Here is a code that can launch a share action.

```
val shareIntent = Intent(Intent.ACTION _ SEND)
shareIntent.type = "text/plain"
shareIntent.putExtra(Intent.EXTRA_SUBJECT, "Click
    to subscribe")
val app_url = " https://www.youtube.com/channel"
shareIntent.putExtra(Intent.EXTRA_TEXT, app_url)
startActivity(Intent.createChooser(shareIntent,
    "Share via"))
```

### 4.1.2 Explicit Intent

An explicit intent specifies the component to start using its fully qualified name. For example, you can open an Activity from another Activity. Using this type of Intent, you can also pass information from one Activity to another. Using the navigation to be implemented in the quiz app, for example, a username will be entered in the welcome screen, which will be required later for displaying the user result on the Result Screen. For the username to get to the result screen, we will use Intent to pass the value from the welcome screen to the quiz questions screen and then to the Result screen because that is the step the navigation will take.

Depending on the data type, different methods are available to the intent object for passing specific information. Each one accepts two parameters, a key and a value, where any key used for sending the data is required for reading the data from the receiving Activity.

## 4.2 STARTING THE QUIZ QUESTIONS ACTIVITY

Opening the Quiz Questions Activity is an example of Explicit Intent. You will have to specify the class name of the Activity and, in turn, get to send any data that can be received from it.

With some idea of how the Intent works, we will write a few codes in the MainActivity to accept the name entered in the input field, carry this name along using Intent, and then start the QuizQuestionActivity when the start button is clicked.

Open MainActivity.kt and create a global binding variable for referencing the views in the activity_main.xml. Remember that this is our welcome screen, so we will use both names interchangeably when referring to the Welcome page.

```
private val binding by lazy {
      ActivityMainBinding.inflate(layoutInflater)
   }
```

The binding variable is created at the top of the class to make it accessible anywhere. If you have not already enabled ViewBinding in the app module build.gradle file, you will be unable to find the binding class, which is ActivityMainBinding. You can reference the necessary step for doing that as mentioned in Section 2.3.1 of Chapter 2.

Within the onCreate method, add the following code.

```
val buttonStart = binding.btnStart
      val nameTxt = binding.etName

      buttonStart.setOnClickListener {
          if (nameTxt.text.toString().
            isEmpty()) {
              Toast.makeText(this, "Please Enter
                Your Name", Toast.LENGTH_SHORT).
                show()
          } else {
              val intent = Intent(this@Main
                Activity, QuizQuestionsActivity:
                :class.java)

              intent.putExtra(Constants.USER_
                NAME, nameTxt.text.toString())
              startActivity(intent)
              finish()
          }
      }
```

Before writing the above code, make sure to update the setContentView argument's value to have the root from the binding variable. Here is what is happening within the code. Using the binding variable, we have referenced the id for the start button and name input field and assigned them to variables buttonStart and nameTxt, respectively. To make the button clickable, you call setOnclickListener on the start button and within its block, check that the input field is not empty before creating an intent that will start the QuizQuestionActivity.

When the start button is clicked, and the input field is empty, show a Toast telling the user to enter their name. How do you know that the field is empty? Using the nameTxt variable we get the value entered in the field, convert it to a string and check if it is empty by calling isEmpty() from the Kotlin standard library. Also, when initializing the Intent, we have explicitly specified it to open QuizQuestionActivity class, which is what Explicit Intent is all about.

A message is shown when the input field is empty using the "Toast" class. This class allows a short-time notification to a user without disrupting the user interaction with the UI. The time duration, although short, can be of two values.

```
"Toast.LENGTH_SHORT" and "Toast.LENGTH_LONG"
```

The first has a shorter time duration than the second.

Moving forward to what happens when a user enters a name and clicks the start button, the Intent class is called with two arguments passed into it. The first argument is the Context that tells the Android system the current environment where the Intent is created or started from, and in this case, the MainActivity, while the second parameter is the Activity that will be started, which is the QuizQuestionActivity. Let's look at the Context in a more detailed aspect.

### 4.2.1 Context

In Android, a Context is an object that provides access to the system resources and services of the Android framework. It represents the current state of the application or the environment it is running. It is an abstract class and can be instantiated by the basic application components:

- **Activity:** Context for an Activity is a user interface component that occupies the screen.

- **Service:** Context for a service is a background component that performs long-running operations.

- **Application:** Context for an application, which represents the entire application and is available for the entire lifetime of the application.

- **Broadcast Receiver:** Context for a broadcast receiver, a component that responds to system-wide broadcast announcements.

Context provides access to many system services, such as resources, preferences, notifications, content providers, location services, and more. It is used to launch Activities, start services, send broadcasts, and access files and databases.

One of its key features is its ability to maintain a reference to the application's resources, such as images, strings, and layouts. This enables the application to easily access these resources, regardless of where the code executes. Context is a fundamental component of the Android framework and is used throughout the development of Android applications. Understanding how Context works and how to use it correctly to build robust and efficient Android applications is important.

Returning to the Intent that starts the QuestionsActivity in Section 4.4, the data is passed and sent to the next screen before this Intent starts. This is accomplished using the putExtra() method. This method passes the username to the QuizQuestionActivity and takes the two arguments, a key and a value. A key is a string to identify the value for each Activity launched with that Intent. In this case, we use the string "user_name" as the key and pass the value from the input field. We'll use this key later to get the name in the QuizQuestionActivity.

After the data is passed into the Intent, we are ready to start the Activity using the startActivity(Intent) method with the Intent passed in as the argument. You should see a finish() method called at the end of the else block. This method ensures that the welcome screen is destroyed when the user leaves the screen. This is to avoid taking the user back to the welcome screen when the back button is pressed from the quiz question screen since we do not expect the user to go back to the welcome screen at that point but rather exit the app.

### 4.2.2 Testing the Start Button

Now that we have the start button setup, you should run the application, click the start button, and watch how the Toast is displayed as seen in Figure 4.1. You can modify the different Toast durations to see how long it stays on the screen.

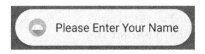

FIGURE 4.1 Toast display when the name field is empty.

After verifying the behavior when the input field is empty, enter a name into the field and click on the "Start" button to proceed with the user interaction.

## 4.3 PREPARING THE QUESTIONS AND OPTIONS

Users should see the first question displayed with its options when they navigate the quiz questions screen. To prepare the question, we need a custom type to group them with the question, flag, options, and the answer as a type. Just as there are basic data types, you can create a class that helps you keep related states and information together for easy data management.

This is the object-oriented feature of Kotlin, where you can divide complex problems into smaller ones by creating an object. Each question contains the same properties, including an image, question, and options but only with different values. They also have the same behavior in that you can select an answer, and there can be right or wrong answers. You will require a Kotlin class to group each question with its properties.

### 4.3.1 Defining a Data Class

Kotlin has made it easy to prepare a class with the required behaviors or properties. In a class, you will need to have a setter and a getter where the first is used to write a value to an object, and the latter is used to read to access the same value. With Kotlin data class, you can create a custom type with properties your use case requires. Let's look at a sample for the Quiz Question class.

Create a new Kotlin class following the directives in the below image. Right-click on the project package and select New > Kotlin Class/File

By selecting the "Data Class" option, as shown in Figure 4.2, the class will be automatically generated with the "data" keyword, which includes all the necessary attributes and methods for data handling.

```
data class Question(
  val id:Int,
  val question:String,
  val image:Int,
  val optionOne:String,
  val optionTwo:String,
  val optionThree:String,
  val optionFour:String,
  val correctAnswer:Int
)
```

FIGURE 4.2   Creating a Kotlin Data class

Then add its properties within the open and closed parenthesis. The above is the complete Question class with an id of type Int, which can be used to identify each question, a question of type String to store the text for each question, and an image of type Int to keep the country flag. Drawable images are Int by default, so we store the image property as one.

Next, we have variables for the four options to hold the option to each question, and finally, we need to specify the correct answer among the four options. We use an Int, in this case, to represent the number to the option that has the correct answer.

With the data class created, we can now create an object of the class for each question to be displayed on the Quiz Question screen.

### 4.3.2  Constants and Dummy Questions

Creating data values that will never change in a separate class is a good programming practice. This is known as constants; the quiz questions will be dummy data that will always remain the same. So, we will create the ten questions where each will be an object of the Question class with a value to each class property. We will use the "object" keyword to create the Constant class for direct access to each question without the need to initialize the class, just like we will do for each Question. The "object" keyword is used in place of the "class" keyword for this purpose. You can create an object just like other Kotlin classes but this time, you will have to select object from the displayed options just like in Figure 4.3.

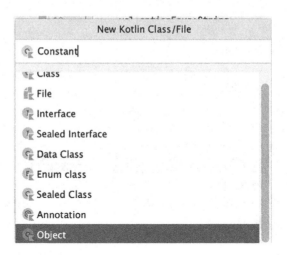

FIGURE 4.3   Creating a Kotlin Object class.

Double-click the Object to get the class created. In the class, we create a function to return a list of questions. This function creates another list to add and keep hold of each question. Each question is an instance of the Question class and is provided with a value for every property. From id, question, country flag, four options, and an integer to represent which of the option is the correct answer.

```kotlin
object Constant {
val questions = listOf(
        Question(
            1, "What country does this flag belong
              to?",
            R.drawable.ic_flag_of_argentina,
            "Argentina", "Australia",
            "Armenia", "Austria", 1
    ), Question(
            2, "What country does this flag belong
              to?",
            R.drawable.ic_flag_of_australia,
            "Angola", "Austria",
            "Australia", "Armenia", 3
    ),
        Question(
            3, "What country does this flag belong
              to?",
```

```
    R.drawable.ic_flag_of_brazil,
    "Belarus", "Belize",
    "Brunei", "Brazil", 4
), Question(
    4, "What country does this flag belong
        to?",
    R.drawable.ic_flag_of_belgium,
    "Bahamas", "Belgium",
    "Barbados", "Belize", 2
),
Question(
    5, "What country does this flag belong
        to?",
    R.drawable.ic_flag_of_fiji,
    "Gabon", "France",
    "Fiji", "Finland", 3
),
Question(
    6, "What country does this flag belong
        to?",
    R.drawable.ic_flag_of_germany,
    "Germany", "Georgia",
    "Greece", "none of these", 1
),
Question(
    7, "What country does this flag belong
        to?",
    R.drawable.ic_flag_of_denmark,
    "Dominica", "Egypt",
    "Denmark", "Ethiopia", 3
),
Question(
    8, "What country does this flag belong
        to?",
    R.drawable.ic_flag_of_india,
    "Ireland", "Iran",
    "Hungary", "India", 4
),
Question(
    9, "What country does this flag belong
        to?",
    R.drawable.ic_flag_of_new_zealand,
    "Australia", "New Zealand",
```

```
                 "Tuvalu", "United States of America", 2
            ),
            Question(
                10, "What country does this flag
                  belong to?",
                R.drawable.ic_flag_of_kuwait,
                "Kuwait", "Jordan",
                "Sudan", "Palestine", 1
            )
        )
```

Take a close look at the options available to each question, and the number provided as the answer is the position of the right country name that owns the flag. For question 1, "Argentina" is the right answer and is the first option out of the four, so the number is used. As the correctAnswer is one (1), looking at the second question, you will notice the same style. The correct answer is Australia, the third (3) among the four options in question two (2), with 2 as the correct answer value. The same applies to the rest of the questions.

After each question is created, it gets added to the questions list, a type of list. An array list is a collection of the same type of data. You can perform various operations using a list that includes adding items. In this case, we add each question after it is created, and after the last question is added, we return the list as the result of the function, which also expects the output of the type of List.

### 4.3.3 MINI Exercise for the QuizQuestionActivity

Now that the questions are ready, we have to display them on the QuizQuestionActivity. In this Activity, we will need to connect the binding layout for this Activity to it for referencing the views from its layout. Try to set up the binding for the QuizQuestionActivity on your own by completing the following steps.

- Create the binding variable for ActivityQuestionQuiz.

- Update setContentView() in its onCreate to connect the layout using the binding variable created above.

If you need help, check out the code on GitHub: https://github.com/tutorialseu/TheQuizApp and compare it to what you have.

## 4.4 DISPLAYING THE QUESTIONS AND OPTIONS ON THE SCREEN

We will first set up the layout widgets to display the questions on the screen. This section assumes you have already connected the binding layout to the Activity, and we will prepare the views by first declaring each one globally within the Activity.

Since there will be different methods to perform specific functions that include setQuestion to set and display each question, defaultOptionsView to prepare and display options, selectedOption that will set the selected option in its default state, and finally, answerView to prepare the options view, and set the appropriate color when selected, the views need to be accessible to every function to allow for synced performance. Also, other variables to keep track of other important values are created like the current position to be used to get the current question, questionsList for keeping track of the complete question, correctAnswers for calculating the number of correct answers, username to retrieve the name entered by the user in the welcome screen and selectedOptionPosition for keeping track of the selected option. Below are the variables.

```
private var progressBar: ProgressBar?=null
private var tvProgress: TextView? = null
private var tvQuestion: TextView? = null
private var ivFlag: ImageView? = null
private var tvOptionOne: TextView? = null
private var tvOptionTwo: TextView? = null
private var tvOptionThree: TextView? = null
private var tvOptionFour: TextView? = null
private var buttonSubmit: Button? = null

private var currentPosition:Int = 0
private val questionsList:ArrayList<Question>
  = arrayListOf()
private var correctAnswers:Int = 0
private var userName:String   = ""
private var selectedOptionPosition:Int = 0
```

In the onCreate method, each view is initialized and assigned to one of the layout widgets, and the questions from the Constants class are added to questionsList.

```
progressBar = binding.progressBar
tvProgress = binding.tvProgress
tvQuestion = binding.tvQuestion
```

```
ivFlag = binding.ivFlag
tvOptionOne = binding.tvOptionOne
tvOptionTwo = binding.tvOptionTwo
tvOptionThree = binding.tvOptionThree
tvOptionFour = binding.tvOptionFour
buttonSubmit = binding.btnSubmit
questionsList.addAll(Constants.
  getQuestions())
```

## 4.4.1 Setting up the Questions

Since the questions comprise four options, we must first prepare the default options style, which will be called every time the user navigates to a new question. A list of the TextView is created, and the four variables created for the options are added to it.

```
private fun defaultOptionsView() {
val options = listOf(
        tvOptionOne,
        tvOptionTwo,
        tvOptionThree,
        tvOptionFour
        )
        for (option in options) {
            option.setTextColor(Color.
              parseColor("#7A8089"))
            option.typeface = Typeface.DEFAULT
            option.background = ContextCompat.
              getDrawable(
                this@QuizQuestionsActivity,
                R.drawable.default_option_border_bg
            )
        }
    }
```

The defaultOptionsView method prepares the default look of the options. The textColor, typeface, and background are always styled to look the same. Notice that the default option drawable, already created in this chapter's earlier sections, is used as the background.

With the already prepared within the onCreate method, each question on the list will be displayed one at a time, and the defaultOptionsView method will be called every time. Since lists are accessed using the index, starting from zero, the index for the first item in the list. The properties of the questions can now be accessed and displayed for each.

In the case of managing the submit button, as soon as the last question is submitted, the submit button is changed to the finish button. The progress bar progress is updated using the value from the current position, indicating how many questions have been answered. This also goes with the TextView that shows the question number, but this time current position increased by one to indicate the correct question since the position starts from zero, but numbering starts from one.

```
private fun setQuestion() {

        val question:Question = questionsList[curr
          entPosition]
        defaultOptionsView()
        if (currentPosition == questionsList.size){
            buttonSubmit?.text = "FINISH"
        } else {
            buttonSubmit?.text = "SUBMIT"
        }

        progressBar?.progress = currentPosition
        val no = currentPosition + 1
    tvProgress?.text = resources.getString(R.string.
      progress_Text,no,progressBar?.max)

        tvQuestion?.text = question.question
        ivFlag?.setImageResource(question.image)
        tvOptionOne?.text = question.optionOne
        tvOptionTwo?.text = question.optionTwo
        tvOptionThree?.text = question.optionThree
        tvOptionFour?.text = question.optionFour
    }
```

In the onCreateMethod, setQuestion is called to initialize each question and view once the Activity is created. Ensure the method is placed below the questions list so that the questions are added and ready before each question is accessed with it.

```
override fun onCreate(savedInstanceState: Bundle?) {
        super.onCreate(savedInstanceState)
        setContentView(binding.root)
        questionsList.addAll(Constants.
          getQuestions())
```

**// A call to the setQuestion method within the onCreate**
```
        setQuestion()
    }
```

## 4.4.2 Choosing the Right or Wrong Answer

There are different states to be considered when answering each question. The first is the selected option, where the style for the chosen option is set to the selected option border, and the defaultOptionsView method is also called. Without the defaultOptionsView method, if a user selects a different option, both will become selected, but the call to "defaultOptionsView" ensures that the previously selected gets deselected. Tracking the number for the selected option is also important. This will be checked against the numbers assigned to each option to decide the correct answer.

```
    private fun selectedOptionView(tv: TextView,
        selectedOptionNum: Int) {

        defaultOptionsView()

        selectedOptionPosition = selectedOptionNum

        tv.setTextColor(
            Color.parseColor("#363A43")
        )
        tv.setTypeface(tv.typeface, Typeface.BOLD)
        tv.background = ContextCompat.getDrawable(
            this@QuizQuestionsActivity,
            R.drawable.selected_option_border_bg
        )
    }
```

The second stage for deciding the right or wrong answer is preparing the option views for changing its background when the submit button is clicked, depending on whether the selected answer is right or wrong. If the selected answer is correct, the background is set to the correct background border, or it is set to the wrong background border. Otherwise, the correct option is set to the correct option background. The rest of the options' background remains the default option drawable.

```
    private fun answerView(answer: Int, drawableView:
        Int) {

        /*
```

**This statement sets a Green or Red background to the option TextView if the answer is right or wrong respectively**

```
*/
            when (answer) {

                1 -> {
                    tvOptionOne?.background =
                      ContextCompat.getDrawable(
                        this@QuizQuestionsActivity,
                        drawableView
                    )
                }
                2 -> {
                    tvOptionTwo?.background = Context
                      Compat.getDrawable(
                        this@QuizQuestionsActivity,
                        drawableView
                    )
                }
                3 -> {
                    tvOptionThree?.background =
                      ContextCompat.getDrawable(
                        this@QuizQuestionsActivity,
                        drawableView
                    )
                }
                4 -> {
                    tvOptionFour?.background = Context
                      Compat.getDrawable(
                        this@QuizQuestionsActivity,
                        drawableView
                    )
                }
            }
        }
```

In the above code, depending on the answer value, the background of the TextView gets changed to the right drawable. The function declares a parameter for this drawable and will be set within the onclick function for the views provided later within the click function.

## 4.4.3 Adding Click Listeners to the Views

You should be familiar with adding click listeners to a view. This time, we will be adding them using an alternative approach. Usually, to add

actions to a view, you call setOnClickListener on it and implement the
process within its block. This time, the implementation will be done on
the Activity directly because over five views require a listener. To keep the
code cleaner, shorter, and properly managed, one onClick method will be
used for all implementations to avoid code repetition.

```
/*

    Implement a ClickListener on the Activity
    and ensure the required views are listening to the click.

*/
    class QuizQuestionsActivity : AppCompatActivity(),
      View.OnClickListener {

      override fun onCreate(savedInstanceState: Bundle?) {
            super.onCreate(savedInstanceState)
            setContentView(binding.root)
    tvOptionOne?.setOnClickListener(this)
            tvOptionTwo?.setOnClickListener(this)
            tvOptionThree?.setOnClickListener(this)
            tvOptionFour?.setOnClickListener(this)
            buttonSubmit?.setOnClickListener (this)
      }


      override fun onClick(view: View) {
          }
      }
```

Looking at the above code, View.OnClickListener is implemented on the
Activity. All widgets are a subclass of the View class, which is why the
TextView and Button can as well inherit from it. Implementing the onClick-
Listener using the View will work on all widgets needing an action within that
Activity. You will have to activate this listener on each view by calling setOn-
ClickListener within the onCreate and passing this within its parenthesis.

Once View.OnClickListener is implemented, and you will be required to
override onClick method where each Views action will be processed. This
is where the control flow statement will become very useful for setting the
action for each view in one method. Starting with the option TextViews,
the option number is collected and kept track of when each one is clicked.
The style is set to selected option border drawable, which has already been
implemented within the selectedOptionView method.

Now you should carefully pay attention to how the submit button works. This button performs three different actions: submit an answer, go to the next question, and finish the quiz after the last question is answered. If the current index is not the last index, it is increased by one, and clicking the submit button changes to go to the next question else the quiz is finished and the ResultActivity is opened. When the question is submitted, the answerView is called which checks the selected option and changes the background of the option views to the required state, that is to show the right answer, the wrong answer, and the default drawable for the nonselected ones.

```
/*
When any Option TextView is selected, it is checked across the correct
answer and the right background is determined depending on if it
is right or wrong using the selectedOptionView method where the
implementations have been created.
*/
override fun onClick(view: View) {
    when(view.id){
        tvOptionOne?.id -> {
          tvOptionOne?.let {
            selectedOptionView(it, 1)
          }
        }

        tvOptionTwo?.id->{
          tvOptionTwo?.let {
            selectedOptionView(it,2)
          }
        }

        tvOptionThree?.id ->{
          tvOptionThree?.let {
            selectedOptionView(it,3)
          }
        }

        tvOptionFour?.id ->{
          tvOptionFour?.let {
            selectedOptionView(it,4)
          }
        }
```

```
/*
```
**When the submit button is clicked, the background for the answer Views and the text is changed to next if there are questions left or changed to finish if it is the last question. If the text is set to finish, clicking it takes the user to the Result Activity.**
```
*/
        buttonSubmit?.id->{

          if (selectedOptionPosition == 0) {

              currentPosition++

              when {

                currentPosition <= questionsList.size -
                  1  -> {

                   setQuestion()
                 }
                 else -> {
                  val intent =
                  Intent(this@QuizQuestionsActivity,
                    ResultActivity::class.java)
                  intent.putExtra(Constants.USER_NAME,
                    userName)
                  intent.putExtra(Constants.CORRECT_
                    ANSWERS, correctAnswers)
                  intent.putExtra(Constants.TOTAL_
                    QUESTIONS, questionsList.size)
                  startActivity(intent)
                  finish()
                }
              }
        } else {
           val question = questionsList[current
             Position]

           if (question.correctAnswer != selected
             OptionPosition) {
              answerView(selectedOptionPosition,
                 R.drawable.wrong_option_border_bg)
           }else{
              correctAnswers++
           }
```

```
answerView(question.correctAnswer,
  R.drawable.correct_option_border_bg)

if (currentPosition == questionsList.
  size-1) {
    buttonSubmit?.text = "FINISH"
} else {
    buttonSubmit?.text = "GO TO NEXT
      QUESTION"
}

selectedOptionPosition = 0
    }
  }
 }
}
```

**Note: Before adding the condition to open the ResultActivity when finish is clicked, ensure to have created an empty Activity and name it ResultActivity.**

Here is what happens when clicking finish at the end of the questions. The username received from the Welcome Activity, the correct answers, and the total questions is passed using the Intent into the ResultActivity. Because putExtra method passing carrying the data requires a constant key for writing and reading the values from the Intent, Strings are created within the Constants class for direct access to the keys when required from any part of the project without requiring initialization. While declaring the ResultActivity as the intent class, we have used the :: operator to get a reference to the class object, and the .java property is used to get the Java class object for the Kotlin class. In Kotlin, ":::" is used to create a reference to a function or property. This is called a member reference or method reference, depending on what it refers to. This can be useful when passing functions as arguments or storing them as variables. Additionally, just in this case, it can also be used to reference a class or a constructor. Now, let's test the applications.

## 4.4.4 Testing the QuizQuestionActivity

Let's see the result of the implementations added to the Question screen. Run the application, enter a name, start the quiz, and start answering the questions. Users can answer each question at this stage and see the right and wrong answers. You will see the difference between each option's state and the actions of the submit button when it is on submit, go to the next question, or finish state.

## 4.5 ADDING FUNCTIONALITY TO THE RESULTACTIVITY

We have arrived at the final screen for this application. Congratulations on getting to this stage. You have learned a lot and are close to completing your second Android application. All the data displayed on this screen will be received from the Intent. The Intent that opened this Activity carried with it the username, the number of correct answers, and the total number of questions. Once the Activity is created, the values are retrieved using specific methods depending on the value type. The username is a String, so we use the getStringExtra method to retrieve its value by passing the key as an argument into the method. This also applies to the number of correct answers and the total number of questions, but his time, we use the getIntExtra method by passing in the key to each value respectively. These keys have been created in the Constants class and were used to write the value into the Intent and can only be used to read them because the Intent will pair them to fetch the correct data.

```kotlin
class ResultActivity : AppCompatActivity() {
  private val binding by lazy {
     ActivityResultBinding.inflate(layoutInflater)
  }
  override fun onCreate(savedInstanceState: Bundle?) {
    super.onCreate(savedInstanceState)
    setContentView(binding.root)

    val tvName: TextView = binding.tvName
    val tvScore: TextView = binding.tvScore
    val btnFinish: Button = binding.btnFinish

/*
Retrieve the username, no of questions, and correct answer from the Intent
using their Key
then start the ResultActivity using the Intent.
*/
    val userName = intent.getStringExtra(Constants.
      USER_NAME)
```

```
tvName.text = userName

val totalQuestions = intent.getIntExtra
  (Constants.TOTAL_QUESTIONS, 0)
val correctAnswers = intent.getIntExtra
  (Constants.CORRECT_ANSWERS, 0)

tvScore.text = resources.getString(R.string.
  score, correctAnswers, totalQuestions)

btnFinish.setOnClickListener {

startActivity(Intent(this@ResultActivity,
  MainActivity::class.java))
        }
    }
  }
```

Within the onCreate, the widgets for displaying each value are referenced from its layout. Each value is retrieved using the Intent and set to the TextViews. Using the String resource file makes it easier to display the values, including an Int, which cannot directly be set on a TextView without being converted to a String. If you need to refresh your memory on formatting String and creating placeholders in a resource file, check out Section 1.6 of Chapter 1. You can also look at the complete code on GitHub to see what the String resource file for this project looks like.

Looking at the implementation for the finish button, the user is taken to the welcome screen to begin the process again when it gets clicked.

### 4.5.1 Testing the App

You can rerun and test the app, starting from the first screen. You should be able to enter a name, navigate to the question screen, and take the quiz. And when you get to the last number, the button takes you into the Result Activity to see the number for correct answers. Finally, you can click Finish to exit the Result screen and navigate back to the beginning of the application. Figure 4.4 shows the testing process.

In Chapter 5, we will explore the powerful features of Android Fragments and ViewPager2. We will learn how to create swipeable views, allowing users to navigate through different screens using one fragment seamlessly.

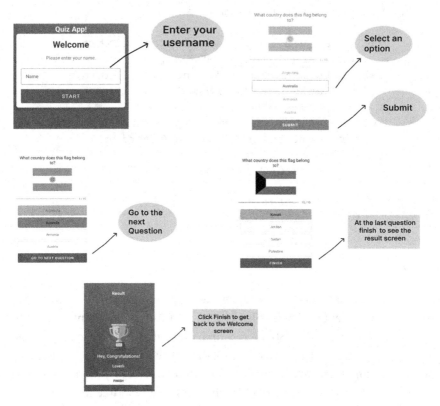

FIGURE 4.4   Testing the application.

## 4.6 SUMMARY

- The Android Intent enables various Android components to communicate with each other.

- You can pass data between Activities using an Intent and there are specific methods available for retrieving sent data depending on its type.

- There are two types of Intent: Explicit and Implicit.

    1. Explicit Intents are used to declare intentions to perform an action using a specific component.

    2. Implicit Intents only declare their intention to perform an action but allow the system to suggest applications that can complete such actions.

- With putExtra method, you can save data to an Explicit Intent using the key-value pair technique.

- To show the progress of a process just like in the quiz, how many questions are left to answer, you can use a <ProgressBar>.

- startActivity is the method used to open another Activity through an Intent.

- You can save images in the Drawable folder within the res folder of the project directory.

# CHAPTER 5

# Android Fragments and ViewPager2

## 5.1 IMAGE SLIDER APP OVERVIEW

There are different cases in an application where you will need to create a swipeable screen. It could be for an onboarding page to introduce several sections within your application or an e-commerce app to display the different sides of an item. Android has a widget called a ViewPager2 which can be used to enable swiping through pages of data on the screen. This widget is typically used in conjunction with a Fragment or a RecyclerView to provide the pages to be displayed. You will learn about using a ViewPager2 and a Fragment in this chapter while we discuss RecyclerView in Chapter 6.

An Image Slider application is a popular way to scroll through several images mainly in a horizontal direction. The user interface will have two buttons, one will display the next image and the other will show a previous one. It will also provide an auto-play feature that will automatically scroll through the images at a set interval with indicators to let you know the current position of the image you are viewing. By the end of this chapter, you will be able to create swipeable pages for your Android screen similar to Figure 5.1.

## 5.2 ANDROID VIEWPAGER AND VIEWPAGER2 EXPLAINED

Android ViewPager is the first widget the Android library provides for creating swipeable views in Android. An updated version of it, the ViewPager2 was created with improved performance and more flexibility

DOI: 10.1201/9781032622538-5

FIGURE 5.1    The image slider app.

with fragments, and an easy integration with RecyclerView. This widget provides a dynamic display for a scrollable list of data. These improvements include the ability to scroll horizontally or vertically with support for the right to left layouts. The Right to Left layout is used for languages read right to left such as Arabic, Hebrew, and Persian.

## 5.3  PREPARING THE LAYOUT FOR THE IMAGE SLIDER

The ViewPager2 widget is part of the Android SDK and can be found in the container section within the palette as seen in Figure 5.2 or by just typing it out within in the layout file. Other views are used together with ViewPager2 depending on the kind of interface and experience you want

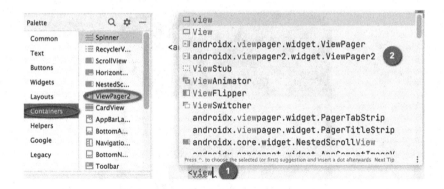

FIGURE 5.2    You can find the ViewPager 2 in the palette section or by typing it out in the layout file.

for your users. It is important to have a form of indicator to help the user know the position of the current image, a means to manually move to the next item or go back to the previous item, and an automatic slider ability for the items to continue swiping on its own.

For our intended interface, there will be an indicator showing a rectangular shape at the current position while the rest shows a circular shape. There will also be two buttons for manually moving to the next image and back to the previous one. Now for the indicator, we will be using a third-party library for this because there is no readily available widget from the built-in library.

### 5.3.1 Android Third-Party Libraries

Android libraries are tools or packaged codes that enable developers to quickly access already made methods and classes to improve their development experience. Since the beginning of this book, we have been using different widgets, classes, and methods for creating the applications in the existing chapters. Some of these tools are built into the Android Software Development Kit (SDK) available to developers on the go after Android Studio installation, a few have their dependencies added by default after you create a new project. You can open the app-level build.gradle file and check out the dependency block as soon a new project completes its build.

Now the dependencies you find in that block by default can be referred to as first-party libraries because the Android team developed them at Google. The likes of ConstraintLayout, and the material dependency which is responsible for most widget styling and themes are part of this category. We talked about having to add the ViewPager2 library before you can have access to its features. This is also a first-party library even though you must add it yourself before you can use them.

Flashback to Chapter 1 where you read about Android and Kotlin being open-source allowing the developers to contribute to the first-party libraries and as well create their own and make them available to the public for use. These libraries created by other developers are called third-party libraries because they are not created by the Google team and therefore not owned by them. However, there are a lot of them published, and very beneficial to the community to avoid reinventing the wheel every time you must implement a certain feature again and again in various applications or even in one project. The Image Slider app will need a third-party library called dots indicator to provide a widget and methods for quick implementation of this feature. Open build.gradle file and enter the following dependencies within the dependencies block.

```
implementation 'com.tbuonomo:dotsindicator:4.2'
```

### 5.3.2 Adding the Widgets for the Image Slider Layout

Create a new Empty Activity project and give it the name Image Slider. The activity_main.xml will be the application's main layout and will have the following widgets: A Guideline, ViewPager2, DotsIndicator, and two buttons for next and previous. The Guideline will position the widgets a few points away from the parent's top with ViewPager2 constrained directly below it. The dots indicator is set directly below the ViewPager2 with the two buttons following suit below the indicator. Below is the code for this layout.

```xml
<?xml version="1.0" encoding="utf-8"?>
<androidx.constraintlayout.widget.ConstraintLayout
    xmlns:android="http://schemas.android.com/apk/
    res/android"
    xmlns:app="http://schemas.android.com/apk/
      res-auto"
    xmlns:tools="http://schemas.android.com/tools"
    android:layout_width="match_parent"
    android:layout_height="match_parent"
    tools:context=".MainActivity">


    <androidx.constraintlayout.widget.Guideline
        android:id="@+id/guideline"
        android:layout_width="wrap_content"
```

```
            android:layout_height="wrap_content"
            android:orientation="horizontal"
            app:layout_constraintGuide_begin="150dp" />


    <androidx.viewpager2.widget.ViewPager2
        android:id="@+id/viewpager"
        android:layout_width="match_parent"
        android:layout_height="0dp"
        android:orientation="horizontal"
        app:layout_constraintTop_toBottomOf="@id/
          guideline"
        app:layout_constraintEnd_toEndOf="parent"
        app:layout_constraintStart_toStartOf=
          "parent" />


    <com.tbuonomo.viewpagerdotsindicator.
      DotsIndicator
        app:layout_constraintTop_toBottomOf="@id/
          viewpager"
        android:id="@+id/dotsIndicator"
        app:layout_constraintStart_toStartOf=
          "parent"
        app:layout_constraintEnd_toEndOf="parent"
        android:layout_width="wrap_content"
        android:layout_height="wrap_content"
        app:dotsColor="@color/white"
        app:dotsCornerRadius="8dp"
        android:layout_marginTop="16dp"
        app:dotsSize="16dp"
        app:dotsSpacing="4dp"
        app:dotsWidthFactor="2.5"
        app:selectedDotColor="@android:color/
          holo_blue_light"
        app:progressMode="true"
        />

    <Button
        android:id="@+id/button_next"
        android:layout_width="wrap_content"
        android:layout_height="wrap_content"
        android:layout_gravity="center"
        android:layout_marginTop="16dp"
        android:layout_marginEnd="32dp"
        android:layout_marginBottom="32dp"
        android:text="Next"
```

```
            android:backgroundTint="@android:
              color/holo_blue_light"
            android:textColor="@color/white"
            app:layout_constraintStart_toEndOf="@
              id/button_prev"
            app:layout_constraintEnd_
              toEndOf="parent"
            app:layout_constraintTop_toBottomOf="@
              id/dotsIndicator" />

    <Button
        android:id="@+id/button_prev"
        android:layout_width="wrap_content"
        android:layout_height="wrap_content"
        android:layout_gravity="center"
        android:layout_marginTop="16dp"
        android:layout_marginEnd="32dp"
        android:layout_marginBottom="32dp"
        android:text="Previous"
        android:backgroundTint="@android:color/
          holo_blue_light"
        android:textColor="@color/white"
        app:layout_constraintEnd_toStartOf="@id/
          button_next"
        app:layout_constraintStart_
          toStartOf="parent"
        app:layout_constraintTop_toBottomOf="@id/
          dotsIndicator" />
</androidx.constraintlayout.widget.Constraint
    Layout>
```

Figure 5.3 shows the design view result after adding the widgets.

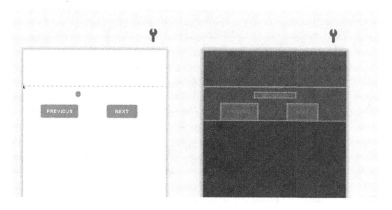

FIGURE 5.3   The activity_main design view.

## 5.4 AN INTRODUCTION TO FRAGMENTS

Before we begin understanding fragments, it's important to have a clear idea of how all the widgets will come together to produce a smooth slider. ViewPager2 requires a PagerAdapter responsible for preparing the data and Views to be displayed on it. These Views will not be directly added to the PagerAdapter but rather through a Fragment with which the adapter is built to work directly to enable reusability.

A fragment is a self-contained modular piece of a larger app usually used as a part of an Activity. A fragment has its lifecycle and can be added or removed when the Activity is still running. There are two types of fragments, the dynamic ones that are not tied to a specific Activity but can be used in multiple activities and the static ones that are tied to a specific Activity and can be used only within that Activity. Fragments have their own lifecycles just like activities have lifecycles tied to the app's lifecycle.

Apply the following steps to create a new fragment within your existing project.

- Right-click on the app folder> New> Fragment >fragment (Blank)

- Within the dialog that appears just like in Figure 5.4, enter Fragment's name as PagerFragment, and click finish.

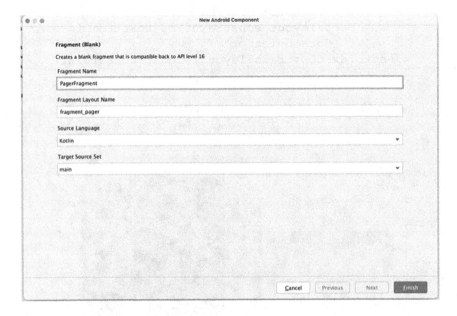

FIGURE 5.4   Creating a new fragment.

When you create a new fragment, a few codes are generated. Because fragments can only exist within an Activity, most times there is the need to pass data between them. That could be why part of the generated code includes a starter sample for receiving and sending data. Above the Fragment class, you will find constant variables created to be used as the keys for the values to be passed around. This is like when we used intent to send and retrieve data within activities in Chapter 4. The key created outside of the class can be directly accessed anywhere in the project without initializing the class.

Also, with Fragment's onCreate method, you will discover the keys being used to retrieve the value with the assumption that they are of the type String. Just like with Activities and Intent where we must retrieve the sent values within the onCreate because it is the first method called for the initial creation of the component, this is also the same with Fragment. There you can use arguments that are part of the Bundle class to return data supplied when Fragment was instantiated.

Towards the end of the class, you will notice the companion object like the object class we discussed while building the quiz app. It is a singleton that allows you to have your properties within its class but is still accessible without requiring the class to be instantiated.

In this object, you will find the fragment class creation using a method with the parameters for data to be sent from its housing component which could be the Activity, an Adapter, or another fragment. A Bundle class is used to pass the data with the help of the available methods depending on the data type.

```kotlin
private const val ARG_PARAM1 = "param1"
private const val ARG_PARAM2 = "param2"

class PagerFragment : Fragment() {

    private var param1: String? = null
    private var param2: String? = null

    override fun onCreate(savedInstanceState: Bundle?) {
        super.onCreate(savedInstanceState)
        arguments?.let {
            param1 = it.getString(ARG_PARAM1)
```

```
        param2 = it.getString(ARG_PARAM2)
    }
}

override fun onCreateView(
    inflater: LayoutInflater, container: ViewGroup?,
    savedInstanceState: Bundle?
): View? {
    return inflater.inflate(R.layout.fragment_pager,
        container, false)
}

companion object {

    @JvmStatic
    fun newInstance(param1: String, param2: String) =
        PagerFragment().apply {
            arguments = Bundle().apply {
                putString(ARG_PARAM1, param1)
                putString(ARG_PARAM2, param2)
            }
        }
    }
}
```

Depending on a fragment use case, not all generated code is required and most times you might be passing a data type that is not string and will have to change the methods or not pass any data at all. For this Image Slider, most of the codes will be removed and only one data will be passed around which will be of the int type. This data is the position of each image in the slide and will be passed through the adapter into a fragment for choosing an image from the list to set on each position of the slide.

```
class PagerFragment : Fragment() {

    private val binding by lazy {
        FragmentPagerBinding.inflate(layoutInflater)
    }
```

```
override fun onCreate(savedInstanceState: Bundle?) {
    super.onCreate(savedInstanceState)
    val position = requireArguments().getInt(slide)
    }
    override fun onCreateView(
      inflater: LayoutInflater, container: ViewGroup?,
      savedInstanceState: Bundle?
    ): View {
      return binding.root
    }

    companion object {
      const val slide = "SLIDES_ARG"
      @JvmStatic
      fun newInstance(position:Int) =
        PagerFragment().apply {
          arguments = Bundle().apply {
            putInt(slide,position)
          }
        }
    }
}
```

The layout of Fragment will contain just an ImageView that will display the image for each slide. The parent of the layout is a FrameLayout that is often used to hold a single view. It places its children in a stack on top of each other and sometimes is used to hold other parent layouts.

```
<FrameLayout xmlns:android="http://schemas.android.com/
apk/res/android"
  xmlns:tools="http://schemas.android.com/tools"
  android:layout_width="match_parent"
  android:layout_height="match_parent"
  tools:context=".PagerFragment">

  <ImageView
    android:id="@+id/image"
```

```
        android:layout_width="300dp"
        android:layout_height="300dp"
        android:scaleType="centerCrop"
        android:layout_gravity="center"
        android:contentDescription="nature"/>

</FrameLayout>
```

## 5.5 PAGER ADAPTER AND ITS COMPONENT

Having prepared each slide component which is Fragment and its layout, an adapter is required for providing Fragment to a ViewPager. The general concept of an adapter is to be a bridge between an Adapter View and the underlying data for that view. There are widgets in Android that fall under an Adapter view like ListView, RecyclerView, and GridView including the ViewPager and ViewPager2. These views generally are important when displaying a dynamic list of items. The adapter will provide the item and re-create the view for each item in the data set.

For a ViewPager2 using a Fragment as its component, its Adapter class will inherit from a FragmentStateAdapter built to help manage the state of a fragment for a ViewPager2. This adapter will keep track of each fragment state and save and restore it when needed. There are two important methods to be overridden from FragmentStateAdapter for our use case: getItemCount and createFragment. The getItemCount() method is used to return the number of items the adapter will manage while createFragment() is used to return a fragment and its position. There are several other methods out of the scope of this chapter available within the FragmentStateAdapter class but are only required per your need.

```
data class Slide(val photo:Int)

val slides = listOf(
  R.drawable.blue_sky_splash,
  R.drawable.bridge_splash,
  R.drawable.green_splash,
  R.drawable.winter_sky_splash,
  R.drawable.mountain_splash,R.drawable.water_fall_splash
)
```

```
class PagerAdapter(activity:AppCompatActivity,
        private val slides:List<Int>):
  FragmentStateAdapter(activity) {

  override fun getItemCount() = slides.size

  override fun createFragment(position: Int):Fragment {
    return PagerFragment.newInstance(position)
    }

}
```

The images are added to the list in the GitHub repository, but you can also use your custom pictures instead. Often the content of a slide will be more than just an image and can include titles with subtitles. Using a model class like the Slide data class allows you to group them as one Object or type and simultaneously read and display each data for every slide item. The PagerAdapter class extends FragmentStateAdaper with a need for context. This context is the environment in which the ViewPager2 lives and in this case is the Activity. Using a constructor, we will pass around the Activity by creating it as a parameter in PagerAdapter and passing it as the value to the FragmentStateAdapter and in turn when the class is called and initialized within the Activity the context will be provided as an argument.

The PagerAdapter class overrides two methods from its superclass: the getItemCount(), which returns the size of the slide to properly manage each item as its added to the adapter, and creatFragment() for providing a fragment component that will display each slide.

## 5.6 SETTING UP VIEWPAGER2 WITH PAGERADAPTER

With the PagerAdapter set up and ready, it will be integrated with ViewPager2 to provide the data and View for constructing each page item. Firstly, you need to connect the pager to the dots indicator; this is very simple and is done using the setViewPager2 method that allows you to pass in the variable of your pager. To control the sliding positions using the button, you can add a callback that is invoked whenever the page changes or is scrolled. Callbacks in Android is like a listener that is used to subscribe to events and provide an implementation in response to it. ViewPager2 has the registerOnPageChangeCallback() with different methods for responding to the changes that occur when swiping through the pages.

Because we want the Next button to show the next slide, within this callback, the current item is increased by one for when the position is not at the end of the slide and for the Previous button, the current item is decreased by one for when the position is not at the beginning. The callback provides the position value for each slide within pager for controlling the smooth scrolling of the widget. An important point to note is that callbacks are a form of subscription that needs to be removed when no longer in use to avoid waste of device resources like memory. Just like the onCreate method that is called first when the Activity is created and is suitable for initializing objects, there are other lifecycle methods like onPause that is called anytime an Activity is no longer in view and at this time the callback needs to be removed because the screen is no longer active. Another important method is the onResume() that is called after the Views are instantiated and the user can start interacting with the Activity; here you can register the callback again to subscribe to the event for continued listening. The complete lifecycle methods will be discussed in detail in Section 5.7.

```kotlin
class MainActivity : AppCompatActivity() {
    private val binding by lazy {
        ActivityMainBinding.inflate(layoutInflater)
    }

    private var viewPager2:ViewPager2? = null
    override fun onCreate(savedInstanceState: Bundle?) {
        super.onCreate(savedInstanceState)
        setContentView(binding.root)

        //The adapter is initialized and attached to the
        //ViewPager
        viewPager2 = binding.viewpager
        val adapter = PagerAdapter(this, slides)
        viewPager2?.adapter = adapter
        binding.dotsIndicator.setViewPager2(viewPager2!!)
        viewPager2?.clipToPadding = false
```

```kotlin
viewPager2?.clipChildren = false
viewPager2?.offscreenPageLimit = 2
val pageMarginPx = resources.getDimensionPixel
  Offset(R.dimen.pageMargin)
val offsetPx = resources.getDimensionPixel
  Offset(R.dimen.ofset)

viewPager2?.setPageTransformer { page, position ->.
  Val viewPager = page.parent.parent as ViewPager2
  val offset = position * -(2 * offsetPx +
    pageMarginPx)
  if (viewPager.orientation == ORIENTATION_
    HORIZONTAL) {
      if (ViewCompat.getLayoutDirection(viewPager)
        == ViewCompat.LAYOUT_DIRECTION_RTL) {
          page.translationX = -offset
        } else {
          page.translationX = offset
        }
    } else {
      page.translationY = offset
    }
}

viewPager2?.registerOnPageChangeCallback(object:
  ViewPager2.OnPageChangeCallback(){
  override fun onPageSelected(position: Int) {
    super.onPageSelected(position)
    if (position == 0){
      binding.buttonPrev.isEnabled = false
      }else{
        binding.buttonPrev.isEnabled = true
      binding.buttonPrev.setOnClickListener {
        viewPager2?.currentItem?.let {
          viewPager2?.setCurrentItem(it - 1, false)
        }
      }
      }
      }
```

```kotlin
                if(position == slides.size - 1){
                    binding.buttonNext.text = "Finish"
                    binding.buttonNext.setOnClickListener {
                        viewPager2?.currentItem = 0
                    }
                }else{
                    binding.buttonNext.text = "Next"
                    binding.buttonNext.setOnClickListener {
                        viewPager2?.currentItem?.let {
                            viewPager2?.setCurrentItem(it + 1,
                                false)
                        }
                    }
                }
                sliderHandler.removeCallbacks(sliderRunnable);
                sliderHandler.postDelayed(sliderRunnable,
                    2000)

            }
        })
    }

    private val sliderHandler: Handler = Handler
        (Looper.getMainLooper())
    /* This will create a thread where each slide
        will automatically be executed once the screen
        becomes visible
    */
    private val sliderRunnable =
        Runnable {
            viewPager2?.let {
                if (it.currentItem == slides.size-1){
                    it.currentItem = 0

                }else {
                    it.currentItem = it.currentItem.plus(1)
                }

            }
        }
```

```
override fun onPause() {
  super.onPause()
  /* This ensures paging is turned off when the
     screen is no longer visible sliderHandler.
     removeCallbacks(sliderRunnable)
  */
}

override fun onResume() {
  super.onResume()
  sliderHandler.postDelayed(sliderRunnable, 2000)
}

}
```

## 5.7  THE LIFECYCLE OF AN ACTIVITY AND FRAGMENT

The Android platform allows you to manage the lifecycle of every screen within your applications through the Activity or Fragment. It provides multiple callback methods you can override to monitor the state changes and take appropriate specific actions within both components. For example, we have mentioned the onCreate many times, which can be used to initialize data because it is called at the point of creating each component. Although a fragment is tied to an Activity in one way or another, it has a lifecycle different from that of an Activity. When an Activity is created, so is Fragment when an Activity is destroyed, and so is Fragmen. However, a Fragment can also be destroyed and recreated while the Activity is still running. Let's look at the lifecycle methods for each component to see how they work and what they do.

### 5.7.1  The Activity

The Activity lifecycle begins with a call to the onCreate method and continues down to the onDestroy method which is the last. There are points between these two methods where the system invokes other callbacks to notify the Activity of some changes.

- **onCreate:** The onCreate method is the first method invoked when an Activity is created. It is the point where the layout of any Activity is usually prepared and the UI is setup using the set-ContentView() method. onCreate is added by default for any new Activity that you create and is only called once in the lifecycle of an Activity unless it is created again. Some actions can trigger the recreation of activities. It can result from configuration changes when the screen orientation changes, a keyboard setting, or multi-window mode. During these changes or recreation, there could be data loss if not properly managed. This will be discussed in a coming section.

- **onStart:** The onStart method is invoked when the Activity becomes visible to the user after the onCreate is called. Also, after the app goes to the background by pressing the back or home button and then opening again from the background apps, the onStart is invoked again.

- **onRestart:** The onRestart is called after the onStart. This is the point where the Activity is restarted. After the app goes to the background and is opened again, this method gets called. It practically is invoked after every onStart.

- **onPause:** This method is called whenever the Activity is no longer visible to the user, mostly before going into the background. At this point, the Activity pauses every UI or service update it performs.

- **onResume:** This method is called after creating the Activity for the first time and when it is returning from the background. After it is invoked, the Activity becomes responsive and ready to be used.

- **onStop:** The onStop method is invoked when the Activity is hidden and immediately after onPause. This could be because it went into the background, or another Activity is called on top of it. At this point, the UI should stop any Activity or service updates that it is performing.

- **onDestroy:** The onDestroy method is invoked when the Activity is destroyed. At this point, the Activity should clear up all processes, release resources, and stop running services.

### 5.7.2 The Fragment

The fragment lifecycle begins with the onAttach method and continues down to the onDetach method. The system invokes several other callbacks to notify Fragment of some changes. Let's look at the most important ones.

- **The onAttach:** As soon as Fragment is added to the Activity, the onAttach method indicates that Fragment is now attached to its Activity. This is the point where you can get a reference to the Activity if required but note that Fragment is not created at this point.

- **The onCreate:** Just like the Activity, this is where Fragment initializes itself, but the layout is not created or set up here because at this point in a Fragment, there is no UI available nor a method for initializing the layout.

- **onCreateView:** At this stage in the lifecycle, Fragment's layout can be set up and inflated using the callback and the parameter provided. After inflating the method must return the view. You can also reference the widgets using the view variable but ensure you have inflated the layout before doing so.

- **onViewCreated:** This callback method is also invoked during the fragment lifecycle's creation, just like the onCreateView. Here is the more appropriate place to perform operations on the Views. However, onCreateView is called first, so the layout is inflated within it to ensure the Fragment views are ready before operations.

- **onStart:** This is called when Fragment is first started and is about to become visible to the user.

- **onPause:** Just like the Activity, this is called when the screen is about to go into the background. It is the right place to save the state of the app's data to ensure it is recovered when the screen becomes visible again.

- **onStop:** This is called once the app goes into the background and the screen is no longer visible.

- **onDestroyView:** At this point in the lifecycle, Fragment has been prepared to be destroyed. The layout views are removed, and the final clean-up of fragment resources is done.

- **onDestroy:** This callback is invoked when Fragment is destroyed. It could be because the app is killed or another fragment is opened on top of it.

- **onDetach:** This call back is invoked when the Fragment is no longer attached to the Activity.

- **Mini Exercise using the Log Class:** Logging in Android is a good way to monitor application processes by logging errors and messages. There is more than one way, but the Log class is the most basic way to achieve this, and there are different methods for different messages. This includes the debug using Log.d(), error using Log.e(), info using Log.i(), verbose using Log.v(), warning using Log.w(), and what a terrible failure using Log.wtf(). Depending on what type of message you need to log, you can use any of the abovementioned methods. There is an option on the Android Logcat to filter out the messages quickly. Let's look at an example.

In the MainActivity, we will add log messages to some of the lifecycle methods to help us understand the points where these callbacks are being called. Within the onCreate, onPause, and onResume, you will set a debug message to be displayed.

```kotlin
override fun onCreate(savedInstanceState: Bundle?) {

    super.onCreate(savedInstanceState)

    setContentView(binding.root)
}
  override fun onPause() {
      super.onPause()
      sliderHandler.removeCallbacks(sliderRunnable)
      Log.d("pause","This is the onPause")
  }
```

```
override fun onResume() {
  super.onResume()
  sliderHandler.postDelayed(sliderRunnable, 2000)
  Log.d("resume","This is the onResume")
}
```

When you rerun the app, open the logcat and select the debug option.

On the app's first launch, onCreate is called followed by onResume. Next, click on home and onPause gets called; at this point, the app is in the background. Now click on overview and select the app again to bring it back to the user view and the onResume will get called again. So, the onResume gets called every time the Activity is visible to the user. Figure 5.5 shows the logcat result.

To observe the rest of the lifecycle methods, override them within each component and add any logging of your choice. Filter the Logcat, enter specific tags as set within the log, and monitor the app to see the point where each of the callbacks gets invoked.

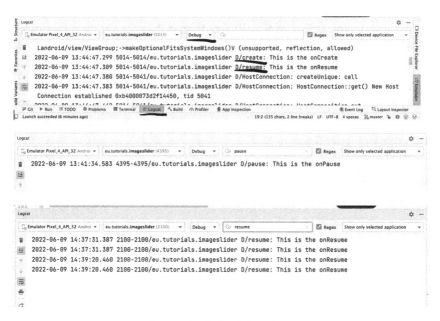

FIGURE 5.5   Logging results to check the lifecycle stages.

FIGURE 5.6   Part of the view is not visible on the screen.

## 5.8 MAKING AN ANDROID SCREEN SCROLLABLE

There are cases when the display on the Android screen looks cut off if they are longer than the device's height. In this case, there is a need to ensure that all the content on the screen can be visible to the user; this is where the ScrollView widgets come in. A ScrollView is an Android widget that helps allow views or displays that fall off the screen to be visible by scrolling. It allows you to enable scrolling either vertically or horizontally. There is also another sub-category called NestedScrollView which is useful mostly when you already have a ScrollView and require its child to have an independent scrolling.

An important aspect of ScrollView is that it can only have one direct child. If you have more than one widget on a UI and discover you need the scrolling feature, then the best way to achieve it is to first add a ViewGroup as the direct child of a ScrollView pand then have the widgets be the children of the ViewGroup. In the ImageSlider app, you will notice that some UI are cut off when you rotate the screen and switch to landscape orientation like in Figure 5.6.

To view those widgets again we will add a ScrollView as the parent layout of the activity_main.xml and then the ConstraintLayout will become its direct child.

```xml
<?xml version="1.0" encoding="utf-8"?>
<ScrollView
  xmlns:android="http://schemas.android.com/apk/res/
    android"
```

```
    android:layout_height="match_parent"
    android:layout_width="match_parent">

<androidx.constraintlayout.widget.ConstraintLayout
    xmlns:android="http://schemas.android.com/apk/res/
    android"
xmlns:app="http://schemas.android.com/apk/res-auto"
xmlns:tools="http://schemas.android.com/tools"
android:layout_width="match_parent"
android:layout_height="wrap_content"
tools:context=".MainActivity">

...
</androidx.constraintlayout.widget.ConstraintLayout>
</ScrollView>
```

When you rerun the app and change to landscape orientation, you can scroll vertically on the screen to see the indicators and buttons.

As seen in Figure 5.7, you will notice that no orientation attribute was added although there are two different orientations for a scroll view, the vertical and horizontal. Vertical is the default one, so if you don't set an orientation, it sets it by default, but if you want the alternative, you can add the following as the scroll view attribute.

FIGURE 5.7 ScrollView shows parts of the display that are not visible.

```
android:orientation="horizontal".
```

In Chapter 6, we will dive into the exciting world of networking in Android app development where you will learn how to connect your app to the internet and handle server requests.

## 5.9 SUMMARY

- An Image Slider is mainly used to showcase the features of your Android application

- The Activity lifecycle starts with the `onCreate` method, passes through some other stages, and ends with the `onDestroy` method.

- The fragment lifecycle starts with `onAttach` method, passes through some other stages, and ends with the `onDetached` method when its host is destroyed.

- ViewPager2 is the Android widget used to create image sliders or swipeable views.

- An adapter in Android is used as a bridge between its view and the data displayed on it. ViewPager2 uses one for managing each slider and its information.

- You can use a Runnable to Implement automatic paging with ViewPager2.

- The ScrollView widget makes an Android screen scrollable and can accept only one direct child.

# CHAPTER 6

# Networking in Android Using Retrofit

## 6.1 THE WEATHER APP OVERVIEW

Before we dive into networking properly, let's get an insight into what the project for this chapter will look like. Anyone with a mobile device, be it Android or IOS, must have come across a weather application before. We will build a similar application to get a user's current location and display the weather forecast. The app will show your current city and country, wind speed, humidity, sunrise and sunset time, and maximum and minimum temperature.

A user's location is regarded as personal information that should require the user's consent before being used by the app. You will learn how to add permissions to your Android project to notify the user of certain features or information that is required to run a certain app effectively. We will dive into networking proper and will not be designing the user interface. You can clone the project for this chapter here to get the content of the activity_main.xml. Figure 6.1 is what the final application UI will look like.

Here is an idea of what the internal application process will be like. As shown in Figure 6.2, firstly, when a user launches the app, there will be an attempt to get the user's location and send it to the weather API fetching the weather forecast. The app will check if the device has already allowed the application to access its location. If not, a popup will appear asking the user to accept permission in three different categories, which we will discuss in detail later in this chapter. Once the user accepts the permission,

FIGURE 6.1   The final weather application.

the device location is picked with its latitude and longitude extracted and sent to the weather API, which it requires to retrieve the weather forecast. As soon as the data is fetched, we display it on the screen with the different values set on the respective widgets.

## 6.2  AN INTRODUCTION TO ANDROID NETWORKING

In the previous chapters, we hardcoded the data displayed on the application with no major changes in the input and output. Networking in Android is a way that most applications show contents that can change over time and, at the same time, can be easily synchronized between different devices, assuming it requires personal data just like your favorite

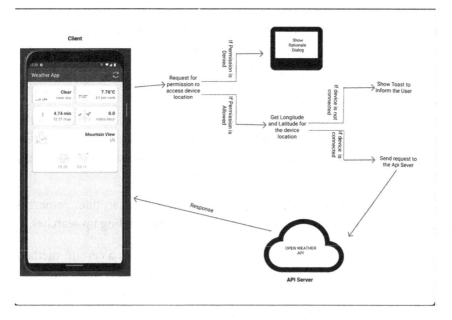

FIGURE 6.2    The weather forecast request and retrieval process.

social networks. This is achieved with the help of HTTP, a hypertext transfer protocol that is the foundation of data communication on the World Wide Web and is used to transfer any data. The most common method to access remote data in Android is by using REST API. A REST API makes it relatively easy to retrieve, send, update, and delete data over a network. It is worth noting that the REST API is based on an HTTP client library, and in Section 6.2.1 we will be gaining an understanding of how the two components work together.

### 6.2.1  What You Need to Know About HTTP and REST APIs

There are two parts to consider when making a request, the client and the server. A client can be any of your devices, such as phone, tablet, laptop, or even a browser, while the server can be any central computer or program that controls or provides the information you need. To make a successful call to a server that can be a REST API, you require a uniform resource locator (URL), a web address used to identify resources on the web. Every REST API has its base endpoint, just like there is a web address used for accessing a normal website. For example, to access the Android website, you must go to https://www.android.com/. So, to connect to a REST API, you require its base URL. HTTPS is the secure type of normal HTTP, and the "S" stands for secure. In addition to the base URL, there are other paths or parameters that point to a particular resource, the base URL being just like a domain name for the general resource.

- **PATH:** This specifies the location of a specific resource within the URL. For example, to get to the Android section of android.com, you will need an additional path like this https://www.android.com/what-is-android/ .

- **Parameter:** A parameter is additional data that can filter resources within the endpoint. This is usually very when setting up searches.

In addition to the request URLs, each process requires a certain method that will communicate the basic action regarding the possible four basic requests while interacting with an endpoint: write, read, update, and delete. Below are the respective HTTP request methods.

- **POST:** A post corresponds to create and is the method for creating a new entry in an endpoint.

- **GET:** A get corresponds to read and is used for retrieving data from an endpoint

- **PUT:** A put corresponds to an update and is used for updating already existing entries within an endpoint.

- **DELETE:** The delete request removes an entry from the endpoint.

### 6.2.1.1 HTTP Response Codes and Meaning

There are also response codes usually sent by the API server to help you determine the response's state when encountering an error. It enables you to confirm the result of the network call and debug issues that might occur in the process or manage the display of data on the UI. Below are the five ranges of code.

- 200 is a response code which means that your request was successful.

- 404 – most people might have experienced often when using a web browser. This means that the information you requested was not found, and the client might have sent a request that does not exist or an incorrect one.

- 500 – Internal Server Error, meaning that the error is happening on the API server itself

- 503 – Service Unavailable could mean that the service requested does not exist or is not available now.

## 6.2.2 Making a Simple Network Call with Standard HTTP URL Connection Class

There are several ways by which you can query a REST API endpoint. This could be using the standard HTTP URL Connection class available in Android or choosing to use libraries like OkHttp, Volley, Retrofit, and others created by other developers to solve specific needs. Each of them has unique features that differentiate them from each other and problems they try to solve. The most popular is the Retrofit library which will be the focus of this chapter. But first, we will use the standard class to fetch the content of the OpenWeather API to get a grasp of some basic operations happening behind the methods available in Retrofit.

### 6.2.2.1 Getting Access to the Weather API

Different API has a level of access given to a user. Some allow you to grab the URL and begin to make network calls without any security checks. Others require that you sign up and get an API key before you can access any of the resources on the API and some even go as far as requesting you pay for all or certain parts of the endpoint. With the OpenWeather API, you can access useful information for free, but you must register and get your own API key.

To create your own account on the OpenWeatherMap, head over to https://openweathermap.org/api, where you will see the interface similar to Figure 6.3.

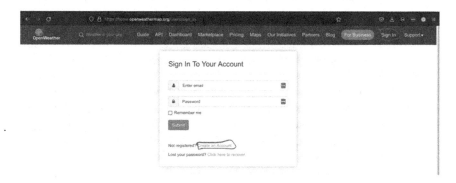

FIGURE 6.3   Creating an account on OpenWeatherMap.

FIGURE 6.4   Generate your API key through the My API keys menu.

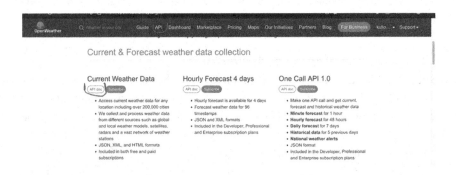

FIGURE 6.5   Navigate to the API docs by clicking on the option.

1. Click on sign in to either sign in if you already have an existing account or create a new account.

2. When you have signed in, you should click on your name to see an option to view the API key as shown in Figure 6.4.

3. To see the API resources, click on API and select API doc under Current Weather data as shown in Figure 6.5. You will see different options and ways to fetch weather forecasts, but we will be focusing on Current Weather data.

4. Within the Current Weather data, you will find the specific URL we will be using as seen in Figure 6.6.

**API call**

```
https://api.openweathermap.org/data/2.5/weather?lat=
{lat}&lon={lon}&appid={API key}
```

FIGURE 6.6 The weather URL to be used for the forecast.

### 6.2.2.2 Main Thread vs Background Thread

Most input and output operation on Android is known to be a long-running operation. This implies that it can take more than five seconds to complete its process, leading to an Android Not Responding (ANR) error. By default, all components in the same application run on the same process and threads called the main thread. The main thread also called the UI thread should be responsible for drawing only your application UIs. To ensure that processes like network operation, do not block the UI and disrupt the responsiveness of your application since it might take more than five seconds to send, for example, a Get request and then receive the data back before displaying the data. They must be run on a different thread called the background thread.

Due to the above reasons, performing long-running operations on the main thread will crash and show the android.os.NetworkOnMainThread-Exception error to prevent you from doing things the wrong way. There are various ways of running network operations outside of the main thread ranging from the standard thread class that comes with the Android SDK to powerful libraries like Coroutine and RxJava. They differ in how easy they make running different operations, doing calculations or manipulations with the results obtained, and switching back to the UI to display. Note that you are not allowed to draw UIs on the background thread. After performing a long-running operation, you will have to switch back to the main thread to display the result; otherwise, the application will throw a Null pointer exception because it cannot find the widget ready to receive the data displayed. We will learn how to use Coroutine's many utility methods to perform these operations in combination with Retrofit. First, we will do a basic network call using the standard HTTP class with the Thread APIs.

### 6.2.2.3 Making Network Calls with HTTP URL Connection

The built-in API for making network calls in Android is the HttpUrl-Connection. This class can be used for all requests by creating a connection object from a URL. For the OpenWeather API, we will make a GET request to fetch the weather forecast of a certain location using the longitude and latitude. The first step is opening a network connection and setting a request property. This property includes the format of the response, which is in JSON. Another important step is to indicate the request type and then use the input stream to read the response from the server.

Note that the process must be executed on a background thread. We will use a basic single thread Executor class to create a thread for the single purpose of fetching the weather forecast. Having mentioned the importance of running network operations on the background thread, an Executor class is a powerful tool in Android that can be used to keep the UI thread free and unblocked while running operations in the background thread of your app. Let's take a long at a simple example.

### 6.2.2.4 A Basic Example Using the Executor Class

We will start by seeing what an ANR error looks like. Let's say you have a button on the screen and a switch widget. The button's action is set to start a long-running operation when it is clicked. This will be implemented in the normal way on the main thread. After this button is clicked, you will also click on the switch to toggle on or off. Doing this simultaneously will trigger the ANR error because the button's action will take more than five seconds to complete. The toggle will not be effective until the process completion. Figure 6.7 shows what the UI will look like where you have the button and switch positioned vertically.

For the button's implementation, we have a thread with sleep set to 7000 millisecond equivalent to 7s. This is to mimic a quick process delay once the button is clicked. Below is the code function.

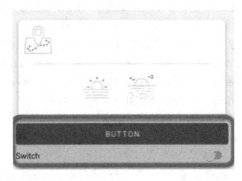

FIGURE 6.7   The button and switch UI display for testing the ANR error.

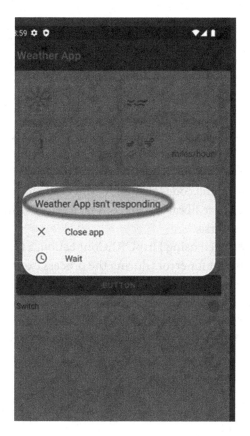

FIGURE 6.8 The ANR error displayed.

```
binding.testButton.setOnClickListener {
            Thread.sleep(7000L)
        }
```

When the button is clicked and the switch is toggled, after 7s, you will get the error as shown in Figure 6.8.

To fix this, we will implement the thread code within the Executor class by updating the code to look like the following.

```
binding.testButton.setOnClickListener {
            Executors.newSingleThread
                Executor().execute {
                Thread.sleep(7000L)
        }
```

With the executor added, rerun and test the app again. This time the switch will be effective and can toggle on and off since the Button action is running in the background and not freezing the main thread. We will do the same when doing a network call using the HttpUrl connection class.

### 6.2.2.5 Fetching the Weather Response

With the response in JSON format, you must extract each data in a form that the Android platform will understand before displaying them on the UI. This is commonly done using libraries like Gson or Moshi by automatically generating the codes that allow you easily to read specific types of JSON content. These libraries can convert a JSON string to a Kotlin or Java code and vice versa.

To catch errors when using HttpURLConnection, a try and catch statement is efficient to test for errors during the process execution. The code is wrapped with the try block, and errors are caught within the catch block if any occur. Finally, it is also introduced that you can disconnect from the network at the end of all operations. Below is the method that sets up the weather forecast URL using the HttpUrlConnection class.

```kotlin
fun getWeatherForecast() {
    Executors.newSingleThreadExecutor().execute {
        var httpURLConnection:HttpURLConnection? =
        null
        try {
// initializing and set the request URL.
val url =
URL("https://api.openweathermap.org/data/2.5/
  weather?lat=35&lon=139&app
  id=da15f28cbf49f1f8a2f030949b85e9a1")

        httpURLConnection = url.openConnection() as
            HttpURLConnection
//specify the property type to which is in a JSON
format.

            httpURLConnection.setRequestProperty(
                "Accept",
                "application/json"
            )
            httpURLConnection.requestMethod =
                "GET"
            httpURLConnection.doInput = true
            httpURLConnection.doOutput = false
```

```kotlin
val responseCode = httpURLConnection.
    responseCode
if (responseCode == HttpURLConnection.
    HTTP_OK) {

//reads the JSON response and converts to a String
    val response = httpURLConnection.
        inputStream.bufferedReader()
            .use { it.readText() }

//Manually parse the response and extract each
//content type.
val json = JsonParser().parse(response).toString()
    val jObject = JSONObject(json)
    val forecast = jObject.getJSONArray
        ("weather")
    val desc = forecast.getJSONObject(0).
        getString("description")
Log.d("weather response :", json)
    } else {
        Log.e("HTTPURLCONNECTION_ERROR",
        responseCode.toString())
    }
    }catch (e:Exception){
        Log.e("error",e.stackTraceToString())
    } finally {
        httpURLConnection?.disconnect()
    }
  }
 }
}
```

### 6.2.2.6 Testing the HttpURLConection Code

We currently use the weather API's default latitude and longitude provided to fetch the weather detail. To enable access to the internet for any Android application, you must add the following code to the AndroidManifest file as seen in Figure 6.9.

```xml
<uses-permission android:name="android.permission.
    INTERNET" />
```

Now run the application. Check the IDEs log, and you will see the JSON response from the provided longitude and latitude just like in Figure 6.10 with the different weather information.

In the next sections, we will properly get a user's current location and use the data for fetching current weather.

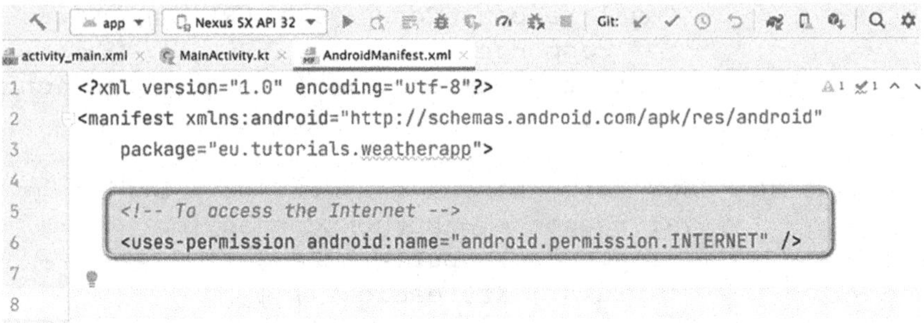

```
1    <?xml version="1.0" encoding="utf-8"?>
2    <manifest xmlns:android="http://schemas.android.com/apk/res/android"
3        package="eu.tutorials.weatherapp">
4
5        <!-- To access the Internet -->
6        <uses-permission android:name="android.permission.INTERNET" />
7
8
```

FIGURE 6.9    Adding the internet permission to the Android manifest file.

2022-06-27 14:09:43.786 4647-4673/? D/weather response ::: {"coord":{"lon":139,"lat":35},
 "weather":[{"id":803,"main":"Clouds","description":"broken clouds","icon":"04n"}],"base":"stations",
 "main":{"temp":297.77,"feels_like":298.48,"temp_min":297.77,"temp_max":297.77,"pressure":1010,
 "humidity":84},"visibility":10000,"wind":{"speed":1.34,"deg":209,"gust":2.24},"clouds":{"all":73},
 "dt":1656331380,"sys":{"type":2,"id":2019346,"country":"JP","sunrise":1656271911,"sunset":1656324110},
 "timezone":32400,"id":1851632,"name":"Shuzenji","cod":200}

FIGURE 6.10    The JSON response from OpenWeatherMap.

## 6.3  USING THE ANDROID LOCATION SERVICE

Location services on Android lets you use features and apps that depend on your device location. Like with the weather forecast, you need to always get the recent location of a user in order to obtain the correct weather detail. To use a location feature, the app must be granted access to it because it's the user's privacy and should not be accessed without their permission.

There are two ways by which you can get the device location, using Geocoder and Fused Location. We will use the latter because it is very efficient in getting the last known location that can serve as its current location. The Fused Location provider is available in Google Play Services and provides simple APIs that can help get high accuracy with low power without much use of the device's battery power.

### 6.3.1  Requestion User Permissions

Before getting the device's location, let's ask for the user's permission first. The first step is to declare the need for location in the Android Manifest just as we did for the internet permission. Two options available can determine the accuracy of the returned location. The Access_Coarse_location that returns the device's approximate location, and the Access_Fine_location returns the possible precise location. It is recommended that the coarse location be requested to respect the user's privacy and only use the approximate location, which is possible for most functionalities. When there is an absolute need for a fine location, both must be requested to give

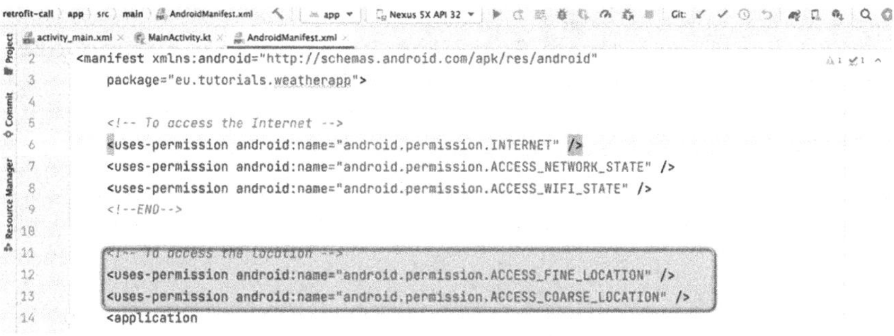

FIGURE 6.11   Adding location permissions to the android manifest file.

the user the option of choosing which option to give the device access. We will add both permissions to the manifest file since we prefer to use the precise location for retrieving accurate weather information. Figure 6.11 shows how the permission is added to the file.

```
<uses-permission android:name="android.permission.
    ACCESS _ FINE _ LOCATION" />
<uses-permission android:name="android.permission.
    ACCESS_COARSE_LOCATION" />
```

Android has a standard API for requesting user permission using the registerForActivityResult. There are different permissions that an application could request, so you will have to specify which one needs to be granted. This is done using the RequestPermission method for single permission, and if your app requires more than one permission, you will use the RequestMultiplePermissions variant. You will check that the user has granted the permission required by the application before you can use the feature, and if they have not, you should request them to do so. Here is the code that checks for permission to use the device location.

```
class MainActivity : AppCompatActivity() {
    override fun onCreate(savedInstanceState:
        Bundle?) {
        super.onCreate(savedInstanceState)
        setContentView(R.layout.activity_main)

   /* call the checkPermission method in the onCreate
      to initiate the process if the location
      permission is not granted or get the location if
      it has previously been granted */
        if (!isLocationEnabled()) {
            Toast.makeText(
```

```
                    this,
                    "Your location provider is turned off.
                      Please turn it on.",
                    Toast.LENGTH_SHORT
                  ).show()
                  checkLocationPermission()
              } else {


              }

         }


/* Retrieve device location is permission request
   is granted else request for
*/
@SuppressLint("NewApi")
private fun checkLocationPermission() {
   when {
      ContextCompat.checkSelfPermission(
        this,
        Manifest.permission.ACCESS_COARSE_LOCATION
      ) == PackageManager.PERMISSION_GRANTED &&
        ContextCompat.checkSelfPermission(
        this, Manifest.permission.ACCESS_FINE_
          LOCATION
      )
          == PackageManager.PERMISSION_GRANTED -> {
      /* check if permission has been denied before
         and show the rationale dialog
      */
      }

      shouldShowRequestPermissionRationale(Mani
        fest.permission.ACCESS_COARSE_LOCATION) -> {
            showRationalDialogForPermissions()
          }
          else -> {
            requestPermissionLauncher.launch(
            arrayOf(
              Manifest.permission.ACCESS_COARSE_
                LOCATION,
              Manifest.permission.ACCESS_FINE_
                LOCATION
            )
          )
        }}}
```

```kotlin
    private fun showRationalDialogForPermissions() {
        AlertDialog.Builder(this)
            .setMessage("It Looks like you have
                turned off permissions required for
                this feature. It can be enabled under
                Application Settings")
            .setPositiveButton(
                "GO TO SETTINGS"

            ) { _, _ ->
                try {
                    val intent = Intent(Settings.ACTION_
                        APPLICATION_DETAILS_SETTINGS)
                    val uri = Uri.fromParts("package",
                        packageName, null)

                    intent.data = uri
                    startActivity(intent)
                } catch (e: ActivityNotFoundException) {
                    e.printStackTrace()
                }
            }
            .setNegativeButton("Cancel") { dialog,
                                        _ ->
                dialog.dismiss()
            }.show()
    }
```

/* This method returns true if the device location has been granted */

```kotlin
private fun isLocationEnabled(): Boolean {

    return ContextCompat.checkSelfPermission(this,
        Manifest.permission.ACCESS_FINE_LOCATION
    ) == PackageManager.PERMISSION_GRANTED &&
        ContextCompat.checkSelfPermission(this,
        Manifest.permission.ACCESS_COARSE_LOCATION) ==
        PackageManager.PERMISSION_GRANTED
}
```

/* Register the permissions that are needed to access the user location and assign to a variable */

```kotlin
val requestPermissionLauncher =
```

```
registerForActivityResult(
   ActivityResultContracts.RequestMultiple
      Permissions()
) { if(it[Manifest.permission.ACCESS_COARSE_
   LOCATION]  == true && it[Manifest.permission.
   ACCESS_FINE_LOCATION] == true){
}else{
   showRationalDialogForPermissions()
}
}}
```

At this point when you run the app, Figure 6.12 will be displayed to ask for user permission.

FIGURE 6.12  System permission dialog requesting the user to choose enable device location.

You should take note of the following principles for requesting permission from a user.

1. Ask for permission when the user starts interacting with the required feature.

2. If the user denies permission, do not block the user, but you can provide the option to cancel an education UI flow that informs the user while they need to grant the permission.

3. Do not force the user to grant permission instead disable the feature that requires the permission.

### 6.3.2  Getting the Device Location

Now that the location permission has been created, you can retrieve the location data using the FusedLocationProviderClient. To make this API available in your project, you will have to add the play service location dependency in build.gradle file. This gives you access to the Location-CallBack available in the FusedLocationProvider API to get the last known location that gives you the value of the latitude and longitude that the network call requires as shown in Figure 6.13. The location request can now be created using high accuracy priority with the help of the LocationCallback and called only if the user grants permission to access the location details. The below dependency and code read the device location and print the latitude and longitude.

```
implementation 'com.google.android.gms:play-
    services-location:18.0.0'

/* Declare and initialize the FusedLocation
    ProviderClient
*/
private lateinit var mFusedLocationClient: Fused
    LocationProviderClient
```

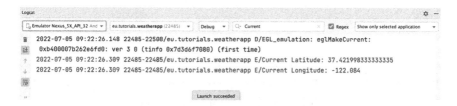

FIGURE 6.13  Logging the latitude and longitude from the current device location.

```
mFusedLocationClient = LocationServices.getFused
  LocationProviderClient(this)

    /*
    Request's location update using a high priority and
      the location callback. The apply method is a
      convenient and concise way to create and configure
      objects when setting properties to it. */

        @SuppressLint("MissingPermission")
        private fun requestLocationData() {

          val mLocationRequest = LocationRequest.
            create().apply {
              priority = LocationRequest.PRIORITY_HIGH_
                ACCURACY
          }

          mFusedLocationClient.requestLocationUpdates(
              mLocationRequest, mLocationCallback,
              Looper.myLooper()
          )
        }

    /* a Location callback that gets the latitude and
      longitude using the last known location */
    private val mLocationCallback = object :
      LocationCallback() {
          override fun onLocationResult(locationResult:
            LocationResult) {
              val mLastLocation: Location = location
                Result.lastLocation

              mLatitude = mLastLocation.latitude
              Log.e("Current Latitude", "$mLatitude")
              mLongitude = mLastLocation.longitude
              Log.e("Current Longitude", "$mLongitude")

          }
      }
```

## 6.4 USING RETROFIT TO SIMPLIFY NETWORKING

Retrofit is a library developed by Square; a company focused on building financial services and digital payments. They have contributed a lot to Android open-source software with several tools and libraries, including

Retrofit, which makes it easy to work with HTTP-based APIs. Previously, we used HttpUrlConection class to make network calls to the weather API which resulted in writing much boilerplate code but with Retrofit, you specify the request method you want to make, and it handles the rest for you. It also supports mapping the JSON response as seen in Figure 6.14, into a Java/Kotlin object and vice versa with the help of a library like Gson.

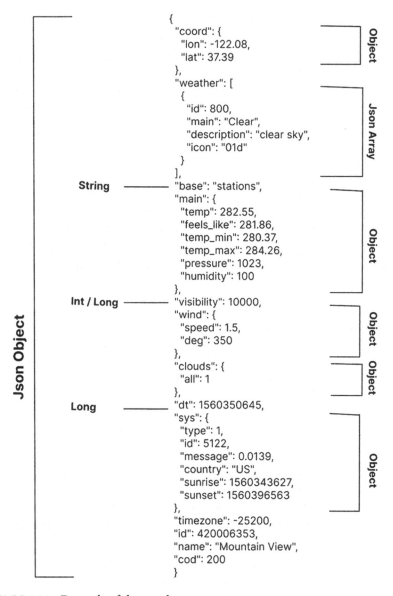

FIGURE 6.14   Example of the weather response.

Gson is a very flexible library that offers a simple API for parsing JSON into Kotlin Object. It is annotation based, meaning it uses annotations to generate extra information for a program. Looking back at the JSON response from the weather API, the result starts with an object and includes inner objects, array, String, Int, and double. When using the HttpUrlConnection, we wrote boilerplate codes to get the Kotlin version of the JSON response, but this time we will use annotations with the help of Moshi to simplify the steps.

To set up Gson with Retrofit, take note of the following steps.

It is required to add a Retrofit dependency and a Retrofit dependency supporting the use of Gson. In the module-level build.gradle file, add the following and click on sync.

```
implementation 'com.squareup.retrofit2:retrofit:
   2.9.0'
implementation 'com.squareup.retrofit2:
   converter-gson:2.9.0'
```

Create a Retrofit instance and add a Gson converter to it. In creating the retrofit instance, you will add the base URL for the API. This is usually the domain name and the most common part in the URL path and not a full URL as we did with the HttpUrlConnection so that it can be easily reused if you have more than one network call to perform within a project. The other specific paths, queries, or parameters will be provided within the request method.

```
object RetrofitApi {
  val retrofit: Retrofit = Retrofit.Builder()
     .baseUrl("https://api.openweathermap.org/data/")
     .addConverterFactory(GsonConverterFactory.
       create())
     .build()
}
```

### 6.4.1 Mapping the JSON Response to a Kotlin Object

The first step to mapping JSON to a Kotlin object using Moshi is to provide a data class to serve as a model like the response. Among all the responses returned from the API, we will select the values that are required to give basic information about the current weather state of a particular location and create a model for them. From the JSON structure, the direct body of the response is an object and the app will need a number of its responses which includes five direct objects, two Strings, four Ints, and an array of weather objects. Below is the Base Response data class with its sub classes.

```kotlin
data class WeatherResponse(
    val coord: Coord,
    val weather: List<Weather>,
    val base: String,
    val main: Main,
    val visibility: Int,
    val wind: Wind,
    val clouds: Clouds,
    val dt: Int,
    val sys: Sys,
    val id: Int,
    val name: String,
    val cod: Int
)
```

Now every object present in the WeatherResponse will have a data class containing its own fields. They can be in separate files or all in the same file.

```kotlin
1. data class Coord(
2.      val lon: Double,
3.      val lat: Double
4. )
5.
```

```kotlin
data class Weather(
    val id: Int,
    val main: String,
    val description: String,
    val icon: String
)
```

```
data class Main(
  val temp: Double,
  val pressure: Double,
  val humidity: Int,
  val temp_min: Double,
  val temp_max: Double,
  val sea_level: Double,
  val grnd_level: Double
)
data class Wind(
  val speed: Double,
  val deg: Int
)
data class Clouds(
  val all: Int
)
data class Sys(
  val type: Int,
  val message: Double,
  val country: String,
  val sunrise: Long,
  val sunset: Long
)
```

The good thing about the mapping library is that in most cases using the annotation is optional. If you use the exact names available in the response as the class variables, then they will be automatically recognized but, in a case, where you prefer to use a different variable name, then you will need to add the annotation on them to specify which of the keys in the JSON file you want to map them to. Here is an example.

```
/* Use @SerializedName annotation to specify the key
   representation in the API response while using a
   different name as a variable name */
    data class Wind(
        val speed: Double,
        @SerializedName("deg") #A
        val degree: Int #A
    )
```

## 6.4.2 Replacing HttpURLConnection with Retrofit

The first step to using Retrofit is adding the dependency and creating the instance to initialize it. We have gone through this process while introducing the library and are now ready to use it in place of the built-in networking class. Retrofit not only simplifies the request but also provides a means to perform the network call outside of the main thread with the help of its callbacks. Here are the basic steps to take when using Retrofit.

- Add the Retrofit dependency with the object mapper library of your choice.

- Initialize Retrofit and add the mapper to it by creating its instance.

- Create data classes that match the expected JSON response.

- Create the request interface using the right request method and the data class.

- Initiate the network call using the Retrofit Callback.

Now we have completed the first two steps and will go-ahead to create the request interface. The request interface will define the HTTP operation by specifying the request type and it will return a Call object that returns both synchronous and asynchronous callback for executing the request. It will also provide the path to specific data including any query that is required. For the current weather API, it will be a Get request, its specific path, the longitude, latitude, and then the API key as the app id which will be a query.

You can identify a value as a query if it comes after the question mark (?) symbol. On the URL provided you will see that the longitude, latitude, and app id come after the symbol and so will be provided as a query. Here is the interface with the getWeather method definition.

```
interface WeatherService {

    @GET("2.5/weather")
    fun getWeather(
        @Query("lat") lat: Double,
        @Query("lon") lon: Double,
        @Query("appid") appid: String?
    ): Call<WeatherResponse>
}
```

Interfaces cannot be initialized and so to prepare the interface class, retrofit has a create method that serves this purpose. Using the instance from the retrofit builder, the WeatherService class can be created to allow access to its methods. This should be done within the Retrofit initializer class like the below code.

```
val service: WeatherService =
    retrofit.create<WeatherService>(Weather
        Service::class.java)
```

### 6.4.2.1 Checking If the Device Is Connected to the Internet

We are ready to send a request to the current weather endpoint but first, there is the need to know when the device is connected to the internet. This can be achieved using the Connectivity Manager class that provides the methods that enable you to find out if the device is connected to the internet and the type of network it is connected to, ranging from WIFI to cellular network or ethernet.

There are currently two different ways of determining the device's internet state depending on its operating system (OS) version or the SDK version. The major difference is that from Marshmallow OS to the current version, you can determine the type of network they are connected to. Other Android OS from Lollipop and below cannot produce this information. Below is the code that checks for internet connection for all operating systems.

```
fun isNetworkAvailable(context: Context): Boolean {
    val connectivityManager = context.getSystem
        Service(Context.CONNECTIVITY_SERVICE) as
        ConnectivityManager
    if (Build.VERSION.SDK_INT >= Build.VERSION_
        CODES.M) {
        val network       = connectivityManager.
            activeNetwork ?: return false
        val activeNetWork = connectivityManager.
            getNetworkCapabilities(network) ?: return
            false
        return when {
```

```
            activeNetWork.hasTransport(Network
              Capabilities.TRANSPORT_WIFI) -> true
            activeNetWork.hasTransport(Network
              Capabilities.TRANSPORT_CELLULAR) -> true
            activeNetWork.hasTransport(Network
              Capabilities.TRANSPORT_ETHERNET) -> true
            else -> false
          }
        } else {
          val networkInfo = connectivityManager.
            activeNetworkInfo
          return networkInfo != null && networkInfo.
            isConnectedOrConnecting
        }
      }
```

### 6.4.2.2 Making the Network Call with Retrofit Callback

With the Retrofit instance created as a separate singleton class, you can reference it from anywhere in your project when it is needed. From the MainActivity, you will initiate the get operation to fetch the current weather information using the device location. There are two methods to take note of when using the Retrofit Call object, the execute and the enqueue method. The first one processes a network operation synchronously and is not a recommended approach since it has the tendency to block the UI if it takes longer time to complete while the second processes operations asynchronously outside of the main thread and is a better approach to use for communicating over HTTP.

Having made that distinction between execute and enqueue, the getWeather interface will be processed using enqueue when there is an internet connection on the device or show a Toast to tell the user to check their internet connection. Enqueue returns two callback methods, onResponse, which gets called if a response is received from an HTTP network calls, and onFailure which gets called if an HTTP error occurs processing the response. For the onResponse callback, the response can still indicate a sort of failure which is why it has a successful method that can be called to indicate success. Below is the code that uses the retrofit library to perform a network call.

```kotlin
private fun getLocationWeatherDetails(){

if (Constants.isNetworkAvailable(this@MainActivity)) {
    val listCall: Call<WeatherResponse> =
      RetrofitApi.service.getWeather(
      mLatitude, mLongitude, Constants.API_KEY        )

    showCustomProgressDialog()
    listCall.enqueue(object : Callback<Weather
      Response> {
        @SuppressLint("SetTextI18n")
        override fun onResponse(
            call: Call<WeatherResponse>,
            response: Response<WeatherResponse>   ) {
            if (response.isSuccessful) {
               hideProgressDialog()
               val weatherList: WeatherResponse? =
                 response.body()
               Log.i("Response Result", "$weather
                 List")
               if (weatherList != null) {
                   setupUI(weatherList)
               }
            } else {
              val sc = response.code()
              when (sc) {
                400 -> {
                  Log.e("Error 400", "Bad Request")
                }
                404 -> {
                  Log.e("Error 404", "Not Found")
                }
                else -> {
                  Log.e("Error", "Generic Error")
                }
              }
            }
        }
```

```
    override fun onFailure(call:
      Call<WeatherResponse>, t: Throwable) {
      hideProgressDialog()
      Log.e("Errorrrrr", t.message.toString())
    }

  })

} else {
  Toast.makeText(
    this@MainActivity,
        "No internet connection available.",
        Toast.LENGTH_SHORT            ).show()
  }

}
```

## 6.5 SIMPLIFYING ASYNCHRONOUS CALLS WITH COROUTINE

A coroutine is a powerful tool that simplifies asynchronous programming in Android. It is lightweight, efficient, and easy to use. A coroutine allows you to write concise code that is easier to read and understand and also less error-prone. It is similar to thread but not bound to any particular one and so may suspend its execution in one thread and resume in another one. Talking about suspension, a coroutine provides different scopes that can run within a suspending function. These scopes are tied to specific lifecycles like the Activities and Fragments and also the ViewModel (this will be discussed in Chapter 8) to allow easy management of memory leaks. Memory leaks occur in Android when memory allocations are made to an object and fail to release the memory when it is no longer been used leading to poor application performance and possible app crashes. Not clearing an inactive coroutine scope can cause memory leaks but with the built-in scopes, the memory is free when the lifecycle it is attached to is destroyed. You can also create custom scopes where applicable but ensure to attach them to a Job that should be cleared at the end of a lifecycle.

### 6.5.1 Suspending Executions and Launching a Coroutine Operation

A suspending function is simply a function with the suspend modifier. The suspend keyword denotes that the operation will be a long-running process and should be run asynchronously. This way it will not block the main thread. There are different dispatchers that are part of the coroutine API making it easier to switch between different threads while running a suspend function.

- **Dispatchers.Main:** This is useful for updating the UI since widgets cannot be drawn outside of the main thread.

- **Dispatchers.IO:** This is used for long-running operations like network calls or local database operations.

- **Dispatchers.Default:** This is useful for central processing unit (CPU)–intensive tasks like reading and writing to a device file.

To get access to the built-in coroutine scopes, you need to add the following dependency to your module-level build.gradle file;

- implementation("androidx.lifecycle:lifecycle-runtime-ktx:2.5.0")

Let's look at a simple coroutine example where we print one million numbers within a for-loop expression. This kind of operation is going to take a longer than normal time to complete and is best processed in a background thread to allow other UI processes to continue being active. In this example, we have a dialog that displays loading progress when a button is clicked and also triggers the for-loop. Within the execute method, the process is launched using the Dispatchers.IO thread and then another method is introduced that cancels the loading and displays a Toast at the end. The runOnUiThread is used to move the processes from the background to the UI, without this the app will crash since drawing UIs are not allowed on the background thread. Here is a basic sample using a coroutine to perform an asynchronous operation.

```
class MainActivity : AppCompatActivity() {
    var customProgressDialog: Dialog? = null
    override fun onCreate(savedInstanceState:
        Bundle?) {
        super.onCreate(savedInstanceState)
        setContentView(R.layout.activity_main)
```

```
    val btnExecute:Button = findViewById(R.
      id.btn_execute)
    btnExecute.setOnClickListener {
      showProgressDialog()
      lifecycleScope.launch {
          execute("Task executed successfully.")
      }
    }


  }
  private suspend fun execute(result:String){
      withContext(Dispatchers.IO) {
        for (i in 1..1000000) {
          Log.e("delay : ", "" + i)
        }
        runOnUiThread {
          cancelProgressDialog()
          Toast.makeText(
            this@MainActivity, result,
            Toast.LENGTH_SHORT
          ).show()
        }
      }
  }

  private fun showProgressDialog() {
      customProgressDialog =
        Dialog(this@MainActivity)
        customProgressDialog?.setContentView
        (R.layout.dialog_custom_progress)
customProgressDialog?.show()
      }

    private fun cancelProgressDialog() {
        if (customProgressDialog != null) {
            customProgressDialog?.dismiss()
            customProgressDialog = null
        }
      }

  }
```

## 6.5.1.1 Testing the App

You can get the complete code from the repository, including the layout and dialog. When you run the app, click the button and open Logcat to see the print results as seen in Figure 6.15. If the loop is still printed with the

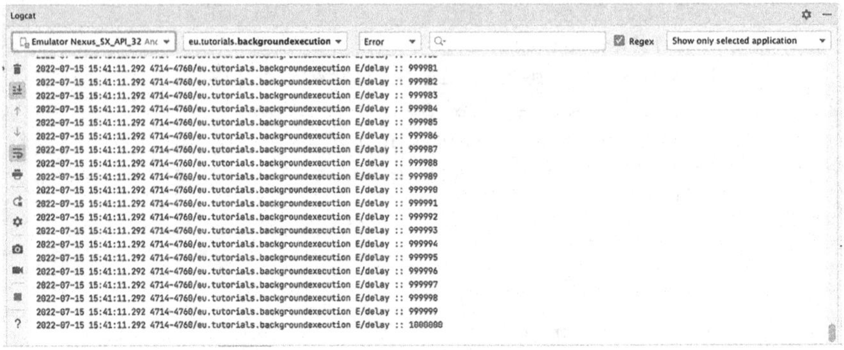

FIGURE 6.15   Logging the coroutine sample results.

```
2022-07-15 15:47:51.870 5011-5052/? E/delay :: 999999
2022-07-15 15:47:51.870 5011-5052/? E/delay :: 1000000
2022-07-15 15:47:51.888 5011-5011/? E/AndroidRuntime: FATAL EXCEPTION: main
    Process: eu.tutorials.backgroundexecution, PID: 5011
    java.lang.NullPointerException: Can't toast on a thread that has not called Looper.prepare()
        at com.android.internal.util.Preconditions.checkNotNull(Preconditions.java:167)
        at android.widget.Toast.getLooper(Toast.java:182)
        at android.widget.Toast.<init>(Toast.java:167)
```

FIGURE 6.16   Error that occurs when running UI-related events on the background thread.

process on the main thread, no other events can happen until it is completed because it will freeze the UI. But with a coroutine being used, UI events can go on while the background events continue through a different process.

Also, remove the runOnUiThread and run again to observe what happens when showing a Toast from the background thread. The app will crash with the exception shown in Figure 6.16.

## 6.5.2  Using Coroutine with Retrofit

We can replace the Retrofit Call object using a suspend function and, in this way, reduce the lines of code with all the callback methods. The get weather interface Call return type will be replaced with suspend keyword, and a lifecycle scope will be used to launch it within the activity using try and catch to check for errors. The following code replaces Retrofit Call with coroutine.

```
private fun getLocationWeatherDetails(){

    if (Constants.isNetworkAvailable(this@
        MainActivity)) {
```

```
        showCustomProgressDialog()
    try {
       lifecycleScope.launch {
          val weatherList = RetrofitApi.
            service.getWeather(
            mLatitude, mLongitude, Constants.
              API_KEY
          )
            Log.i("Response Result",
              "$weatherList")
            if (weatherList != null) {
            }
            hideProgressDialog()
         }

      }catch (e:Exception){
         hideProgressDialog()
         Log.e("response error", e.message.
           toString())
      }
    } else {
      Toast.makeText(
        this@MainActivity,
        "No internet connection available.",
        Toast.LENGTH_SHORT
      ).show()
   }
}
```

## 6.6 DISPLAYING THE WEATHER INFORMATION ON THE UI

It is time to connect the weather details from the API to the user interface. You can get the complete UI setup from the repository provided at the beginning of this chapter. Firstly, you should create a binding variable for referencing the layout views. There is an icon for each weather property like the clouds, temperature, wind, country, sunset, and sunrise. Each image has a TextField to display the value from the forecast. You can reference each one and set the respective value to it only If the weather list returned from the response is not null. Using the weather forecast data retrieved from the API we will update the UI with the following method.

```
private fun setupUI(weatherList: WeatherResponse) {


  for (z in weatherList.weather.indices) {
```

```
Log.i("NAMEEEEEEEE", weatherList.weather[z].
   main)

binding.tvMain.text = weatherList.
   weather[z].main
binding.tvMainDescription.text =
   weatherList.weather[z].description
binding.tvTemp.text =
    weatherList.main.temp.toString() +
      getUnit(application.resources.
      configuration.toString())
binding.tvHumidity.text = weatherList.main.
   humidity.toString() + " per cent"
binding.tvMin.text = weatherList.main.temp_
   min.toString() + " min"
binding.tvMax.text = weatherList.main.temp_
   max.toString() + " max"
binding.tvSpeed.text = weatherList.wind.
   speed.toString()
binding.tvName.text = weatherList.name
binding.tvCountry.text = weatherList.sys.
   country
binding.tvSunriseTime.text =
   unixTime(weatherList.sys.sunrise.toLong())
binding.tvSunsetTime.text =
   unixTime(weatherList.sys.sunset.toLong())
when (weatherList.weather[z].icon) {
    "01d" -> binding.ivMain.setImageResource
       (R.drawable.sunny)
    "02d" -> binding.ivMain.setImageResource
       (R.drawable.cloud)
    "03d" -> binding.ivMain.setImageResource
       (R.drawable.cloud)
    "04d" -> binding.ivMain.setImageResource
       (R.drawable.cloud)
    "04n" -> binding.ivMain.setImageResource
       (R.drawable.cloud)
    "10d" -> binding.ivMain.
       setImageResource(R.drawable.rain)
    "11d" -> binding.ivMain.
       setImageResource(R.drawable.storm)
    "13d" -> binding.ivMain.
       setImageResource(R.drawable.snowflake)
    "01n" -> binding.ivMain.
       setImageResource(R.drawable.cloud)
    "02n" -> binding.ivMain.
       setImageResource(R.drawable.cloud)
```

```
"03n" -> binding.ivMain.
    setImageResource(R.drawable.cloud)
"10n" -> binding.ivMain.
    setImageResource(R.drawable.cloud)
"11n" -> binding.ivMain.
    setImageResource(R.drawable.rain)
"13n" -> binding.ivMain.
    setImageResource(R.drawable.snowflake)
        }
    }
}
```

### 6.6.1 Testing the App

Run the application, accept the location request, and wait for the weather forecast to be retrieved. Figure 6.17 shows the weather result.

FIGURE 6.17  The expected final weather app UI.

## 6.7 SUMMARY

- Android networking involves connecting an Android device to a remote URL and performing designated operations.

- Four basic HTTP operations include Create, Read, Update, and Delete CRUD mechanisms.

- JSON types can be mapped or converted to Kotlin Objects using the Gson library.

- Using the Connectivity Service API, you can check for the internet connection state on your Android device.

- Using sensitive information required by an application will require permission requests granted by the user.

- Android location service can get a device's current location through its latitude and longitude.

- The Android main thread, also known as the UI thread, is mainly used to draw user interfaces and does not allow long-running operations to be processed.

- The background thread is also known as a worker thread and is ideal for performing long-running operations.

- The coroutine API in Android simplifies long-running operations with concise and easy-to-read providing three main dispatchers: Dispatchers.IO, Dispatchers.Main, and Dispatchers.Default.

# CHAPTER 7

# Google Firebase Services

## *Project 5 – Tour Guide App*

## 7.1 THE TOUR GUIDE APPLICATION OVERVIEW

The primary objective of this chapter is to develop a simple app that assists users in discovering beautiful travel destinations. Upon launching the app, users can view each place's image, location, and description. However, to post detailed information about a particular location, users must first register an account and log in. Another vital feature of the application is the ability to select or capture an image using the camera. We will also explore this functionality in detail. Below are the application screens.

After registration, users will be able to create new tour posts and share, edit, update, or delete posts they have created. The app will display tour lists using a Recycler View, a dynamic list display widget in the Android SDK. This widget is adapter based and more advanced than a standard view. Like ViewPager2, it effectively maintains a limited number of views while showing a vast data set. Additionally, we will use fragments to display destinations within the tour app instead of multiple activities. We will also delve into the navigation framework, which facilitates connections between these destinations, making it easier to navigate between them. Figure 7.1 shows the screen flow for this application.

DOI: 10.1201/9781032622538-7

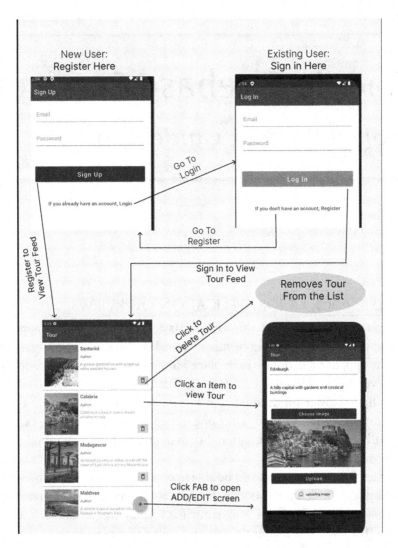

FIGURE 7.1   The Tour application flow.

## 7.2  INTRODUCING THE ANDROID NAVIGATION COMPONENT

The Android Navigation component is a navigation architecture that simplifies movement between app destinations using fragments. In previous chapters, we used activities to display different app screens and only introduced fragments in Chapter 5 using ViewPager2. We only needed one fragment for the use case in that chapter, so we integrated it into the app using the traditional method.

Navigating between fragments is not only about moving from one to another but also involves implementing other processes, such as passing data, handling deep links, managing back stacks, and more. These processes can become complicated when there are many fragments, using only the FragmentManager. This is where the navigation component comes in. To successfully integrate this framework, it is essential to understand the following terms:Navigation Graph: An XML file that defines different destinations, including the actions needed to move from one destination to another.

- **NavHostFragment:** A container within the main layout that provides an area for navigation.

- **NavController:** Used for initiating destination actions to move from one screen to another.

Add the following dependencies to the module-level build to access the navigation APIs.gradle file:

```
implementation 'androidx.navigation:navigation-
   fragment-ktx:2.5.0'
 implementation 'androidx.navigation:navigation-
   ui-ktx:2.5.0'
```

## 7.2.1 Creating the Navigation Graph

We need a navigation graph to connect to the Tour app's different destinations.

The navigation file is an XML file that defines the different screens or destinations in an Android application and how they are connected to each other. In this file, each destination is represented by a <fragment> tag, and each action that connects one destination to another is represented by a <action> tag.

The root element of the navigation file is , which contains attributes for the ID and start destination of the navigation graph. The start destination is the initial screen displayed when the app is launched.

Each <fragment> tag has fragment ID, label, and layout attributes. The fragment ID is a unique identifier for the destination, the label is a human-readable name for the destination, and the layout specifies the XML layout file that should be inflated for the destination.

Each <action> tag represents a connection between two destinations and has attributes for the action ID and destination ID. The action ID is a unique identifier for the action, and the destination ID is the ID of the destination that the action connects to. Figure 7.2 is a fragment tag specifying examples of these identifiers.

This file belongs in the res folder and should be created as a new resource file with the type set as Navigation to ensure its root element is of type navigation. The fragments for each destination will be added to the file, and actions to move from one to another will be created. To create the navigation graph, right-click on the res folder and select New>Android Resource File. Enter the file name and choose Navigation as the resource type. Figure 7.3 shows the new resource file information. Click Ok to see the generated code.

```
<fragment
    android:id="@+id/LoginFragment"        2
    android:name="eu.tutorials.tour.LoginFragment"
    tools:layout="@layout/fragment_login">

    <action
        android:id="@+id/action_LoginFragment_to_TourFragment"  1
      3  app:destination="@id/TourFragment" />
</fragment>
```

FIGURE 7.2 A Fragment tag showing action id, current fragment id, and destination id.

FIGURE 7.3 Creating a new navigation graph resource file.

The navigation graph file consists of a design and code views. To add fragments that will be part of the navigation, select the design view and click on the plus icon on the window's left side as seen in Figure 7.4. From here, you can choose the desired fragment to add. Once the fragment is added, you can click on it to see a connection dot. This dot allows you to click and drag to another fragment, creating a destination action that connects the two. Figure 7.5 shows the connecting dot. This action defines the movement from one fragment to another within the app.

FIGURE 7.4   The design view showing the plus icon for adding new fragment.

FIGURE 7.5   You can drag the dot to another fragment to create a connection.

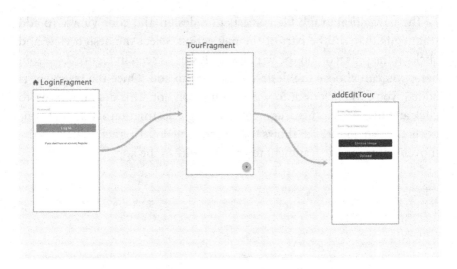

FIGURE 7.6   The tour has three destinations within the navigation graph.

Additionally, the design view also provides other tools that can be used to configure the navigation, such as adding arguments and specifying transitions between fragments. These options are available by selecting the desired fragment and navigating to the attribute panel on the right-hand side of the window.

The basic destination action for the Tour app is navigation from login fragment to Tour Fragment and from Tour Fragment to AddEditTour Fragment, which can be achieved by connecting the LoginFragment to the TourFragment and TourFragment to AddEditToutFragment. Figure 7.6 shows what the navigation graph design view should look like.

And in the code view, you will find the XML tags added and updated to reflect the three fragments with the destination and action IDs. The layouts of each fragment are displayed on the graph by adding the tools attribute within each fragment tag with the layout name as the attribute value. Here is what the code view will look like.

```
<!—The startDestination attribute indicates the first
    screen to be displayed. -->
<navigation xmlns:android="http://schemas.android.com/
    apk/res/android"
    xmlns:app="http://schemas.android.com/apk/res-auto"
    xmlns:tools="http://schemas.android.com/tools"
    android:id="@+id/nav_graph"
    app:startDestination="@id/LoginFragment" >
```

```
<!—The android:id is for the fragment id while the
   app:destion is the destination id. The android name
   is the fragment name while the tools:layout shows
   the fragment layout on the design view-->
  <fragment
       android:id="@+id/LoginFragment"
       android:name="eu.tutorials.tour.LoginFragment"
       tools:layout="@layout/fragment_login">

       <action
           android:id="@+id/action_LoginFragment_to_
             TourFragment"
           app:destination="@id/TourFragment" />
  </fragment>
  <fragment
       android:id="@+id/TourFragment "
       android:name="eu.tutorials.tour.TourFragment"
       tools:layout="@layout/fragment_tour">

       <action
           android:id="@+id/action_TourFragment_to_
             addEditTour"
           app:destination="@id/addEditTour" />
  </fragment>
  <fragment
       android:id="@+id/addEditTour"
       android:name="eu.tutorials.tour.AddEditTour"
       tools:layout="@layout/fragment_add_edit_tour"
         /> #D
</navigation>
```

## 7.2.2 Adding the NavHostFragment

Once the Navigation Graph is created, the next step is to define a container where the navigation will occur. The container can be created using the NavHostFragment in the layout of the main screen, where ours is the MainActivity layout. To do this, a FragmentContainerView is added to the layout, which will serve as the host for the destinations.

The FragmentContainerView is a widget with specific attributes that are unique to navigation. The android:name attribute is set to androidx.navigation.fragment.NavHostFragment, which indicates that it is the NavHostFragment. The app:NavGraph attribute specifies which navigation graph it will use. The app:defaultNavHost attribute is particularly important if there are multiple navigation graphs, as it specifies the default navigation container. Below is the code for the tour host container layout.

```
<androidx.constraintlayout.widget.ConstraintLayout
  xmlns:android="http://schemas.android.com/apk/res/
    android"
  xmlns:app="http://schemas.android.com/apk/res-auto"
  android:layout_width="match_parent"
  android:layout_height="match_parent"
  app:layout_behavior="@string/appbar_scrolling_view_
    behavior">

  <androidx.fragment.app.FragmentContainerView
    android:id="@+id/nav_host_fragment_content_main"
    android:name="androidx.navigation.fragment.
      NavHostFragment"
    android:layout_width="0dp"
    android:layout_height="0dp"
    app:defaultNavHost="true"
    app:layout_constraintBottom_toBottomOf="parent"
    app:layout_constraintEnd_toEndOf="parent"
    app:layout_constraintStart_toStartOf="parent"
    app:layout_constraintTop_toTopOf="parent"
    app:navGraph="@navigation/nav_graph" />
</androidx.constraintlayout.widget.ConstraintLayout>
```

If the layout is set up correctly with the right navigation graph, you should see the first destination screen as the interface on the design view of the above layout just like in Figure 7.7.

FIGURE 7.7   The start destination to be displayed is the login screen.

### 7.2.3 Setting up the NavController

The NavController is an Android Navigation component object responsible for navigating between different screens or destinations within an app. It manages the navigation stack, which keeps track of the current state of the app and allows users to move back and forth between screens.

The NavController is created by the Navigation component and is typically associated with the NavHostFragment in the app's UI. When a user performs an action that triggers a navigation event, such as clicking on a button or selecting an item from a menu, the NavController performs the navigation and updates the navigation stack accordingly.

If the Tour app was to have any menus, such as an options menu on the toolbar, a drawer menu on the left side with a hamburger icon, or a bottom navigation menu, the NavHostFragment in the MainActivity must be set up to properly connect with these menus and the controller that manages them and their back stack.

To achieve this, we first need to get a reference to the Fragment-ContainerView and create it as a NavHostFragment. Then, we connect the nav controller with any of the menus. The code below will setup the NavHost fragment with the app menu.

```
/* The code above retrieves the NavHostFragment from
   the supportFragmentManager and assigns it to
   navHostFragment variable.
*/
   val navHostFragment = supportFragmentManager
   .findFragmentById(R.id.nav_host_fragment_content_
      main) as NavHostFragment

/* The NavController is obtained from the NavHost
   Fragment and assigns it to navController.
*/
        val navController = navHostFragment.
           navController

/* The ActionBar and BottomNavigationView is setup
   with the NavController to enable navigation within
   the app.
*/
        appBarConfiguration = AppBarConfiguration
           (navController.graph).
```

```
setupActionBarWithNavController
    (navController, appBarConfiguration)

setupActionBarWithNavController(navController,
    drawerLayout = drawerLayout)

binding?.bottomNav?.setupWithNavController(nav
    Controller = navController)
```

Since we are not using any of the menus for the Tour app, we will only need to use the findNavController within any current destinations to navigate to the next one by calling the action id. For example, when the FloatingActionButton is clicked, the action to move from TourFragment to the AddEditTourFragment will be called. If the Sign-in button is clicked, the action to move from the LoginFragment to the TourFragment will be called. We will see the code for navigating between the destinations later in this chapter but first, let's dive into the Google Firebase platform.

## 7.3 AN INTRODUCTION TO GOOGLE FIREBASE SERVICES

Firebase Services by Google is a platform that enables developers to build and deploy applications quickly and easily. It is a Backend as a Service (BaaS) platform that provides several services and APIs for developers to create sophisticated applications. While Firebase is popular among mobile developers, it supports website frameworks.

Firebase Services provides developers with powerful tools to manage user data and files, including the ability to perform complete CRUD operations. In this chapter, we will use several Firebase Services, including Firebase Authentication, Cloud Firestore, and Cloud Storage.

- Firebase Authentication is a flexible and easy-to-use system that enables developers to add authentication to their applications. It supports multiple authentication methods, including email and password, phone numbers, and social providers like Google, Facebook, and Twitter (X). With Firebase Authentication, developers can quickly and easily authenticate users in their applications without building a custom authentication system.

- Cloud Firestore is a cloud-based NoSQL database that offers powerful and easy-to-use features for data management. It is designed to keep your data in sync across all client apps using real-time listeners and offers offline support for mobile and web applications. This enables developers to build responsive applications regardless of network latency or internet connectivity.

- Cloud Storage is a service that supports applications with file management, such as photos, videos, music, and other files. It allows developers to upload and retrieve files from anywhere for free during development and allows them to pay as they go as users increase. With Cloud Storage, developers can store large files and access them from anywhere, making it a convenient option for applications that require file management.

## 7.3.1 Adding Your Project to Google Firebase

- To use Google Firebase, you require a Google account which you will use to sign up for an account. Head over https://firebase.google.com/ and click on Go to the console menu as seen in Figure 7.8.

- After clicking on Go to console, a window will pop up and ask you to select a Google account to continue. Next, you will see a Firebase page where you can create a project as seen in Figure 7.9.

- Click on Add project to create one. Click on the + icon and another screen will appear prompting you to create a project by entering the name.

FIGURE 7.8    Firebase "Go to Console" Button.

FIGURE 7.9    Firebase Projects page to be seen after signup.

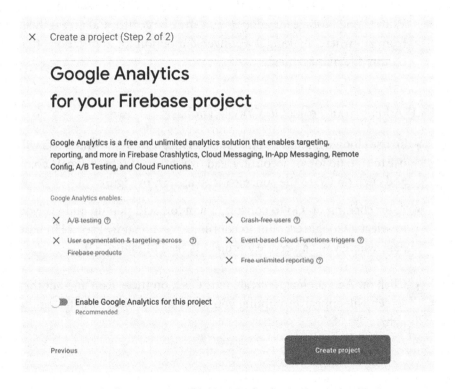

FIGURE 7.10    The "create project" button to finalize a new project setup.

- After you have entered the project name, click continue then disable Google Analytics which is one of the services that Firebase provides but will not be covered in this chapter. Then you can click on Create Project to complete the process. Figure 7.10 shows the project creation screen.

- The creation process will begin and when completed you will see a continue button that leads to your project dashboard.

FIGURE 7.11  Project page showing the different app icons Firebase can be integrated into.

These steps create a general project overview providing you with options to set up a specific application type or framework you intend to develop for. As seen in Figure 7.11, you will find the different icons for each one including Android which you will need to select to create an Android project.

To add Firebase to an Android app, the first step is to register it using the package name. Remember the package name should be unique since it will be used for identifying this specific application. It is the application id that you entered while creating the new project in Android Studio and you can find it in the build.gradle file. Figure 7.12 shows the registering info screen.

After adding the package name, you can ignore the App nickname and sign-in certificate as they are not required for this project. Register the app to generate a config file. Download the file then copy and paste it into the app folder. To see the file after you have moved it into the app folder make sure to select the Project view rather than Android as seen in Figure 7.13.

Note that this file is an important part of your Firebase project and should be kept private and secured. The next step is to add the Firebase SDK dependency; still, on the project setup page, click next to copy the classpath dependency and add it to the project level build.gradle file while the implementation goes into the app level build.gradle file. And make sure to apply the plugin at the top of the file.

## 7.3.2 Project Level Dependencies

```
buildscript {
    dependencies{
        classpath 'com.google.
gms:google-services:4.3.13'
    }
}
```

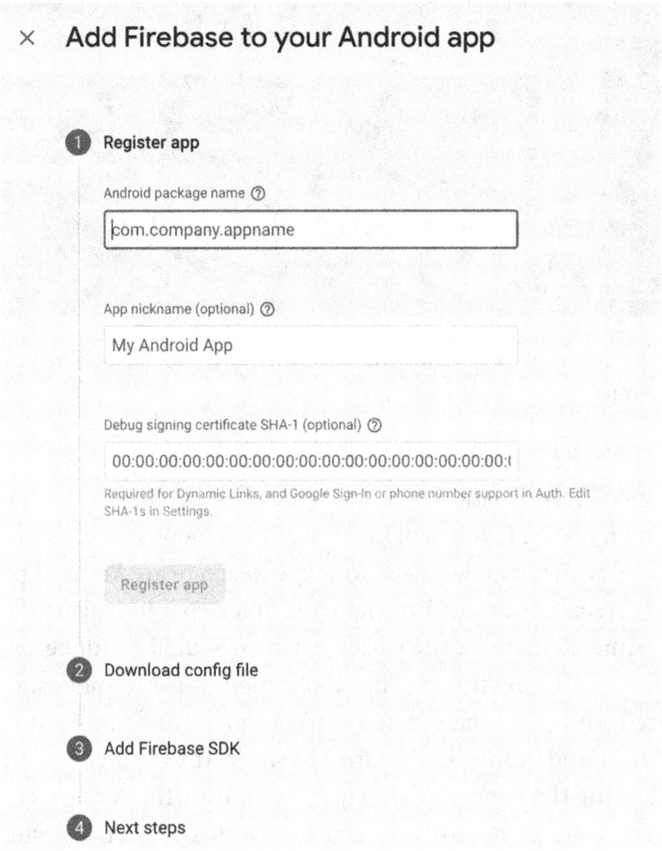

FIGURE 7.12   Add an Android app to a Firebase project.

### 7.3.3 App-Level Dependencies

```
plugins {
    id 'com.google.gms.google-services'
}
```

implementation platform('com.google.firebase:firebase-bom:30.2.0')

Sync the added dependencies and continue to the project console. Rebuild the project and ensure it completes without errors to confirm the setup's success.

## 7.4 FIREBASE AUTHENTICATION WITH EMAIL AND PASSWORD

Authentication is the crucial process of verifying a user's identity with specific credentials, such as an email and password. As mentioned earlier,

FIGURE 7.13  Add google-services.json file to the project level app folder.

Firebase offers several authentication methods, but this chapter will focus on email and password authentication. To start using Firebase authentication, you must first enable the authentication method you intend to use.

To enable the authentication method, navigate to the Firebase project dashboard and click the Build menu to access the product services. From there, you can select Authentication, which will open the Authentication page, where you can enable the authentication method you want to use.

Firebase Authentication provides a flexible and user-friendly system that enables developers to add authentication to their applications without worrying about user management and security. This service supports multiple authentication methods, including email and password, phone numbers, and social providers like Google, Facebook, and Twitter (X).

With Firebase Authentication, you can quickly implement email verification, password resets, and multifactor authentication features. This ensures your users' data is secure and protected from unauthorized access. Figure 7.14 shows the different services available to Firebase project.

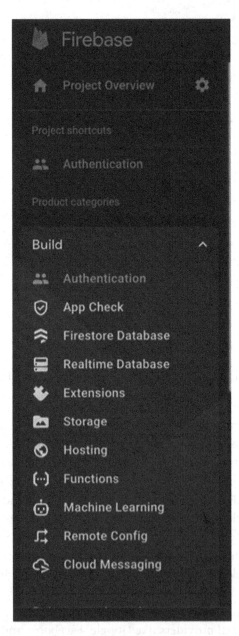

FIGURE 7.14   The Firebase services available to a project.

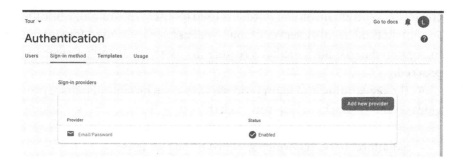

FIGURE 7.15    Enabling the email and password authentication method.

You can click on authentication and select Email/password provider to see the option to enable or disable. After you have enabled the email provider you should see it added to the Sign-in providers with status enabled as seen in Figure 7.15.

The Firebase Assistant available on Android Studio is a helpful tool that allows easy and quick integration with Firebase services. Open the Firebase assistant, choose authentication, click Add Firebase authentication to your app, and accept the changes. Check the dependencies section in build. gradle to see the authentication SDK added.

```
dependencies {
implementation platform('com.google.firebase:firebase-
   bom:30.2.0')
}
```

The Firebase BOM (Bill of Materials) added above is a dependency management tool provided by Google to make it easier for developers to manage their Firebase dependencies in their Android projects. It provides a simple way to specify the versions of the Firebase libraries that your app uses, so you don't have to update them every time a new version is released manually. Instead, you can specify the version of the Firebase BOM that you want to use in your project, and it will manage the versions of the Firebase libraries for you. This helps ensure that your app uses compatible versions of Firebase libraries, which can help prevent conflicts and other issues. With this dependency added, we will now look at what registering a user with email and password entails.

### 7.4.1  Registering a User to Firebase Authentication

First, Firebase authentication provides two methods to handle user registration and login using email and password. The first method, createUserWithEmailAndPasword(), is used for user registration, while the second method, signInUserWithEmailAndPassword(), is used for signing in registered users. Both methods require the user's email and password to proceed.

As the registration and login processes are asynchronous, Firebase provides several callbacks to help you track their state. These callbacks include:

- onFailureListener(), which is called if the task fails.

- onSuccessListener(), which is called if the task is successful.

- onCancelledListener(), which is called if the task is canceled.

- onCompleteListener(), which is called when the task is completed.

It is important to note that task completion does not guarantee task success; the task can result in any of the three actions mentioned above, that is, success, failure, or cancellation.

You can use the onCompleteListener() to manage each state, which returns a TaskResult. The TaskResult can be used to determine the outcome of the task, and you can perform different actions depending on the result. For example, if the task is successful, you can proceed to the next step, such as navigating to the user's profile page. On the other hand, if the task fails, you can display an error message to the user or retry the operation.

### 7.4.2 Implementing the Authentication Flow

The Tour application has a Login UI allowing users to sign-in or register. We will utilize the Constraint Group widget to efficiently manage each case from a single screen. This widget is particularly helpful when working with multiple child widgets to create complex layouts. In our case, we will use it to group the widgets for registration and login in two parts. When the login text is clicked, the login group becomes visible while the register group becomes hidden and vice versa. Let's look at the coding solution.

To enable users to sign-in or register in the Tour application, we will create a dedicated class to handle all the Firebase operations. Within this class, we will create an instance of the FirebaseAuth object and use its built-in methods to register and sign-in users.

By separating the Firebase operations from the UI, we can ensure organized code implementation, making it easier to maintain and debug in the future. Additionally, this approach allows us to reuse the same Firebase code in other parts of the application, minimizing code redundancy and promoting a more scalable codebase. Below is the Firebase service class with the register and sign-in methods.

```
class FirebaseServices(
    private val firebaseAuth:FirebaseAuth =
    FirebaseAuth.getInstance()) {

    fun registerUser(
        userEmail: String,
        userPassword: String,
        onUserCreated:(Task<AuthResult>)->Unit
    ){
            firebaseAuth.createUserWithEmailAndPassword
              (userEmail, userPassword)
                .addOnCompleteListener {
                    onUserCreated(it)
                }
    }


    fun signInUser(
        userEmail: String,
        userPassword: String,
        onUserSignIn:(Task<AuthResult>)->Unit
    ){
        firebaseAuth.signInWithEmailAndPassword(user
          Email, userPassword)
            .addOnCompleteListener {
                onUserSignIn(it)
            }
    }
}
```

Each method above provides a parameter for passing the email and password. In the Fragment class, the registerUser and signInUser methods from the service class will be called using the right buttons for each process. If the task is successful, a success message is displayed on the screen, and the user is taken to the Tour screen. The function below checks that the email and password are not empty and either signs a user in or registers them before navigating into the tour screen.

```kotlin
private fun setUpViewActions(){
    val emailEditText = binding.emailEt.text.
      toString()
    val passwordEditText = binding.passwordEt.text.
      toString()
    binding.apply {
        loginBtn.setOnClickListener {
            if (emailEditText.isNullOrEmpty() ||
passwordEditText.isNullOrEmpty()) {
                Toast.makeText(
                    requireContext(),
                    "Fields cannot be empty",
                    Toast.LENGTH_LONG
                ).show()
            } else {
                firebaseServices.SignInUser(
                    emailEditText,
                    passwordEditText
                ) {

/*
  When signup or login is successful, we check that
the current destination is not already TourFragment
before calling the navigate method. This ensures that
no crash can occur when multiple clicks or calls are
made to the same destination.
*/
                    if (it.isSuccessful) {
if (findNavController().currentDestination?.id !=
R.id.action_LoginFragment_to_TourFragment){

    findNavController().navigate(R.id.action_Login
      Fragment_to_TourFragment) }
                    } else {
                        Toast.makeText(
                            requireContext(),
                            it.exception.toString(),
                            Toast.LENGTH_LONG
                        ).show()
                    }
                }
            }
        }
        signUpBtn.setOnClickListener {
```

```
                 if (emailEditText.isNullOrEmpty() ||
                   passwordEditText.isNullOrEmpty()) {
                     Toast.makeText(
                         requireContext(),
                         "Fields cannot be empty",
                         Toast.LENGTH_LONG
                     ).show()
                 } else {
                     firebaseServices.registerUser(
                         emailEditText,
                         passwordEditText
                     ) {
                         if (it.isSuccessful) {
                             Toast.makeText(
                                 requireContext(),
                                 "User Registered",
                                  Toast.LENGTH_LONG
                             ).show()
if (findNavController().currentDestination?.id !=
  R.id.action_LoginFragment_to_TourFragment){
      findNavController().navigate(R.id.action_
      LoginFragment_to_TourFragment)}

                             Log.d("LoginActivity",
                                it.result.user?.email.
                                toString())
                         } else {
                             Toast.makeText(
                                 requireContext(),
                                 it.exception.toString(),
                                  Toast.LENGTH_LONG
                             ).show()
                             Log.d("LoginActivity", it.
                                exception.toString())
                         }
                     }
                 }
             }

        loginInstruction.setOnClickListener {
            loginHideGroup.visibility = View.GONE
            signUpHideGroup.visibility = View.
              VISIBLE
            (activity as MainActivity).title =
              getString(R.string.login)
        }
```

```
signUpInstruction.setOnClickListener {
    loginHideGroup.visibility = View.VISIBLE
    signUpHideGroup.visibility = View.GONE
    (activity as MainActivity).title =
        getString(R.string.signUp)
    }
} }
```

### 7.4.2.1 Testing the Authentication process

Now you can run the application and click on the TextView that takes you to the signup screen since you are yet to register. Enter an email and password to get registered. The Tour screen will be opened if the fields are not empty and the registering is successful. Now rerun the app and use the registered account to try in.

Figure 7.16 shows the registered user in the authentication dashboard within Authentication menu.

## 7.5 MANAGING THE TOUR IMAGES WITH FIREBASE CLOUD STORAGE

Users need to add tours to the app when they access the tour screen. We will begin with image upload, which requires quite a step to be completed successfully. The location for storing files like images in Firebase differs from where typical data like texts are stored.

Firebase cloud storage is a cost-effective storage service where you can store and retrieve user-generated content like images and videos from your Firebase project. Not only does it provide a storage platform, but it also has APIs in place that enables developers easily integrate it into their applications.

FIGURE 7.16  Viewing a registered user via the Users menu.

In your Firebase project dashboard, you will find the option for storage. Before you can start using the service, you need to enable it by clicking on the Get Started button and choosing to start in the production mode to ensure that only registered users can upload files. Finally, select the default file location suggested by it and click done. To upload and retrieve images from storage, there are two essential functions, putfile() and download-Url. The putFile function is used to upload an image into storage, while the downloadUrl is used to get a URL to the image for displaying on the Android application. Just like every Firebase service, you must get an instance of the specific service which you can use to access the utility methods like the putfile and downloadUrl. In the FirebaseService class, we will add the following code for uploading and downloading the image.

```
/*
The selectedImageUri is the parameter for receiving
the image to be uploaded while onUploadSuccess is a
lambda method with a string parameter to receive the
image access URL after the download is successful.
*/
fun uploadImageToFirebaseStorageAndAddTour(
        selectedImageUri: Uri,
        onUploadSuccess: (String)->Unit
    ){

/* The storageRef which is the instance of the storage
service is used to create a path with a name for each
uploaded image. tourImages is the folder where each
image will be named using the time it got uploaded in
milliseconds.
    */
            val uploadTask = storageRef.child
                ("tourImages/${ Calendar.getInstance().
                time.time}")

/*
The putFile method is used to get the image selected
from the device and uploaded to storage. If it is
successful, the downloadUrl will be retrieved and
passed to the receiving lambda.
*/
uploadTask.putFile(selectedImageUri).addOnComplete
    Listener {
                if (it.isSuccessful){
```

```
uploadTask.downloadUrl.addOnSuccess
    Listener { uri ->
        if (uri.toString().isNot
        Empty()) {

            Log.d(
                "AddTourFragment",
                "TourImage link get
                    DownloadImageUrl:
                    $uri"
            )

        onUploadSuccess(uri.toString())
        } else {
            Log.d("AddTourFragment",
            "Image Url is null")
        }
    Log.d("AddTourFragment", "Image
    File Location:// $uri")
    }}}}
```

### 7.5.1 Selecting Image from the Device

To pick an image that will be uploaded to Firebase storage from the device, READ_EXTERNAL_STORAGE permission must be granted. Android permission has already been discussed in Chapter 6 so you can refer to it for more clarity. The first step is to add the specific permission to the manifest file and thereafter implement the code to request the user to enable access for reading files from external storage. Setting up the ActivityResultLauncher in fragments differs slightly from how it is done in the Activity. Instead of creating and initializing the launcher globally, the initialization needs to be made within the fragments onCreate method to ensure that the fragment has been created and the request properly initialized at the point of launching the permission. But also, because some other methods and implementations might require checking if the access has been granted before picking an image, it will be declared as a global variable and initialized within the onCreate.

Two launcher requests are needed to pick images from the device. The first will request permission to access the external storage, while the second will open the external storage for the image selection. As for selecting the image, we discussed implicit intents in Chapter 4, and this is applicable when picking an image from the device because it will not specify the specific app component to start but rather specify the action and provides some data with which to perform the action.

Lets' look at the code below.

```
//This intent action will open the device media file.
    galleryIntent = Intent(
            Intent.ACTION_PICK,
            MediaStore.Images.Media.EXTERNAL_
            CONTENT_URI
        )


/*
 A permission to request access to media files is
registered and if the result is OK then an image was
selected. The data will be received, and image upload
will be processed.
*/
        requestPermissionLauncher =
           registerForActivityResult(
              ActivityResultContracts.Request
                 Permission()
           ) { isGranted: Boolean ->
              if (isGranted) {
                 showToast("Storage permission
                    granted")

                 startActivityLaunch.launch(gallery
                    Intent)
              } else {
                 showToast("Storage permission
                    denied. You can also allow it
                    from settings.")
              }

           }
        startActivityLaunch =
         registerForActivityResult(ActivityResult
           Contracts.StartActivityForResult()) {
              val resultCode = it.resultCode
              val data = it.data

              if (resultCode == AppCompatActivity.
                 RESULT_OK && data != null) {
                 try {
                    selectedImageFileUri = data.
                       data
```

```
                              selectedImageFileUri?.let {
                                it1 ->

/* The Firebase storage upload method that adds the
   image to Firebase.
*/

firebaseServices.uploadImageToFirebaseStorageAndAddTo
   ur(it1){
                                    Log.d("image link",it)
                                }
                            }
                            binding.previewImageView.
                                visibility = View.VISIBLE
                            binding.previewImageView.set
                                ImageURI(selectedImageFile
                                Uri)

                            Log.d(TAG, "Selected
                                Image Uri file ||| ===
                                ${selectedImageFileUri}")
                            Log.d(TAG, "Showing image Uri
                                $selectedImageFileUri")

                        } catch (e: IOException) {
                            e.printStackTrace()
                            showToast("Image selection
                                Failed! ${e.message}")
                        }
                    }else{

/* If the permission is not enabled, the permission
   request will be launched.
*/
                        requestPermissionLauncher.
                            launch(Manifest.permission.
                            READ_EXTERNAL_STORAGE)
                    }
                }
```

There is a choose image button on the UI that, when clicked, checks if the permission is granted and opens the external storage or requests permission If it has not been granted. The checkPermissions method below is called anytime the read external storage permission needs to be checked.

```
private fun checkPermissions(context: Context) {
        if (ContextCompat.checkSelfPermission(
                context,
                Manifest.permission.READ_EXTERNAL_
                STORAGE
            )
            == PackageManager.PERMISSION_GRANTED
        ) {
            startActivityLaunch.launch(galleryIntent)
        }else{
            requestPermissionLauncher.launch(Manifest.
                permission.READ_EXTERNAL_STORAGE)
        }

    }

binding.chooseImageBtn.setOnClickListener {
        showToast("clicked")
        checkPermissions(requireContext())
    }
```

*7.5.1.1 Testing the Image Upload and Retrieval from Firebase Storage*
Before you run the app, you must bypass needing to sign-in every time it is
started. You need to check if there is an existing registered user on the app
and navigate straight into the tour feed. Firebase authentication has the
currentUser method that is used to retrieve the existing user. The Login
screen is a suitable place to check if the current user is not null then navigate them into the Tour screen. Here is what the code should look like, having in mind that all Firebase data should be in the Firebase service class.

```
FirebaseService class
    val hasUser = firebaseAuth.currentUser != null
Run the application and login into the

LoginFragment

if (firebaseServices.hasUser)
            findNavController().navigate(R.id.action_
                FirstFragment_to_SecondFragment)
```

Run the application, grant the request to read the external storage, and
pick an image from the file.

Check the log cat to view the image URL which you can click to view in
a browser.

FIGURE 7.17   Uploaded image file on the Storage dashboard.

```
2022-07-21 08:21:49.909 9674-9674/eu.tutorials.tour D/image
    link: https://firebasestorage.googleapis.com/v0/b/tour-
    36acf.appspot.com/o/tourImages%2F1658388103167?alt=media
    &token=abe7e5dd-69a0-4262-b99f-9ea985d40067
```

Open the storage dashboard in the Firebase project to see the uploaded image as seen in Figure 7.17.

## 7.6  SAVING AND READING DATA WITH FIREBASE FIRESTORE

Now that we have implemented image upload and retrieval, we can move on to complete the tour section of our app by using Cloud Firestore. Cloud Firestore is a powerful NoSQL database that allows for flexible data storage and retrieval. Unlike a traditional relational database, Cloud Firestore does not require a specific structure within its tables, allowing for documents in collections to contain varying sets of information.

To create a collection in Cloud Firestore, you can either manually create a name or let Firestore automatically generate one for you once the first data is added. Each document in the collection should be structured as a key-value pair, with the key serving as an identifier when reading from the database. In Kotlin, it is best practice to create an object class that groups the content of each document, including a conversion to a map that can be easily called when writing into Cloud Firestore.

For our tour section, each document will include the name of a place, a description, an image, and the author's ID. The ID will be important when updating and deleting a tour, as it will ensure that only the creator of a tour can make modifications to it. Here is an example of what the Tour class might look like:

```
data class Tour(
    var id: String = UUID.randomUUID().toString(),
    var placeName: String = "",
    var description: String = "",
    var userId: String = "",
```

```
    var placeImage: String = "",
)  {

    fun toMap() =
        mapOf(
            "tourId" to tourId,
            "placeName" to placeName,
            "description" to description,
            "userId" to userId,
            "placeImage" to placeImage
        )

}
```

We are using a data class rather than a regular class to create the tour model. If you know Java, you will notice the difference between a POJO class used to hold data and the Kotlin data class. A data class is a special type of class that is designed to hold data. It provides a concise way to create classes that contain only properties and the associated getters and setters without having to write any additional boilerplate code. They are useful when you define a simple class primarily used for storing data and can make your code more readable and maintainable.

For each property in the Tour model, there is an empty String as the value, which is not required for a typical model in Kotlin. We have provided them in this use case because if all the primary constructor parameters have default values, the compiler will generate an additional empty constructor which essential for a Firebase operation.

Now that we have a data class, we will use it to perform Firebase operations, starting with saving data to the database.

### 7.6.1 Saving a Tour into Firestore

To use Firestore, you first need to add its dependency to your project's build.gradle file and enable it on the Firebase console dashboard. To do this, you can select it from the Firebase menu, click on the "Create Database" button, and set the rules to be in production mode with the read and write value set to true.

After enabling Firestore, you can initialize an instance of it and use it to reference the method for adding a tour document. There are two methods used for adding documents to a tour: the set method and the add method. The set method is used when you want to specify a certain type of data as an ID for the document, while the add method is used when you want the database to automatically generate an ID for each created document.

Here's the code snippet for the FirebaseService class to add a Tour document:

```
fun saveATour(tour:Tour,onTourSaved:(Task<Void>)->Unit){
    databseReference.document().set(tour).
            addOnCompleteListener {
                if(it.isSuccessful){
                    onTourSaved(it)
                }else{
    Log.d("Firebase Services","${it.exception}")
                }
            }
    }
```

Within the AddEditFragment, we retrieve the value of each input view and the image and use it to create a Tour object. If any of the values are not null or empty, the Tour object will be saved to Firebase. The following is an implementation of the code:

```
binding.uploadBtn.setOnClickListener {
    val userId = firebaseServices.user?.uid.to
      String()
    val name = binding.placeName.text.toString()
    val image = selectedImageFileUri.toString()
    val desc = binding.placeDescription.text.
      toString()
    if (userId.isNullOrEmpty() || name.isNullOr
      Empty() ||
        image.isNullOrEmpty() || desc.isNullOr
          Empty()){
        showToast("Field cannot be empty")
    }else{
    firebaseServices.saveATour(Tour(placeName =
      name,
        description = desc,userId= userId,
          placeImage = image)) {
        if (it.isSuccessful){
            showToast("Tour successfully uploaded")
        }else{
            showToast(it.exception?.message.
              toString())
        }
        }
    }
    }
}
```

### 7.6.1.1 Testing the add tour feature to firestore

Now run the app, click the floating action button, and add text to the input fields. Select an image and finally click upload. Also, try clicking on the upload button without entering any value. Toast will be displayed to inform you that some or all fields are empty. Figure 7.18 shows the testing flow for adding a tour.

## 7.6.2 Fetching Data from Firestore

To retrieve data from Firestore, you need to know the name of the collection and document you want to access. In the case of the Tour documents, you'll be retrieving each document as an object of the Tour class and adding them to a list to populate the tour feed. It's important to use listeners

FIGURE 7.18   Testing the add tour feature.

available within the Firestore API to ensure that any changes made to the document are reflected in real time within the application. Our collection is named tours and, in the function below, we use the addOnCompleteListener() to fetch the documents from it.

```kotlin
fun getAllTour(onSuccess:(tours:List<Tour>)->Unit){
    val toursList = ArrayList<Tour>()
    val response = database.collection("tours").
      get().addOnCompleteListener {
        if(it.isSuccessful){
        for (document in it.result.documents) {
            val tour = document.toObject(Tour::
              class.java)
            if (tour != null) {
                toursList.add(tour)
            }
            onSuccess(toursList)
            Log.d(
                "TourFragment",
                "All Tours Info:|:|:|:${document.
                  id} => ${document.data}")
        }
    }}

}
```

The method getAllTours() should be added to the FirebaseService class and will be called from the TourFragment to retrieve the tour list returned by the onSuccess function. To access the method, we will instantiate an object of the FirebaseService class and invoke the method within the onViewCreated method. We will then add a log statement to print the retrieved tours.

```kotlin
firebaseServices.getAllTour {
            Log.d("tours", "$it")
        }
```

### 7.6.2.1 Testing the Read data from Firestore

The tour feed is going to be displayed on a widget which we will be discussing in the next topic. But for now, the reading process will be tested by logging in on the terminal. Run the application and open the logcat to see the tours printed on it as seen on Figure 7.19.

Now click on the add button and create a new tour, navigate back to the tour screen, and check to see the new our added to the displayed list.

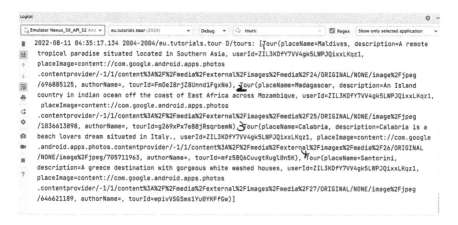

FIGURE 7.19   Logging the tours from the database.

## 7.7  DISPLAYING A DYNAMIC LIST USING A RECYCLERVIEW

In today's mobile app development, presenting users with a list of items is a common design pattern. Social media apps such as Facebook and Instagram display a list of posts from users, while email apps show a list of emails. To effectively manage such lists where item position changes periodically, the RecyclerView widget was created in Android. The RecyclerView widget is designed to replace the traditional ListView and GridView as they become more difficult to use with the display of dynamic items.

The RecyclerView is a container that displays large data sets that can be scrolled very efficiently by maintaining a limited number of views. This widget is ideal for data collections whose elements change frequently based on user actions or events. It requires an adapter which is responsible for providing and reusing only one view for all items on the list and a ViewHolder that provides the layout for each item on the list.

Additionally, it also includes a LayoutManager that tells the Recycler-View the direction to display its children. There are three default layouts provided by the RecyclerView widget: LinearLayoutManager, GridLayout-Manager, and StaggeredGridLayoutManager. Figure 7.20 shows the data display using a RecylerView.

- The LinearLayoutManager arranges items in a single column or row depending on the orientation set.

- The GridLayoutManager displays items in a grid of rows and columns.

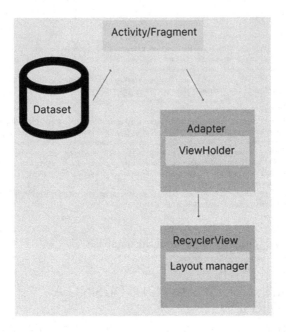

FIGURE 7.20   The RecyclerView data flow with ViewHolder and adapter.

- The StaggeredGridLayoutManager is like the GridLayoutManager but arranges items in a staggered pattern, allowing for items with different heights and widths to be displayed.

For a working Recyclerview, the following widgets and objects are required.

- The RecyclerView
- An Item layout
- ViewHolder
- Adapter
- LayoutManager

### 7.7.1  Adding the Recyclerview to the Tour Fragment Layout

With the understanding of the Recyclerview, the tour data will be retrieved from the Firestore and displayed on a RecylerView. Since it will be a dynamic list that will keep changing as more tour is added to the database. The first step is to add the View to the layout of the Tours Fragment with its width set to match_parent, constraint top set to the top of parent, and layout height set to wrap_content.

```
<androidx.recyclerview.widget.RecyclerView
    android:id="@+id/tourRv"
    android:layout_width="match_parent"
    app:layout_constraintTop_toTopOf="parent"
    android:layout_height="wrap_content"/>
```

### 7.7.2 Creating the Item Layout

After adding the RecyclerView to the layout of the Tours Fragment, the next step is to define a layout that will be used for each item within the list. This layout should contain an ImageView for the image, a TextView for the place name, and another TextView for the description.

To create the item layout, you can use a ConstraintLayout, which allows you to define the position of each view relative to the others. For example, you can constrain the ImageView to the start of the parent, set the name TextView to the top of the parent and its start to the end of the ImageView, and set the description TextView to the bottom of the name TextView and its start to the end of the ImageView.

Here's the code for the Recyclerview's item layout:

```
<androidx.constraintlayout.widget.ConstraintLayout
    xmlns:android="http://schemas.android.com/apk/res/
    android"
    xmlns:app="http://schemas.android.com/apk/
        res-auto"
    android:layout_width="match_parent"
    android:layout_height="wrap_content"
    android:orientation="horizontal"
    android:padding="10dp">

    <ImageView
        android:id="@+id/placeImageView"
        android:layout_width="126dp"
        android:layout_height="150dp"
        android:scaleType="centerCrop"
        app:layout_constraintBottom_toBottomOf=
            "parent"
        app:layout_constraintStart_toStartOf="parent"
        app:layout_constraintTop_toTopOf="parent"
        android:src="@drawable/water_villa" />
```

```xml
<TextView
    android:id="@+id/placeNameTextView"
    android:layout_width="wrap_content"
    android:layout_height="wrap_content"
    android:layout_marginStart="8dp"
    android:ellipsize="end"
    android:text="@string/place"
    android:maxLines="1"
    android:textSize="18sp"
    android:textStyle="bold"
    app:layout_constraintStart_toEndOf="@+id/
      placeImageView"
    app:layout_constraintTop_toTopOf="@+id/
      placeImageView" />

<TextView
    android:id="@+id/dateTextView"
    android:layout_width="wrap_content"
    android:layout_height="wrap_content"
    android:layout_marginTop="8dp"
    android:ellipsize="end"
    android:text="@string/date"
    android:maxLines="1"
    android:textStyle="bold"
    app:layout_constraintStart_toStartOf="@+id/
      placeNameTextView"
    app:layout_constraintTop_toBottomOf="@+id/
      placeNameTextView" />

<TextView
    android:id="@+id/authorNameTextView"
    android:layout_width="wrap_content"
    android:layout_height="wrap_content"
    android:layout_marginTop="8dp"
    android:ellipsize="end"
    android:text="TextView"
    android:maxLines="1"
    app:layout_constraintStart_toStartOf="@+id/
      dateTextView"
    app:layout_constraintTop_toBottomOf="@+id/
      dateTextView" />

<TextView
    android:id="@+id/descriptionTextView"
    android:layout_width="wrap_content"
    android:layout_height="wrap_content"
```

```
android:layout_marginTop="8dp"
android:ellipsize="end"
android:maxLength="200"
android:text="TextView"
android:maxLines="3"
android:textColor="@android:color/darker_gray"
app:layout_constraintStart_toStartOf="@+id/
    authorNameTextView"
app:layout_constraintTop_toBottomOf="@+id/
    authorNameTextView" />
```

```
</androidx.constraintlayout.widget.ConstraintLayout>
```

### 7.7.3 Creating the Adapter and the ViewHolder

In this step, we will create an adapter that will provide the list for the Recyclerview. The adapter will extend the RecyclerView.Adapter class and with the help of a RecyclerView.ViewHolder, it will inherit the onCreateViewHolder method that will inflate the item layout, and the onBindViewHolder method that binds each item on the list with the item layout. That been said, the Adapter class has three main methods: onCreateViewHolder(), onBindViewHolder(), and getItemCount().

- **onCreateViewHolder()**: This method is responsible for inflating the layout for each item in the list and creating a ViewHolder for it. This method is called when the RecyclerView needs a new ViewHolder to display an item. It inflates the layout for the item and creates a new instance of the ViewHolder.

- **onBindViewHolder()**: This method is responsible for binding the data to the ViewHolder when it is displayed on the screen. This method is called every time a new item is displayed on the screen. It gets the data for the item and sets the values of the views in the ViewHolder to display the data.

- **getItemCount()**: This method returns the number of items in the list. The RecyclerView uses this method to determine the size of the list and how many items it needs to display.

Furthermore, when binding the views within the onBindViewHolder(), the image URL will be loaded using Glide, a library that efficiently loads images from the internet into an ImageView. To use Glide, its dependency must be added to the build.gradle file since it is a third-party tool:

implementation 'com.github.bumptech.glide:glide:4.13.2'

Below is the TourAdapter class prepared for the tour screen.

```kotlin
class ToursAdapter(
    private val tourItems: ArrayList<Tour>,
    private val listener: (Tour) -> Unit
) : RecyclerView.Adapter<ToursAdapter.ToursView
Holder>() {

    override fun onCreateViewHolder(parent: ViewGroup,
        viewType: Int): ToursViewHolder {
        val binding = TourItemViewBinding
            .inflate(LayoutInflater.from(parent.
                context), parent, false)
        return ToursViewHolder(binding)
    }

    @RequiresApi(Build.VERSION_CODES.O)
    override fun onBindViewHolder(holder:
      ToursViewHolder, position: Int) {
        with(holder) {
            with(tourItems[position]) {
                val context = holder.itemView.context

                binding.placeNameTextView.text =
                    placeName
                binding.descriptionTextView.text =
                    description
                binding.authorNameTextView.text =
                    context.getString(R.string.author,
                    placeName)

                Log.d("TourAdapter Image =|=|=",
                    "===$placeName")

                Glide.with(holder.itemView.context)
                    .load(placeImage)
                    .into(binding.placeImageView)

                holder.itemView.setOnClickListener {
                    listener.invoke(tourItems[position])
                }
            }
        }
    }
}
```

```
override fun getItemCount() = tourItems.size

inner class ToursViewHolder(val binding:
  TourItemViewBinding) :
    RecyclerView.ViewHolder(binding.root)
```
}

### 7.7.4 Binding the Adapter to the RecyclerVIew

In the TourFragment, we will now display the tour list on the RecyclerView by binding the adapter created above to it. This is done by initializing the Adapter class and passing the list fetched from the Firebase as the data into its constructor. It is also important to add a layout manager at this point as this is an easily forgettable step that can keep you from achieving the intended result. Below is the function for setting up the adapter with the RecyclerView

```
private fun initializedAdapter(toursList:
  ArrayList<Tour>) {
    val tourAdapter = ToursAdapter(toursList)
    val dividerItemDecoration = DividerItemDec
      oration(requireActivity(), RecyclerView.
      VERTICAL)
    if (toursList.isNotEmpty()) {
        binding.apply {
            binding.tourRv.adapter = tourAdapter
            binding.tourRv.layoutManager = Linear
              LayoutManager(requireActivity())
            binding.tourRv.addItemDecoration
              (dividerItemDecoration)
            toursList.reverse()
            binding.tourRv.visibility = View.
              VISIBLE
        }
    } else {
        binding.apply {
            binding.tourRv.visibility = View.
              INVISIBLE

        }
    }

}
```

In the onViewCreated method, where the getAllTour method from the Firebase is called, reference the above function and pass in the list from the lambda.

```
firebaseServices.getAllTour {
            Log.d("tours", "$it")
            initializedAdapter(ArrayList(it))
        }
```

### 7.7.5 Testing the Tour List Display on RecyclerView

To test the RecyclerView display, run the app to see the existing tours in the database showing on it as seen in Figure 7.21. Click on the add icon to create a new tour and see it added to the list display.

## 7.8 UPDATING EXISTING DATA IN FIRESTORE

Updating existing data in Firestore can be achieved using the update method provided by Firestore. This method allows you to modify the content of an already existing document by passing in the document's unique ID and the updated entries.

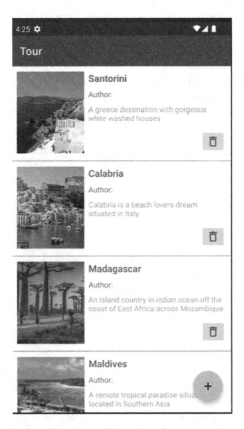

FIGURE 7.21   Displaying Tour from Firestore on RecyclerView.

To implement the update operation, you first need to retrieve the document ID for the item you want to update. This was done within the getAll-Tours() method in the FirebaseService while fetching the list.

With the document ID, you can update the document in Firestore with data changes. It's important to note that when using the update() method, only the fields that are explicitly specified will be updated, leaving the rest of the fields unchanged.

Here's an example code snippet for the updated getAllTours() method in the

```
fun getAllTour(onSuccess:(tours:List<Tour>)->Unit){
        val toursList =  ArrayList<Tour>()
        database.collection("tours").get().addOn
          CompleteListener {
            if(it.isSuccessful){
            for (document in it.result.documents) {
                val tour = document.toObject(Tour::
                  class.java) #A
                val newTour =  tour?.copy(tourId =
                  document.id)          #A
                if (newTour!= null) {
                    toursList.add(newTour)
                }
                onSuccess(toursList)
                Log.d(
                    "TourFragment",
                    "All Tours Info:|:|:|:${document.
                      id} => ${document.data}")
            }
        }}

    }
```

In the update method, the tourId is passed in as the reference for the update which will be received from the list when the item is selected.

```
fun updateTour(tourId:String,tour: Tour,onUpdate
  Success:()->Unit){
        databseReference.document(tourId).
          update(tour.toMap()).addOnComplete
          Listener {
            if (it.isSuccessful){
                onUpdateSuccess()
            }
```

```
        }
        Log.d(
            "AddTourFragment",
            "Tour DocumentSnapshot updated with
                ID: ${tour.tourId}"
        )
    }
```

Before making a call to the update method, we will need to select the item we want to edit from the Recyclerview to open it on the edit screen, edit it, and save it back into the database. Setting a click listener on a RecyclerView item can be done through the adapter using a lambda method. The method triggers the click event and invokes the item object through the Adapter constructor which gets received by the calling class for further actions which can be editing and updating.

### 7.8.1 Implementing a ClickListener within the Adapter

To enable item clicks within the TourAdapter class, a lambda method needs to be declared in the constructor to listen to click events. This method will take a Tour object as its parameter and will be invoked within the onBindViewHolder method to receive the object argument from the clicked position.

Here's an example implementation.

Add the following variable, a listener as a second parameter to its constructor

```
    private val listener: (Tour) -> Unit
Update the onBindViewHolder by setting a clickListener
on each item through the root view
holder.itemView.setOnClickListener {
            listener.invoke(tourItems[position])
        }
```

Now to pass the tour to the edit screen, first we will send it to the TourFragment because that is where the adapter is initialized and then onto the edit screen from there.

### 7.8.2 Send the Object to the Edit Screen

Before a class can be passed around, it needs to be a parcelable object which automatically converts it to a byte size during the sending process and converts back to the original object during the retrieval process.

This means that the tour class must be converted to a parcelable object, and this can be done in three simple steps.

Add the parcelize plugin at the top of the module-level build.gradle file

```
id 'kotlin-parcelize'
```

Annotate the Tour class with @Parcelize keyword and make sure to import the Kotlin version and not the Android one.

Extend the Parcelable class.

```
@Parcelize
data class Tour(
    var placeName: String = "",
    var description: String = "",
    var userId: String = "",
    var placeImage: String = "",
    var tourId:String = UUID.randomUUID().toString()
):Parcelable   {
      fun toMap() =
        mapOf(
            "tourId" to tourId,
            "placeName" to placeName,
            "description" to description,
            "userId" to userId,
            "placeImage" to placeImage
        )
}
```

In the TourFragment class, we create the following method to send the object to the edit screen when an item is clicked. A bundle class is used for passing data between fragments just like intents are used for passing data between activities.

```
private fun itemOnClick(tour: Tour) {
      val args = Bundle()
      args.putParcelable(Constants.TOUR_KEY, tour)
      findNavController().navigate(R.id.action_
        SecondFragment_to_addEditTour, args)

   }
```

Where the Adapter is initialized, you receive the lambda, call the itemOn-click method and pass in the object received as the method's argument

```
val tourAdapter = ToursAdapter(toursList){
        itemOnClick(it)
    }
```

### 7.8.3 Receiving the Object and Displaying on the Screen

To read values from a fragment you can use the arguments method which returns the data supplied to a fragment during navigation. The data can be of any type and requires that the right one is used. Because the Tour object is sent as a parcelize stream, the parcelable method will be used in reading from the arguments just like the below code.

```
val tour = arguments?.getParcelable<Tour>(TOUR_KEY)
```

Now we create a method that reads the values and displays them on the views. Since the tour can be null, to avoid a null pointer exception we check that the tour value is not null before reading its properties. Within the same method, we ensure that only the author of a post can edit it by disabling the fields and the buttons if the user opening an item did not create it. Let's look at the code below.

```
private fun onTourSelected(tour: Tour){

    binding.apply {
        placeName.setText(tour.placeName)
        placeDescription.setText(tour.description)
        placeImageView?.let {
            Glide.with(requireContext())
                .load(tour.placeImage)
                .placeholder(R.drawable.water_villa)
                .into(it)
        }

        if (tour.userId != firebaseServices.user?.
          uid) {
            placeName.isEnabled = false
            placeDescription.isEnabled = false
            uploadBtn.isEnabled = false
            chooseImageBtn.isEnabled  = false

        }else{
            placeName.isEnabled = true
            placeDescription.isEnabled = true
            uploadBtn.isEnabled = true
```

```
        chooseImageBtn.isEnabled   = true
    }
    }
}
```

## 7.8.4 Implement the Update Method

If the selected item is opened by the author of the post, the views will be enabled for editing and updating. We will create a method that will use the upload button for the same purpose but will only call the update method when the Tour object contains data and call the add method when the Tour object is null or has no data. Below is the method that performs the operation.

```
private fun saveAndUpdateTour(tour: Tour?) {
        val userId = firebaseServices.user?.uid.
          toString()
        val name = binding.placeName.text.toString()
        val image = selectedImageFileUri.toString()
        val desc = binding.placeDescription.text.
          toString()
        if (userId.isNullOrEmpty() || name.isNullOr
          Empty() ||
            selectedImageFileUri.toString().isNullOr
              Blank() || desc.isNullOrEmpty()
        ) {
            showToast("Field cannot be empty")
        } else {
            if (tour != null) {
                firebaseServices.updateTour(
                    tourId =tour.tourId,
                    tour.copy(
                        placeName = name,
                        description = desc, userId =
                          userId, placeImage = image
                    )
                ){
                    showToast("Tour successfully
                      updated")
                }
            } else {
                firebaseServices.saveATour(
                    Tour(
                        placeName = name,
```

```
                    description = desc, userId =
                        userId, placeImage = image
                )
        ) {
            if (it.isSuccessful) {
                showToast("Tour successfully
                    uploaded")
            } else {
                showToast(it.exception?.
                    message.toString())
            }
        }}}}
```

The method is called within the onViewCreated and the received object from the bundle is passed in as an argument.

```
tour?.let {
        onTourSelected(it)
    }
```

### 7.8.5 Testing the Edit and Update Feature

You can run the app to test the implementations. First, test as an author of the post, and click on a Tour post you created to open the edit screen. Modify the entries and click upload. Check the same item on the list to see that the changes are reflected.

Second, test as a second user by creating a new account to use the app. Click on any tour to see if the views are enabled for modification. Create your own tour and also make an update to it. Figure 7.22 shows the edit and update feature test process.

## 7.9 DELETING DATA FROM FIRESTORE

Deleting an item is like updating it: they require the document ID for successful completion but do not need any additional tour value as a parameter. On the item layout, we will have a button that, when clicked deletes the object in that position. In the TourAdapter, two new parameters are added, one is a current user id which will be checked against the user ID for the Tour object to be deleted which will ensure that a user can only see the delete button for tours that they created. The second parameter is a lambda method like the item click listener which will be added as a parameter to pass the object on the position when the delete button is clicked. Also, a click listener is set to the delete button and the delete

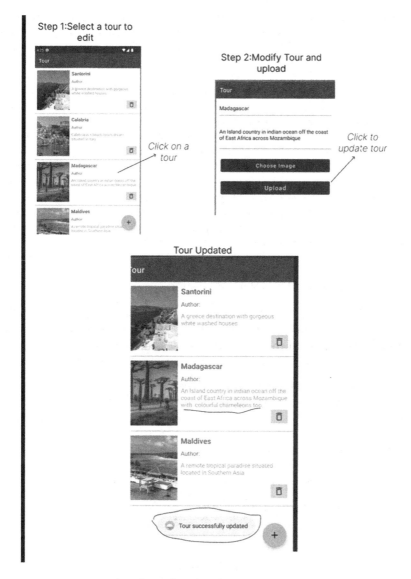

FIGURE 7.22   Testing the edit and update feature.

method is invoked within its block with the tour object passed as an argument. Below is the updated Adapter constructor.

```
class ToursAdapter(
private val currentUserId:String,
    private val tourItems: ArrayList<Tour>,
    private val onDeleteClicked: (Tour) -> Unit,
    private val onItemClicked: (Tour) -> Unit)
```

Within the onBindViewHolder, the check before showing the delete button is performed and the click listener is set to it.

```
if (currentUserId == userId){
                binding.deleteButton.visibility =
                    View.VISIBLE
            }else{
                binding.deleteButton.visibility  =
                    View.INVISIBLE
            }
        }
        itemView.setOnClickListener {
            onItemClicked.invoke(tourItems
                [position])
        }
```

### 7.9.1  Implementing the Delete Operation

In the Firebase service class, we will add the delete method with a parameter to the document id for the position to be deleted and a lambda method to be called if the deletion is successful. Within the method, the delete function from the Firebase is called to delete the data associated with the document id. When the operation is successful, the onSuccess method is invoked. Below is the delete method for the Firebase service class.

```
fun deleteATour(docId: String, onSuccess: () ->
    Unit){
        Log.d("TourDetailsFragment", "Document
            Snapshot id::: $docId")
databseReference.document(docId).delete().addOn
    CompleteListener {
                onSuccess()
            Log.d("TourDetailsFragment", "Tour
                deleted successfully")
        }}
```

Back into the TourFragment, we will create a method for the onDelete-Clicked operation which will have three parameters—a tour object, a tour list, and the tour adapter. The delete method from the service class will be called here, and the tour id is passed in as its argument. If the delete operation is successful, the object will be removed from the tour list and the adapter will be notified that a change occurred within the list so that the items will be updated within it as well. Here is the onDeleteClicked method for the TourFragment.

```
private fun onDeleteClicked(tour: Tour,toursList:
    ArrayList<Tour>,toursAdapter: ToursAdapter?){

    firebaseServices.deleteATour(tour.tourId){
        toursList.remove(tour)
        toursAdapter?.notifyDataSetChanged()
        showToast("Tour has been deleted")
    }
}
```

One last process is to call the above method in the TourAdapter constructor within the onDeleteClicked method. Remember the adapter basically provides the data for a RecycleView and therefore contains the item view for its list. We have set the onClickListener for the delete button within the onBindViewHolder and invoked a lambda method to trigger the delete action. Below is the updated adapter constructor which can be found within the initializedAdapter method.

```
var tourAdapter:ToursAdapter? = null
    tourAdapter = ToursAdapter(firebaseServices.
        user?.uid,toursList, onDeleteClicked = {
        onDeleteClicked(it,toursList,tourAdapter)
    }){
        itemOnClick(it)
    }
```

## 7.9.2 Testing the Delete Operation

You can run the application now and click the delete button for any of the tour items which you can only see if you are the author of the post. Figure 7.23 shows the deletion process.

The Google Firebase platform is a powerful and flexible service that offers real-time data management for different types of applications. Here, we have learned how to use email authentication, storage, and cloud Firestore. We also learned to store and retrieve images and to read, write, update, and delete data. If you want Android applications that require user data management, Firebase has the resources and capabilities you need to succeed. In the next chapter, we will take the same project to the next level by integrating an architecture into it.

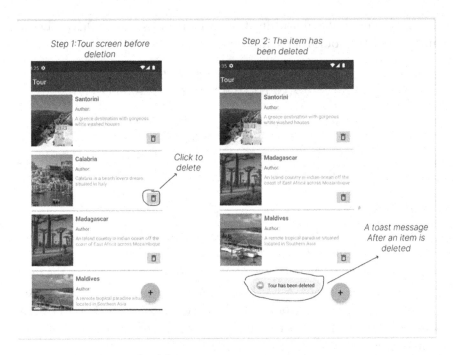

FIGURE 7.23   Testing the delete operation.

## 7.10  SUMMARY

- The Google Firebase platform provides services that enable developers to have access to various data management tools that help them build their apps relatively fast and easily.

- Firebase Authentication is a service with different methods for adding user management to an application. The methods include email and password, Google, Facebook, Twitter (X), etc.

- Firebase Firestore is a database option that provides APIs for performing CRUD operations in your application.

- Firebase Storage allows you to store files like images, media, etc., required for use within the application.

- A RecyclerView widget is useful for displaying and efficiently managing dynamic lists using the adapter design.

- With the Navigation component, moving from one destination to another is less complicated, especially within a large project.

# CHAPTER 8

# Android MVVM Architecture

## *Project 5 – Tour Guide Part 2*

## 8.1 THE ANDROID ARCHITECTURAL PATTERNS

The importance of using an architectural pattern for writing your application includes creating a scalable, extensible project and promoting easy code modification, especially when it has to do with feature addition or removal. If you do not use a proper architecture, then a code change could lead to a significant code break which can, in turn, lead to a longer project delivery.

This means that a change to an existing function stops it from working for its intended use case, which worked well before it was modified.

Another advantage of an architectural pattern is to promote efficient team collaboration. Applying a specific pattern to a project enables better productivity when there is more than one project contributor and helps a new member adapt faster to the development style. A third importance is that using an architecture makes testing your codes possible since it promotes the separation of concerns and allows each app component to be tested separately. There are four commonly used architecture patterns you can find today in different Android projects, including the following.

DOI: 10.1201/9781032622538-8

### 8.1.1 MVC

MVC stands for Model View Controller and has been the traditional approach for writing Android applications. This pattern separates a project into three components: the Model, the View, and the Controller. The model is used to represent the data-related logic, the View is for all UI-related logic mostly applied to the app widgets, which is commonly found in Activities and Fragments, and the Controller is like an intermediary between the model and the view. It processes the logic from the model, manipulates it when required, and interacts with the view to display the result. It connects the model and views together. Figure 8.1 shows the flow of data using this pattern.

### 8.1.2 MVP

The Model View Presenter architecture is a pattern with a better testability approach than MVC. With MVC, most times, the data logic ends up in the View, that is, the Activities and Fragment, but with MVP, the presenter strictly has the responsibility of communicating the Views requirement to the Model while providing Views with the events and data required for an interface. So, in MVP, the presenter replaces the MVC controller with a more testable class. Figure 8.2 shows the flow of data using this pattern.

### 8.1.3 MVVM

The Model View ViewModel architecture is currently the Google recommended architecture for Android development. Its model and view are similar to MVP but with the Presenter replaced with a ViewModel. The ViewModel also introduces two important features, reactive programming,

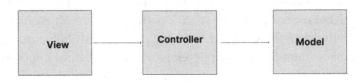

FIGURE 8.1 The MVC architecture progress flow.

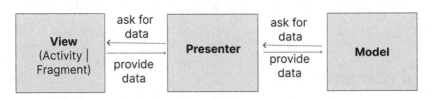

FIGURE 8.2 The MVP architecture process flow.

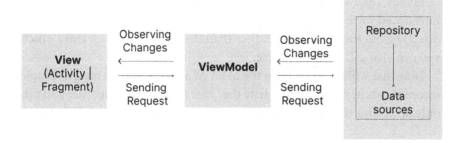

FIGURE 8.3    The MVVM architecture process flow.

where the UI data is being held in observables that get called to update the UI when changes occur, and lifecycle awareness which makes it easier to manage data retention when there is a change from one lifecycle state to the other without the data state been returned to an initial state. Figure 8.3 shows the flow of data using this pattern.

## 8.2  REFACTORING THE TOUR PROJECT

We will be learning about the MVVM pattern in this chapter among the listed architectures. This is not just because it is the recommended architecture by Google but also because of the two listed features above, which help to reduce the lines of code required in the View (Activity and Fragment) while trying to retain the state of data during the lifecycle changes. First, we will modify the application to include some data display states. These states will include a loading screen to show when the data is still being processed from the remote server, an error screen to show if an error occurs, and an empty state if no tour data is displayed.

In addition to data display states, we will introduce interfaces into the business logic layers, including the Repository and the data source class where the repository will act as an intermediary between the data source and the ViewModel class. As seen in Figure 8.4, the data flow will be modified to include a ViewModel class. Although application testing will not be a part of this book, interfaces used in the business logic layers make testing easier without requiring complete construction of the class involved.

FIGURE 8.4    Data flow with the MVVM architecture included.

Finally, the ViewModel class will be created with LiveData objects introduced for holding the UI states. The View will now receive its data directly from the ViewModel rather than the Firebase Service class which you can also call the data source.

Note that while we are using the MVVM architecture, although Google recommends it, it is not necessarily the "best architecture" because you can only determine the right one for the project at hand depending on its needs.

## 8.3 REFINING THE DATA LAYERS

As we initially mentioned, testing will not be covered in this book, but the data source must be loosely coupled with classes that depend on it. Coupling in programming means a class depends on another class to complete its operation. There are two types of coupling, tight coupling, where class B needs to construct class A to complete its operation, and loose coupling, where class B can get class A from the outside when needed. From the Tour Project, the TourFragment is tightly coupled to the FirestoreService class, an interface is a great approach to having loosely coupled dependencies, and we will modify the service class to become one.

An interface is said to be a contract between two classes. It contains the abstract behaviors of a class by defining the methods and properties that another class must implement. The class implementing an interface must provide implementations for every method and property defined in the interface. We will modify the service class to become an interface with only method definitions. The method signatures will be updated to include an error lambda for catching errors during the firebase operation processes. Before making these changes to the service class, let's get an insight into Lambda expressions.

### 8.3.1 Lambda Expressions and Higher-order functions

In Kotlin, lambda functions are special functions that allow you to write concise code. You can write them without declaring their return type because it is automatically inferred explicitly. This type of function can also be used as a higher-order function. A higher-order function can take in other functions as parameters. This functional programming pattern promotes conciseness as it makes code transformation possible when the function is called. Below are different ways a lambda function can be created and used.

1. A Lambda block with a variable, two parameters, and an explicit type.

```
val sum:(a:Int,b:Int) -> Int = { a: Int, b: Int ->
          a + b
     }
```

The parameters and return types are declared explicitly

2. A Lambda block with a variable, two parameters and an inferred return type.

```
val sum = { a: Int, b: Int ->
          a + b
     }
```

The parameters are not explicitly declared but provided within the block and the type of the last value is the return type.

3. A Lambda function can be used as higher-order function where they can be used as a parameter and in the body of a function.

```
fun average(a:Int,b:Int, sum:(a:Int,b:Int)->Int):Int {

return sum(a,b) / 2
     }
```

The average function has a lambda as a parameter that is returned as a value. When calling the average function, you can pass another function as an argument like the below code

```
average(10, 20, sum)
```

Lambda functions are very useful for creating short and concise codes, especially when you need to pass a small piece of code as an argument to another function. Now let's make the changes to the Firebase service class by creating its interface with method definitions and including lambda methods for catching errors.

```
interface FirebaseService {
    fun registerUser(userEmail: String,
                     userPassword: String,
                     onUserCreated:(Task<
                         AuthResult>)->Unit)
    fun SignInUser(
        userEmail: String,
```

```
            userPassword: String,
            onUserSignIn: (Task<AuthResult>)->Unit
        )
        fun uploadImageToFirebaseStorageAndAddTour(
            selectedImageUri: Uri,
            onUploadSuccess:(String)->Unit
        )

        fun saveATour(onError:(Throwable?)->Unit,tour:
          Tour,onTourSaved:(Task<Void>)->Unit)
        fun getAllTour(onError:(Throwable?)->Unit,
          onSuccess:(List<Tour>)->Unit)

        fun updateTour(onError:(Throwable?)-
          >Unit,tourId:String,tour:
          Tour,onUpdateSuccess:()->Unit)
        fun deleteATour(onError:(Throwable?)->Unit,
          docId: String, onSuccess: () -> Unit)
    }
```

The interface will be implemented in a class where all the methods will be overridden, and the body created. This class will become the interface initializer created outside the object that depends on it. Now wherever the class is required, the interface will be injected rather than the implementation to reduce frequent object creation. This process is called dependency injection, which we will see once we create the ViewModel class. Below is the service implementation class with the interface methods overridden and the method body implemented.

```
/* This class implements the FirebaseService
   interface and overrides all its methods.
*/
    class FirebaseServiceImpl: FirebaseService {
        private val firebaseAuth:FirebaseAuth =
          FirebaseAuth.getInstance()
        private val storageRef = Firebase.storage.
          reference
        private val database = Firebase.firestore
        private val databseReference = database.
          collection("tours")

        override fun registerUser(
            userEmail: String,
            userPassword: String,
            onUserCreated:(Task<AuthResult>)->Unit
        ){
```

```kotlin
            firebaseAuth.createUserWithEmailAnd
              Password(userEmail, userPassword)
               .addOnCompleteListener {
                   onUserCreated(it)
               } }

  val user = firebaseAuth.currentUser
   val hasUser = user != null

  override fun SignInUser(
      userEmail: String,
      userPassword: String,
      onUserSignIn:(Task<AuthResult>)->Unit
  ){
      firebaseAuth.signInWithEmailAndPassword
        (userEmail, userPassword)
          .addOnCompleteListener {
              onUserSignIn(it)} }

   override fun uploadImageToFirebaseStorageAnd
     AddTour(
       selectedImageUri: Uri,
       onUploadSuccess:(String)->Unit
   ){
         val uploadTask = storageRef.
           child("tourImages/${Calendar.
           getInstance().time.time}")
         uploadTask.putFile(selectedImageUri).
           addOnCompleteListener {
             if (it.isSuccessful){
                 uploadTask.downloadUrl.addOn
                   SuccessListener { uri ->
                     if (uri.toString().
                       isNotEmpty()) {
                     onUploadSuccess(uri.
                       toString())
                     }
                 }
             }
         }


     }

  override fun saveATour(onError:(Throwable?)-
    >Unit,tour:Tour, onTourSaved:(Task<Void>)-
    >Unit){
```

```
/* The addOnCompleteListener listens to event changes
and when a tour is successfully created in the
database, the onToursaved is called and the task
result is shown. if a tour creation fails, the onError
method is called with the exception message shown.
    */
            databseReference.document().set(tour).
                addOnCompleteListener {
                    if(it.isSuccessful){
                        onTourSaved(it)
                    }else{
                        onError(it.exception?.
                            fillInStackTrace())
                    } } }

        override fun getAllTour(
        onError:(Throwable?)-
          >Unit,onSuccess:(List<Tour>)->Unit){
            val toursList =  ArrayList<Tour>()
          database.collection("tours").get().
            addOnCompleteListener {
              if(it.isSuccessful){
                for (document in it.result.documents) {
                    val tour = document.
                      toObject(Tour::class.java)
                    val newTour  =  tour?.copy(tourId
                      = document.id, authorName =
                      user?.displayName.toString())
                    if (newTour != null) {
                        toursList.add(newTour )
                    }
                    onSuccess(toursList)
                }
                }else{
                    onError(it.exception?.fillInStack
                      Trace())
                }}

            }

    /* The success function is called if the update
        operation is successful. If not, the error
        function is called.
    */
    override fun updateTour(onError:(Throwable?)->Unit,
        tourId:String, tour: Tour, onUpdateSuccess:()->Unit){
```

```
            databseReference.document(tourId).
              update(tour.toMap()).
              addOnCompleteListener {
                  if (it.isSuccessful){
                      onUpdateSuccess()
                  }else{
                      onError(it.exception?.
                        fillInStackTrace())
              }}}
```

```
/*The success function is called if the delete
  operation completes successfully. If not, the error
  function is called.
*/
    override fun deleteATour(onError:(Throwable?)-
      >Unit,docId: String, onSuccess: () -> Unit){
          Log.d("TourDetailsFragment", "Document
            Snapshot id::: $docId")
          databseReference.document(docId).delete().
            addOnCompleteListener {
                if (it.isSuccessful) {
                    onSuccess()
                }else{
                    onError(it.exception?.
                      fillInStackTrace())
                }
          } }
```

In the ViewModel class, these methods will be accessed through its interface using constructor injection, which is a means of Dependency injection. Dependency injection is providing the object of a class from the outside when needed rather than initializing it inside the class depending on it. Generally, this can be managed best using libraries like Dagger, Dagger Hilt, and Koin for larger projects, but we will do that manually in this book. Each lambda function will be implemented in the ViewModel class, and values received will be used when required. Before we can look at the ViewModel class, we will first dive into data state management.

Repositories are usually part of the data layer, but we will skip them. This is because they are more relevant when there are different data sources, like a remote source and a local source, and you need to manage both data flow through one class. A Repository is a class responsible for merging two or more data sources and providing one data source to the ViewModel class.

## 8.3.2 Testing the Change in the Data Layer

Without having the ViewModel class, we can run the app to confirm that the functionalities are still working as expected. Starting with the AddEditFragment you can make temporary solutions for the error states within the saveTour and the updateTour methods. Here is what the updated code will look like.

To save a tour:

```
firebaseServices.saveATour(onError = {},
                Tour(
                    placeName = name,
                    description = desc, userId
                        = userId, placeImage =
                        image
                )
        ) {
                if (it.isSuccessful) {
                    showToast("Tour
                        successfully uploaded")
                    findNavController().
                        popBackStack()
                } else {
                    showToast(it.exception?.
                        message.toString())
                }

        }
```

To update a tour:

```
firebaseServices.updateTour(onError = {},
                tourId =tour.tourId,
                tour.copy(
                    placeName = name,
                    description = desc, userId
                        = userId, placeImage =
                        image
                )
        ){
                showToast("Tour successfully
                    updated")
                findNavController().
                    popBackStack()
        }
```

You also need to do the same in the TourFragment by modifying the deleteATour and getAllTour method.

To delete a tour:

```
firebaseServices.deleteATour(onError = {},tour.
    tourId){
            toursList.remove(tour)
            toursAdapter?.notifyDataSetChanged()
            showToast("Tour has been deleted")
        }
```

To get all tour:

```
firebaseServices.getAllTour(onError = {}) {
                Log.d("tours", "$it")
                initializedAdapter(ArrayList(it))}
Creating the Data States
```

Handling the state of data in Android is important in providing a better user experience when displaying them on the UI. This can help the user ascertain the current state of a feature process and what to do next, especially if a problem occurs and what might be caused. To manage this state, we will use a sealed class. Sealed classes are a restricted class hierarchy that allows you to create subclasses of any type, like an object, data class, or a regular class. With this ability, you can represent different states using the parent class with the subclass having multiple instances. Let's look at an example where an object is used as the inner class.

```
sealed class Result{
    object A:Result()
    object B:Result()
    object C:Result()
}
```

With a sealed class, when statement can be used to cover all the possible cases since it's an exhaustive case. It will execute the corresponding blocks of code for each subtype. Here is a code example.

```
fun score(result: Result) {
            when (result) {
                is Result.A -> {
                    println("Excellent")
                }
```

```
            is Result.B -> {
                println("Merit")
            }
            is Result.C -> {
                println("Passed")
            }
        }
    }
```

Now we will define a Resource class for the different data states to manage three different use cases. One indicates the Loading state, another indicates the Success state while the third shows the Error state. We want to show UI states for the three processes and with a sealed class, the parent will be used to access each state making it possible to account for all by using a when statement. Below is the code block with a data class as the subtype.

```
sealed class Resource<out T> {
    data class Loading<out T>(val data: T? =
      null):Resource<T>()
    data class Success<out T>(val data: T? = null,
      val message: String = ""):Resource<T>()
    data class Failure<out T>(val message: String)
      : Resource<T>()
}
```

Each state will be represented in the ViewModel class when data processing requires values to be allocated. More of this is in Section 8.4.

## 8.4 THE PRESENTATION LAYERS

From Figure 8.4, you will see that the presentation layer includes the state holders and user interface. The ViewModel class is the state holder and will be holding the data for the tour Fragment class, which represents the UI. This class will receive data from the service class, prepare its three states, and present it to the UI. The data will be in the form of a LiveData, which is observable and will always notify the UI when there is a change. In turn, the UI will observe this LiveData and modify its display with every change in data.

What generally happens in the presentation layer of the tour Feed? When there is a change in an event, like the addition of a new tour, this notifies the ViewModel class, which then prompts the service class to update the tour list LiveData with the new tour. Because the Fragment is observing the changes in the LiveData, the tour feed will automatically get the new data added to the UI. This is also similar to create, update, and delete. Each UI attempt to perform any operation will trigger its ViewModel method to notify the FirebaseService class to modify the database.

### 8.4.1 Adding MVVM to the App

The ViewModel is a part of the Android Architecture components, a collection of libraries introduced by Google in 2107 to help ease the architecting process of your application. Also included in this component is the LiveData, which is lifecycle-aware, meaning that it only triggers a UI update if it is in the correct lifecycle state. Usually, you will need to clean up data processes happening within your app when it is not in a useful state. In an earlier chapter, we discussed both the Activity and Fragment lifecycle states where a method like onDestroy is called when the application is no longer alive. But this does not guarantee that the app's memory is completely cleared of its data processes depending on the data management pattern. It can cause memory leaks because the reference to the app's data remains. Since memory leaks can reduce app performance, it is important that all processes no longer in use are cleared out of the memory. Therefore, LiveData is built with the ability to dispose of unused data when the Activity or Fragment is destroyed, saving you the stress of having to do that yourself for each data the UI is subscribed to.

Now for the ViewModel, it helps your application data survive configuration changes that occur when there is a restart behavior within the app. The restart behavior is designed to help your app adapt to new configurations by automatically reloading it with alternative resources that match the new configuration. Configuration changes can occur due to screen orientation, keyboard availability, or enabling multiwindow mode. When configuration changes happen, your data will be recreated to return to its creation state rather than the last state before the changes. You will need to keep track of every data, save, and retrieve it after the restart. With ViewModel, this is done automatically, and the last data value remains the same after any configuration change.

For the Tour app, the ViewModel class will have a LiveData wrapped around a Resource type for each CRUD process. Each method will be processed from the saveTour, updateTour, getAllTOur, and deleteATour. Also, the image downloadUrl will have its LiveData for each uploaded image. All CRUD method from the service class is processed within the ViewModel class, and for each resource state, the required value is posted to the UI for updating its display state. For example, within the getAllTour method, the loading Resource state is posted to show the loading UI before its method from the service class is called. Within the error lambda, the Failure state is posted, and any occurring error is shown, and finally, within the success lambda, the retrieved data is posted for display on the required View.

Below is the code for the TourViewModel class.

```kotlin
class TourViewModel(private val firebaseService:
    FirebaseService) : ViewModel() {

    private val downloadUrl = MutableLiveData<Reso
        urce<String>>()
    val downloadUrlLiveData: LiveData<Resource
        <String>>
        get() = downloadUrl

    private val tours = MutableLiveData<Resource
        <List<Tour>>>()
    val tourLiveData: LiveData<Resource<List
        <Tour>>>
        get() = tours

    private val saveTour = MutableLiveData
        <Resource<Nothing>>()
    val saveTourLiveData: LiveData<Resource
        <Nothing>>
        get() = saveTour

    private val updateTour = MutableLiveData
        <Resource<Nothing>>()
    val updateTourLiveData: LiveData<Resource
        <Nothing>>
        get() = updateTour

    private val deleteTour = MutableLiveData
        <Resource<Nothing>>()
    val deleteTourLiveData: LiveData<Resource
        <Nothing>>
        get() = deleteTour

    /* This method fetches all tour from the database
       and passes to a LiveData variable
    */

    fun getAllTour() {
```

```
        tours.postValue(Resource.Loading())
        firebaseService.getAllTour(onError = {
            tours.postValue(Resource.Failure(it?.
              message.toString()))
        }) {
            tours.postValue(Resource.Success(it))
        }
    }
```

/* **This method uploads selected image and gets the download URL. The URL is passed to a livedata.**
\*/

```
    fun uploadImage(uri: Uri) {
        downloadUrl.postValue(Resource.
          Loading())
        firebaseService.uploadImageToFirebase
          StorageAndAddTour(uri) {
            downloadUrl.postValue(Resource.
              Success(it,"image uploaded"))
        }
    }
```

/\***This saves a tour to the database. if an error occurs, the error message is passed to a livedata variable. If successful, the success message is passed instead.**
\*/

```
    fun saveTour(tour: Tour, uri: Uri) {
        saveTour.postValue(Resource.Loading())
        firebaseService.saveATour(onError = {
            saveTour.postValue(Resource.
              Failure(it?.message.toString()))
        }, tour) {
            if (it.isSuccessful) {
                saveTour.postValue(Resource.
                  Success(message = "Tour saved
                  successfully"))
            } else {
                saveTour.postValue(Resource.
                  Failure(it.exception.
                  toString()))
            }
        }
    }
```

```
/* This method updates an existing tour. If an error
occurs in the process, the error message is passed to
a livedata and if successful, the success message is
passed instead.
*/
    fun updateTour(
        tourId: String,
        tour: Tour
    ) {
        updateTour.postValue(Resource.Loading())
        firebaseService.updateTour(onError = {
          updateTour.postValue(Resource.
            Failure(it?.message.toString()))
        }, tourId, tour, onUpdateSuccess = {
            updateTour.postValue(Resource.
              Success(message = "Update
              successfull"))
        })
    }


/* This deletes a tour from the database. If an
error occurs, the error message is passed to a
livedata and if successful, a success message is
passed to the livedata.
*/
    fun deleteTour(docId: String) {
        deleteTour.postValue(Resource.Loading())
        firebaseService.deleteATour(onError = {
            deleteTour.postValue(Resource.
              Failure(it?.message.toString()))
        }, docId) {
            deleteTour.postValue(Resource.
              Success(message = "Tour has been
              deleted"))
        }
    }
}
```

As already mentioned, LiveData is an observable data holder. Each of the posted values will always be held in the state posted when any change occurs for the UI to observe and update the screen.

To complete the ViewModel setup, we require a factory class. This class is provided by Android which we can create a subclass for any of our ViewModel classes. Towards the end of the code above, we will add an inner class extending ViewModelProvider.Factory for creating the TourViewModel where the service class is also provided within its constructor. When we are using ViewModel, we cannot pass arguments to that ViewModel. In some cases, like our app, we must pass our arguments to ViewModel. This can be done using ViewModelFactory.

Below is the factory class.

```
class TourViewModelFactory(private val service:
  FirebaseService) : ViewModelProvider.Factory
  {
    override fun <T : ViewModel>
      create(modelClass: Class<T>): T {
        return TourViewModel(service) as T
    }
}
```

## 8.4.2 Connecting the ViewModel to the UI Classes

One of the aims of refactoring this app is to practice dependency injection (DI), which promotes getting the dependency a class needs from the outside to promote loose coupling. Remember that for a bigger project, consider using any existing DI library that suits your architecture plan rather than doing it manually, as we will do for the Tour App.

In the MainActivity, we will create the service class and provide it as a dependency on the ViewModel. Since all the existing fragments have access to this Activity, they can get a reference to the ViewModel class when they need to call any of the methods. We will make changes in the MainActivity by adding the following global codes.

```
val firebaseServices by lazy {
      (application as TourApp).firebaseServices
  }
  val factory by lazy {
      TourViewModel.TourViewModelFactory(firebas
        eServices)
  }
  val viewModel by lazy {
      ViewModelProvider(this, factory)
        [TourViewModel::class.java]
  }
```

Starting with the Tour fragment, you will connect to the tourLiveData for observing any available update. But before that you need to make a call to getAllTour to fetch the tour that will be posted in the UI. Below are the code changes to be made for displaying all Tour within the TourFragment.

```
activity.viewModel.getAllTour()
                        activity.viewModel.
                        tourLiveData.
                        observe(requireActivity())
                        { result->
                            when(result){
                                is Resource.
                                    Loading ->{
                                        show
                                            Progress
                                            Bar()
                                }
                                is Resource.
                                    Success -> {
                                        hideProgress
                                            Bar()
                                        initialized
                                            Adapter
                                            (ArrayList
                                            (result.
                                            data))
                                }

                                is Resource.
                                    Failure ->{
                                        hide
                                            Progress
                                            Bar()
                                        showToast
                                            (result.
                                            message)
                                }
                            }
                        }
                        }
```

### 8.4.2.1 Testing the Tour Display Feature

Now you can rerun the app to see what has changed with the tour display UI. First, you will see the loading progress, which appears when the data is still being fetched, then the tours get displayed on the UI when they are available.

We will take a similar step for the delete operation. Within the onDeleteClicked method, the call to FirebaseService class will be replaced with its equivalent reference from the ViewModel class, and the LiveData is observed to keep track of State changes. Below is the updated onDeleteClicked method.

```
private fun
   onDeleteClicked(tour:
   Tour,toursList:
   ArrayList<Tour>,toursAdapter:
   ToursAdapter?){

      activity.viewModel.
         deleteTour(tour.tourId)

      activity.viewModel.
         deleteTourLiveData.
         observe(require
         Activity()){resources->
            when(resources){
               is Resource.
                  Loading ->{
                     showToast
                        ("operation
                        in
                        progress")
               }
               is Resource.
                  Success ->{
                     toursList.
                        remove
                        (tour)
                     toursAdapter?.
                        notifyData
                        SetChanged()
                     showToast
                        (resources.
                        message)
               }
               is Resource.
                  Failure->{
                     showToast
                        (resources.
                        message)
               }
}}    }
```

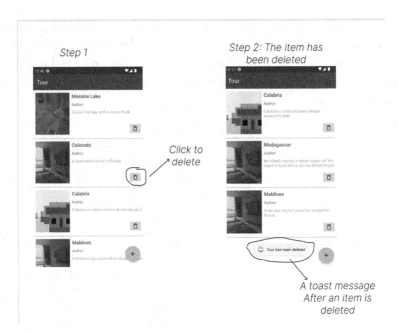

FIGURE 8.5   Deleting an item with a toast message.

### 8.4.2.2 Testing the Delete state from the ViewModel

When you click the delete button for a certain tour, you see a toast when the operation begins, and once deleted, you get another toast that the tour has been deleted successfully. Figure 8.5 shows the expected result for a successful delete action.

Next, to refactor AddEditFragment to use the TourViewModel, the uploadImageToFirebaseStorage method from the service class will be replaced with the uploadImage method from the ViewModel class. This will add a progress state in form of a toast to indicate when the upload begins and then another one when the upload completes. The below code changes are required.

```
selectedImageFileUri?.let { it1 ->
                        activity.viewModel.
                           uploadImage(it1)

                }
```

Then observe its LiveData to get the download URL for saving into the database. This will be processed at the top layer of onCreate and below is the required code.

```
activity.viewModel.downloadUrlLiveData.
   observe(requireActivity()){resource->
```

```
when(resource){
    is Resource.Loading->{
        showToast("uploading image")
    }
    is Resource.Success ->{
        showToast(resource.message)
        placeImage = resource.data.
            toString()
    }
    is Resource.Failure ->{
        showToast(resource.message)
    }
}
```

We will do the same for the saveATour and updateTour methods, respectively, where the method called from the FirebaseService class is replaced with ones from the TourViewModel and their LiveData are observed within the onCreate. Here is an update for the saveAndUpdateTour method with the calls from TourViewModel rather than the service class.

```
private fun saveAndUpdateTour(tour: Tour?) {
    val userId = activity.firebaseServices.
        user?.uid.toString()
    val name = binding.placeName.text.
        toString()
    val image = placeImage
    val desc = binding.placeDescription.text.
        toString()
    if (userId.isNullOrEmpty() || name.
        isNullOrEmpty() ||
        selectedImageFileUri.toString().
            isNullOrBlank() || desc.
            isNullOrEmpty()
    ) {
        showToast("Field cannot be empty")
    } else {
        if (tour != null) {
            activity.viewModel.updateTour(
                tourId =tour.tourId,
                tour.copy(
                    placeName = name,
                    description = desc, userId
                        = userId, placeImage =
                        image
                ))
```

```
            } else {
                activity.viewModel.saveTour(
                    Tour(
                        placeName = name,
                        description = desc, userId
                            = userId, placeImage =
                            image
                    )) } }
    }
```

Then observe the LiveData for each operation within the onCreate as follows:

```
activity.viewModel.saveTourLiveData.
    observe(requireActivity()){resource->
            when (resource) {
                is Resource.Loading ->{
                    showToast("saving Tour in
                        progress")
                }
                is Resource.Success ->{
                    showToast(resource.message)
                    findNavController().
                        popBackStack()
                }

                is Resource.Failure ->{
                    showToast(resource.message)
                }

            }
        }

        activity.viewModel.updateTourLiveData.
            observe(requireActivity()){ resource->
                when(resource){
                    is Resource.Loading->{
                        showToast("update in
                            progress")
                    }
                    is Resource.Success->{
                        showToast(resource.message)
                        findNavController().
                            popBackStack()
                    }
                    is Resource.Failure ->{
```

```
                                      showToast(resource.message)
                        }
            }}
```

### 8.4.2.3 Testing the save And Update method refactor

You can run the app to test the save and update. When the upload button is clicked for either process, a progress toast is shown to notify the user and when it is complete, another is shown before navigating back into the Tour display screen. Figure 8.6 shows the save and update test result.

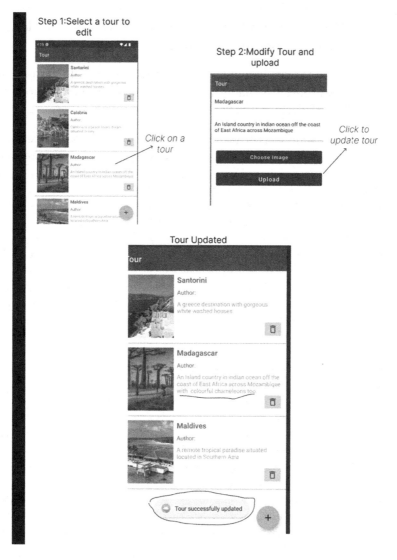

FIGURE 8.6  Save and update the refactor process.

## 8.5 SUMMARY

- Architecting your app promotes cleaner code, testable code, and easy team contributions.

- The common architecture patterns within Android development are MVC, MVP, MVVM, and MVI.

- Google introduced the MVVM Android architecture using its component libraries, ViewModel and LiveData, and recommends it for building your application.

- The ViewModel class helps your app data retain its state during a restart mostly caused due to configuration changes.

- A Repository class is an intermediary between the data source(s) and the ViewModel class but is most important when there is more than one data source.

- With a Resource class, you can manage the data process state while displaying them to keep the users aware of what is happening on the UI.

# CHAPTER 9

# Basic Jetpack Compose Elements

## 9.1 INTRODUCTION TO JETPACK COMPOSE

The Jetpack Compose libraries are powerful APIs that allow you to create native user interfaces using Kotlin functions. It leverages the declarative programming pattern to simplify components' reusability by allowing you to abstract away logic required for an element to perform an action. It also fastens development due to its reactive nature with the ability to display immediate changes and propagate data flow to child composable. A Compose element is usually referred to as a composable function or just composable. This is a regular function with a Composable annotation on it. Look at the example shown below.

```
@Composable
fun Greeting(name: String) {
    Text(text = "Hello $name!")
}
```

The Greeting composable is a function that displays a text with a Hello followed by any name entered as an argument when calling the function. Text is a built-in composable API and allows you to display text to the application user. Just like we have Views and ViewGroup when using XML, some elements can serve as a parent Composable, and others that cannot accept child elements.

DOI: 10.1201/9781032622538-9

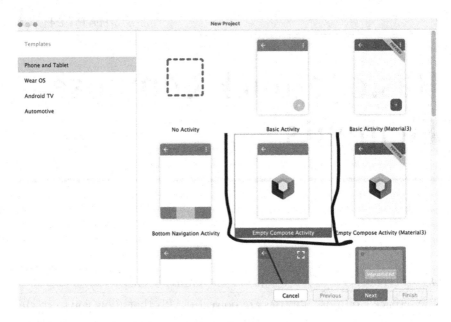

FIGURE 9.1   The compose activity template.

## 9.1.1  Creating a New Compose Project

From the Android Studio Arctic Fox and later versions, you will find the Jetpack Compose feature enabled by default. To create a compose project, you will find a template made specifically for it from the list of existing new project templates. This will generate a greeting composable for you with just one Activity. Just like you will create a regular Android project, go to File> New > New Project and choose the "Empty Compose Activity" as seen in Figure 9.1.

When the project is ready, you can look at the MainActivity.kt file. In the MainActivity file, there are three different compartments, the MainActivity class, the Greeting composable, and the preview function.

### 9.1.1.1  The MainActivity Class

You will need at least one Activity class when working with Composables because they remain the entry point into any application even with the Compose framework. Starting with the Activity class, you will find that the method that sets the UI of the application within the onCreate method which is the setContent() accepts expressions within its body because it was created with a lambda parameter which is different from the traditional setContentView() used when drawing an XML layout. Below is the MainActivity class.

```
class MainActivity : ComponentActivity() {
    override fun onCreate(savedInstanceState:
    Bundle?) {
        super.onCreate(savedInstanceState)

// The setContent block that draws the UI of a
   Compose app
        setContent {
            TipCalculatorTheme {
                Surface(
                    modifier = Modifier.
                    fillMaxSize(),
                    color = MaterialTheme.colors.
                    background
                ) {
//A Call to the Greeting Composable.
                    Greeting("Android")
                }
            }
        }
}}}
```

### 9.1.1.2 The Greeting Composable

The second content of the MainActivity file is the Greeting composable which has a String parameter. It also has the Composable annotation and a Text Composable call within the function. A call to this method displays a text with the entered argument. Also, note that a Composable can only be called within another composable hence having to annotate the Greeting function as composable before adding the Text into it. Below is the sample code

```
@Composable
fun Greeting(name: String) {
    Text(text = "Hello $name!")
}
```

### 9.1.1.3 The Preview Feature

Finally, we have the preview function which is annotated with the Preview annotation. Such a function is another way you can be able to see what your app looks like without using the run button with the ability to see immediate results from UI changes. An important point to note about the Preview function is that it does not accept arguments and therefore will not produce the expected result if you pass one to it. Below is the Preview function and the display result as shown in Figure 9.2.

FIGURE 9.2   The preview feature display.

```
@Preview(showBackground = true)
@Composable
fun DefaultPreview() {
    TipCalculatorTheme {
        Greeting("Android")
    }
}
```

### 9.1.1.4 Lambda Expressions and Higher-Order Function in Jetpack Compose

We talked about lambda expressions in Chapter 8 showing examples on how they are defined. Having mentioned that compose allows logic to be abstracted and only provided at the point where they are needed, lambda makes this possible with its first-class feature that allows them to be used as values and variables. To refresh our memories a bit, let's look at some of the composable elements and properties using this feature.

```
val onClick = { name:String ->
             Toast.makeText(this,name,Toast.LENGTH_
             LONG).show()
        }
```

In the above method, the anonymous function begins with the opening braces, the name is a String parameter for the function and then there is a toast statement to be completed. This function is assigned to a variable called onClick, which can be called as a method with a value for the name assigned to it like below.

```
onClick("Android")
```

In Compose, you will mostly come across these high-order functions that accept other functions as parameters where these parameters are lambdas.

To provide its argument, you can either set an opening and closing braces to process the implementation or pass in another lambda function. An example of the onClick lambda function above is the inbuilt implementation for the button click. Let's look at its parameter definition and how the argument can be implemented.

The onClick parameter definition

```
    @Composable
fun Button(
    onClick: () -> Unit,
    )
```

The argument implementation 1

```
    Button(onClick = {
// The function implementation block
    })
```

As we explore the elements in the Compose API, we will explain more about the lambda use cases where they apply.

### 9.1.2  Basic Compose Layouts

Two basic layouts are available in the compose API, the Row and Column composable. The Row is a composable that is used to align elements horizontally on the screen just like the horizontal linear layout in XML. The Column is a composable that can be used to align elements vertically on the screen just like the vertical linear layout. Figure 9.3 shows examples using each layout.

### 9.1.3  Element Decoration

Now the UI could look more appealing and will require a decoration to customize how it looks. You might also want to align the elements to the center or other positions on the screen. Layout composables have properties

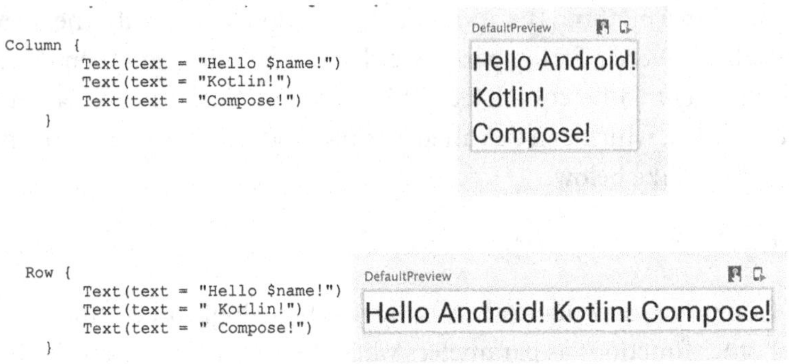

```
Column {
        Text(text = "Hello $name!")
        Text(text = "Kotlin!")
        Text(text = "Compose!")
    }
```

DefaultPreview

Hello Android!

Kotlin!

Compose!

```
Row {
        Text(text = "Hello $name!")
        Text(text = " Kotlin!")
        Text(text = " Compose!")
    }
```

DefaultPreview

Hello Android! Kotlin! Compose!

FIGURE 9.3 The row and column composable.

that can be called to achieve such alignments like verticalArrangement for positioning their children vertically within a Column and a horizontalArrangement for positioning their children horizontally within a Row with both expecting values from the Arrangement object. Then there is the horizontalAlignment for positioning the content of a Column horizontally and verticalAlignment for positioning the content of a Row vertically. Below is an example of where and how they can be used.

```
Row(horizontalArrangement = Arrangement.Center,
        verticalAlignment = Alignment.
        CenterVertically) {
    Text(text = "Hello TutorialsEu")
    Text(text = " Kotlin!")
    Text(text = " Compose!")
}

Column(verticalArrangement = Arrangement.Center,
        horizontalAlignment = Alignment.
        CenterHorizontally) {
    Text(text = "Hello TutorialsEu")
    Text(text = " Kotlin!")
    Text(text = " Compose!")
}
```

Each object has different values that can be used to place child elements on other parts of the screen aside in the center but without a Modifier, there is no reflection of any of the changes made with either of the two properties as they will remain the same as the result from 9.1.2 without the alignment. When you refresh the preview there will be no noticeable changes in the current UI and this is because there is no specified size for the UI screen which is required to determine the correct placement, and this is where the Modifier comes in.

### 9.1.3.1 Compose Modifier

A Modifier is an object that all compose elements have access to and which provides them with properties that can be used to customize or beautify them. One of these properties includes size where you can specify a width and height for the element or make it take up the max and min size with other alternative options. Add the Modifier to the Column layout for the Greeting Composable and use the dot operator to find all the available sizing options like in Figure 9.4.

When the fillMaxSize() option is applied, the Column takes up the size of the screen horizontally and vertically.

```
@Composable
fun Greeting(name: String) {
    Column(verticalArrangement = Arrangement.
      Center,
            horizontalAlignment = Alignment.
            CenterHorizontally, modifier =
            Modifier.fillMaxSize()) {
        Text(text = "Hello TutorialsEu")
        Text(text = " Kotlin!")
        Text(text = " Compose!")
    }
}
```

With the size property is added, you should see the Arrangement and Alignment reflect on preview, as shown in Figure 9.5. You need to refresh the preview if you don't see the changes.

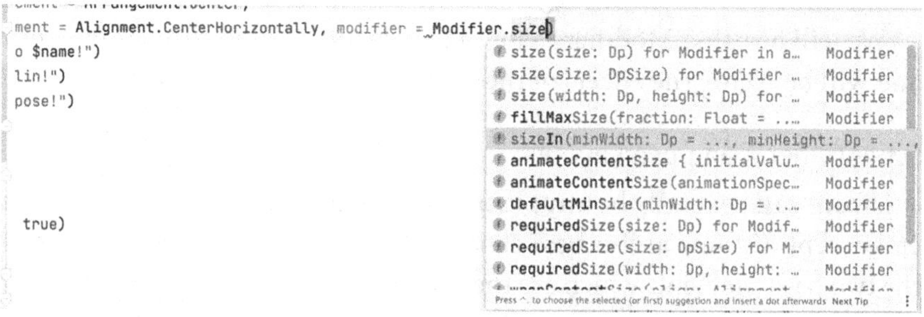

FIGURE 9.4   Different element sizing available with the Modifier.

FIGURE 9.5   The screen display result when fillMaxSize property is added to a column alignment.

We will be using Modifiers a lot in this chapter and in the coming ones and will be seeing the effects of the properties they can provide.

### 9.1.4  Other Compose Layouts

A Layout can generally be any element that accepts a child element. Some can accept just one and others can accept more than one. We have seen the two basic elements which are the Row and Column, but others can also be used on a case-by-case basis. There is also the Box layout which stacks up children on top of each other and the ConstraintLayout that helps you create a little more complex UIs with ease by constraining elements to each other.

### 9.1.4.1 The Box Layout

To see an example of what you can do with the Box layout, we will create a simple UI that will stack up three boxes just like a game of cards. The first Box will be the parent box with a fillMaxSize property to take up the maximum height and width of the screen. There are going to be three child boxes where they all have the same height and width, an alignment to the center using a Modifier, padding start, and end with 10dp difference from each other, and padding bottom for the second and third boxes.

In Jetpack Compose, margins and paddings are defined using the Modifier class, which is used to modify the layout and behavior of Composable UI elements.

You can use the padding() Modifier to add padding to a composable element, which takes four arguments for left, top, right, and bottom padding, respectively.

Figure 9.6 shows the code and the resulting interface.

As seen in the code above, colors are hardcoded in Compose UI using the Color class, where Color(0XFF4c4c4c) represents the color value in hexadecimal format (0xFF for alpha channel and 4C4C4C for the RGB channels).

```
Box(Modifier.fillMaxSize()) {
    Box(
        Modifier.size(400.dp,500.dp).
        align(Alignment.Center)
            .padding(start = 35.dp,
            end = 35.dp)
            .background(Color(0XFF4c4c4c))
    )
    Box(
        Modifier.size(400.dp,500.dp).
        align(Alignment.Center)
            .padding(bottom = 30.dp,
            start = 25.dp, end = 25.dp)
            .background((0XFF969696))
    )
    Box(
        Modifier.align(Alignment.Center)
            .size(400.dp, 500.dp)
            .padding(bottom = 60.dp,
            start = 15.dp, end = 15.dp)
            .background(Color(0XFF1d1d1d))
    )
}
```

FIGURE 9.6   Using the box layout.

### 9.1.4.2 The Constraint Layout

In the View system, ConstraintLayout was introduced to reduce the use of multiple nested layouts. This is because it can cause performance issues like UI lagging which are more noticeable when used for large projects. Although such issues are not a concern in compose since it is built to handle nested layout hierarchies, it does not matter much if you prefer to use them for your application. ConstraintLayout is still useful when you want to place composables relative to other composables on the screen to conform to complicated UI requirements. It also provides positioning using guidelines that are useful for positioning elements at a certain dp or percentage on the screen, barriers that are useful for referencing multiple composables to create a virtual guideline or chains that are very useful for grouping composables in a single axis horizontally or vertically. Below is a basic example using a ConstraintLayout.

## 9.2 YOUR FIRST COMPOSE INTERFACE

Having gotten familiar with the compose basic layout elements, let's create our first real UI that shows a user profile. This will contain a profile image with a name, location, and contact icons so we will use three nonlayout elements which are the Image, Text for the name and location display, and Icon for the contact icons. We will also be using different layout elements but first, let's look at the final result.

From the UI displayed in Figure 9.7, we can have two different layouts, Row and Column. The image, name, country, and Row will be placed directly within the Column while the Row will be the layout for the contact

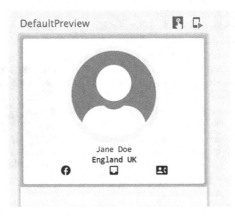

FIGURE 9.7   A profile UI created with composables.

icons. The UI also looks Card-like, which can be achieved using a Card composable. The Card element can contain a single element and has properties like elevation that creates a shadow around it. Below is what the code looks like. Add this in the MainActivity file, outside of the MainActivity class.

```
@Composable
fun Profile() {
    Column(modifier = Modifier.fillMaxSize()) {
        Card(
            elevation = 6.dp, modifier = Modifier
                .background(color = Color.
                  LightGray)
                .fillMaxWidth()
                .padding(6.dp)
        ) {
            Column(
                horizontalAlignment =
                Alignment.CenterHorizontally,
                verticalArrangement = Arrangement.
                 SpaceBetween,
                modifier = Modifier.
                 wrapContentSize()
                    .padding(vertical = 16.dp)
            ) {
                Image(
                    painter = painterResource(id
                    = R.drawable.
                    default_no_profile),
                    contentDescription =
                    "picture", modifier =
                    Modifier
                        .size(200.dp)
                        .clip(CircleShape)
                )

                Text(text = "Jane Doe",
                    fontFamily = FontFamily.
                    Monospace)
                Text(text = "England UK",
                 fontFamily = FontFamily.
                 Monospace,
                 fontWeight = FontWeight.ExtraBold
                )
```

```
              Row(horizontalArrangement =
              Arrangement.SpaceEvenly,
              modifier = Modifier.
              fillMaxWidth()) {
                  Icon(imageVector = Icons.
                  Default.Facebook,
                      contentDescription =
                      "Facebook")
                  Icon(imageVector = Icons.
                  Default.Inbox,
                      contentDescription =
                      "Inbox")
                  Icon(imageVector = Icons.
                  Default.ContactPhone,
                      contentDescription =
                      "Facebook")
      } } }}}
```

## 9.3 TIP CALCULATOR APP OVERVIEW

We have covered some composable elements that are most frequently used but still haven't seen them in action. Here you will be building a tip calculator app that will allow users to tip people at the end of a service. The tip calculator app will enable you to learn about states and events in compose by introducing you to two composables that cannot be used without these two concepts which are TextField and Button. You will also learn about the Slider element that enables users to select a tip percentage from a range of values along a bar. Figure 9.8 is what the app will look like.

When a user enters the total bill amount into the TextField, they can use the slider to select a tip percentage by moving up and down the bar for a change of the value. They can also choose how many people they would like to split the tip by using the buttons provided to either increase or decrease before clicking the calculate button for the final amount. We will be breaking each element requiring state and event into different composable functions so we can manage their values better and avoid a long unreadable function.

## 9.4 BUILDING THE UI OF THE APP

To get started creating the tips calculator, you can create a new empty compose activity project and rename the Greeting function to TipCalculator. The parent layout will be a Column that will have its children centered in

FIGURE 9.8   The tip calculator final result.

the middle of the screen. In the Column, the Text for displaying the Tips per person will come first, followed by the TextField for entering the bill's total, we will create a separate composable function that will be placed below the tips Text as shown in Figure 9.9.

### 9.4.1 TextField

The compose TextField is an element for accepting inputs from a user and it provides properties like a label to be displayed inside the container to show the expected value. It also provides two other important properties value and onValueChanged. The value is the input text to be shown in the TextField while the onValueChanged is a callback that keeps track of the input changes as they occur.

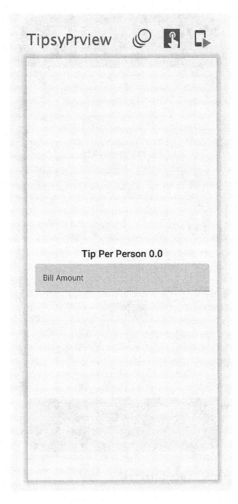

FIGURE 9.9   UI display for the bill amount input.

You will create a separate composable function called BillTotalField with parameters for value, and onValueChanged to be provided later in the state section. Within the function, add a TextField and pass in the parameters created respectively for the required values. Below is what the function should look like.

```
@Composable
fun BillTotalField(
    value: String = "",
    onValueChanged: (String) -> Unit = {},
    modifier: Modifier = Modifier
) {
```

```
    TextField(
        value = value, onValueChange =
         onValueChanged,
        label = { Text(text = "Bill Amount") },
        modifier = modifier.fillMaxWidth()
    )
}
```

In the TipsCalculator function, you can add the tips per person Text and call the BillTotalField composable just like the code below and preview the display.

```
@Composable
fun TipCalculator() {
    Column(
        modifier = Modifier
            .fillMaxSize()
            .padding(16.dp),
        verticalArrangement = Arrangement.Center
    ) {

        Text(
            text = "Tip Per Person 0.0",
            modifier = Modifier
                .align(Alignment.
                   CenterHorizontally)
                .padding(bottom = 8.dp),
            style = MaterialTheme.typography.h6
        )
        BillTotalField(
        )
    }
}
```

### 9.4.2 The Slider Widget

Below the bill TextField, the Slider widgets including the Tip and percentage value text will be placed. This will also be created as a separate function with a Column as the layout composable and three composables as its children placed vertically after each other. The Slider also has a value property and onValueChanged where just like the TextField, the value is the current value of the slider while onValueChanged tracks the change in value and keeps it updated. There is a Slider property called steps that helps to distribute the value across the range and in our case it will be 5

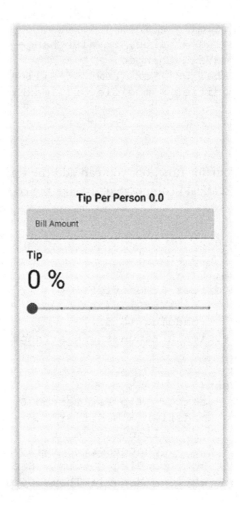

FIGURE 9.10   The slider and tip percentage added to the UI.

steps. Below is the code for the slider widget and Figure 9.10 shows the display result.

```kotlin
@Composable
fun TipPercentSlider(
    value: Float, onValueChanged: (Float) -> Unit,
    modifier: Modifier = Modifier
) {
    Column {
        Text(
            text = "Tip",
            modifier = modifier
```

```
            .align(Alignment.Start)
            .padding(top = 16.dp),
        style = MaterialTheme.typography.h6
    )
    Text(
        text = "${(value * 100).toInt()} %",
        modifier = modifier.align(Alignment.
          Start),
        style = MaterialTheme.typography.h3
    )
    Slider(
        value = value, onValueChange =
          onValueChanged,
        steps = 5
    )
    }
}
```

You can call the above composable within the TipCalculator function just below the BillTotalField to get the following result.

### 9.4.3 The Split Elements and Calculate Button

To split tips between more than one person, we have an increase and decrease button with Text to show the value. The button will also be a separate function with a card-like feature to be reused for increment and decrement. It will be a circle in shape achievable using Modifiers' clip property and applying the circle shape. Since the function will be reusable, it will have parameters for values that will be different for both events like the Image and the content description. Below is what the function looks like.

```
@Composable
fun SplitButton(
    modifier: Modifier = Modifier,
    imageVector: ImageVector,
    onClick: () -> Unit = {},
    desc: String
) {
    Card(modifier = modifier
        .size(
            40.dp
        )
        .clip(CircleShape)
```

```
            .clickable { onClick() }
            .padding(4.dp),
        shape = CircleShape
    ) {
        Icon(
            imageVector = imageVector,
            contentDescription = desc
        )
    }
}
```

Within the TipCalculator and directly below the TipPercentSlider, you can complete the UI by first adding the Split Text label before a Row layout to place the decrement and increment buttons by the left and right of the split value Text respectively. Finally, the calculate button will be placed last after the Row. Below is the final code of the TipCalculator UI with Figure 9.11 showing the complete UI preview.

```
@Composable
fun TipCalculator() {
    Column(
        modifier = Modifier
            .fillMaxSize()
            .padding(16.dp),
        verticalArrangement = Arrangement.Center
    ) {

        Text(
            text = "Tip Per Person 0.0",
            modifier = Modifier
                .align(Alignment.
                    CenterHorizontally)
                .padding(bottom = 8.dp),
            style = MaterialTheme.typography.h6
        )
        BillTotalField(
        )

        TipPercentSlider()

        Text(text = "Split")
        Row(modifier = Modifier.padding(top =
          8.dp)) {
            eu.tutorials.tipcalculator.
              SplitButton(
```

```
            imageVector = Icons.Default.
             Remove,
            onClick = {   },
            desc = "Decrease"
        )
        Text(
            text = "1",
            modifier = Modifier.padding
             (horizontal = 4.dp),
            style = MaterialTheme.typography.
             h5
        )
        eu.tutorials.tipcalculator.
         SplitButton(
            imageVector = Icons.Default.Add,
            onClick = {   },
            desc = "Increase"
        )
    }
    Button(
        onClick = {
```

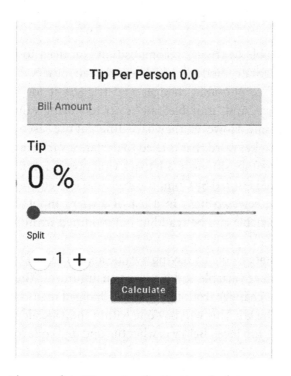

FIGURE 9.11    The complete UI preview for the tip calculator.

```
        },
        modifier = Modifier
            .align(Alignment.
                CenterHorizontally)
            .clip(RoundedCornerShape(8.dp))
    ) {
        Text(text = "Calculate")
} }}
```

## 9.5  STATE IN JETPACK COMPOSE

To make the application functional, we need to introduce state and events. A state is any value that can change over time but in compose this is handled differently from XML since composables don't automatically remember their value state, so you have to make it keep track of changes in value. When a value changes, for example, entering a text in the TextField, something called recomposition occurs which causes a rerun of the UI thereby changing the value to the initial state. For a composable to be able to store a state across compositions you can use the remember object available within the API because it stores the value and returns it after recomposition.

Also, to be able to trigger recomposition you need to hold the value with the mufigState method which creates an observable holder that keeps track of composable changes and triggers it for recomposition. Both "remember" and "mutableState" refer to storing values that can be changed over time. However, they have different use cases and behaviors. "remember" is a keyword that is used to declare a variable that retains its value across recompositions in a Jetpack Compose UI. It is a form of persistent state that is stored by Compose itself and is used to store UI-related data, such as a selected item in a list or a user's input. The value of a "remember" variable can be read but not modified within a composable function.

For all the state elements having a value and onValueChanged, we will create a remember variable and pass it as an argument. The same variable will receive the changes from the onValueChanged method and then display them on the UI. This will be done within the TipCalculator compose function, at the top level. Below is what the updated code looks like.

```
@Composable
fun TipCalculator() {
```

```kotlin
var amountInput by remember {
    mutableStateOf("")
}

var percentValue by remember {
    mutableStateOf(0.1f)
}

var numberOfPerson by remember {
    mutableStateOf(1)
}

var tipPerPerson by remember {
    mutableStateOf(0.0)
}
Column(
    modifier = Modifier
        .fillMaxSize()
        .padding(16.dp),
    verticalArrangement = Arrangement.Center
) {

    Text(
        text = "Tip Per Person $tipPerPerson",
        modifier = Modifier
            .align(Alignment.
                CenterHorizontally)
            .padding(bottom = 8.dp),
        style = MaterialTheme.typography.h6
    )
    BillTotalField(
        value = amountInput,
        onValueChanged = {
            amountInput = it
        }
    )

TipPercentSlider(value = percentValue,
 onValueChanged = {
        percentValue = it
    })

    Text(text = "Split")
    Row(modifier = Modifier.padding(top =
     8.dp)) {
```

```
                     eu.tutorials.tipcalculator.
                      SplitButton(
                          imageVector = Icons.Default.
                           Remove,
                          onClick = { numberOfPerson-- },
                          desc = "Decrease"
                      )
                     Text(
                          text = "$numberOfPerson",
                          modifier = Modifier.
                           padding(horizontal = 4.dp),
                          style = MaterialTheme.typography.
                           h5
                      )
                     eu.tutorials.tipcalculator.
                      SplitButton(
                          imageVector = Icons.Default.Add,
                          onClick = { numberOfPerson++ },
                          desc = "Increase"
                      )
                 }
                 Button(
                      onClick = {

                      },
                      modifier = Modifier
                          .align(Alignment.CenterHorizontally)
                          .clip(RoundedCornerShape(8.dp))
                 ) {
                      Text(text = "Calculate")

             }}}
```

You can create a remember variable using either the by keyword or the "=". With the by keyword, you will need to make two imports.

```
    import androidx.compose.runtime.getValue
import androidx.compose.runtime.setValue
```

Now you can run the app, and you should be able to interact with the TextField, Slider, and Split buttons. The final step is to use the values to calculate the final tip.

## 9.6 CALCULATING THE TIPS PER PERSON

To get the final value for the Tip, two calculations are broken down using functions. The first is to calculate the total tip, and the second is to calculate the tip per person. In calculating the total tip, you will create a function to multiply the tip percent with the total bill as the tip percent is the slider value multiplied by 100. The function requires two parameters, the first is the amount that will be gotten from the input value and the second is the tip percent which will be gotten from the slider value. Below is what the function looks like.

```
private fun calculateTip(amount: Double,
  tipPercent: Double = 10.0): Double {
    return if (amount.toString().isNotEmpty() &&
    amount > 1.0) {
        amount * tipPercent
    } else {
        0.0
    }

}
```

With the tip function ready you can now calculate the final value to be displayed per person using the output from the above function. Because it is dependent on the function above it will also receive the same parameters with the addition of the split number to be gotten from the split value. Below is what the function will look like.

```
private fun calculateTipPerson(
    amount: Double,
    tipPercent: Double = 10.0,
    numberOfPerson: Int
): Double {
    return kotlin.math.round(
        calculateTip(
            amount,
            tipPercent
        ) / numberOfPerson
    )
}
```

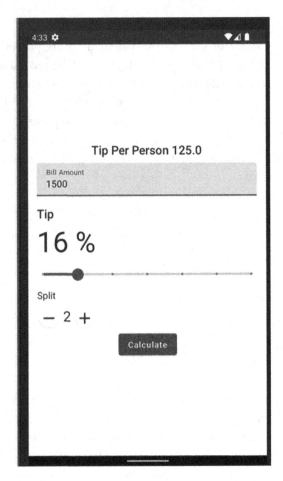

FIGURE 9.12   Testing the tip calculator.

Within the calculate button onClick function, we will call the calculateTipPerson, run the app, and test again. This time enter the bill amount, select a slider value, choose the split number, and click the calculate button. Figure 9.12 shows a test result with a tip calculation performed.

## 9.7 SUMMARY

- Jetpack Compose is a reactive framework that uses Kotlin to build user interfaces rather than XML for Android.

- Composables are just like normal functions but with composable annotations.

- Row and Column are the basic layout elements in Jetpack Compose.

- The Row composable is used to position elements in the horizontal direction.

- The Column composable is used to position elements in the vertical direction.

- All Composables have access to the Modifier object that provides properties for beautifying and customizing each one.

- For a Composable state to be updated after recomposition, you need to hold the value using the remember object.

CHAPTER **10**

# More on Compose Elements

## 10.1 THE COUNTDOWN TIMER PROJECT OVERVIEW

A countdown timer is an essential application that is used in various forms to count down from a specific date or time, indicating the end or beginning of an event. In this chapter, we will guide you through the process of creating a timer ticker, where you can enter the time in hours, minutes, or seconds, then click the button to start counting. While the timer is in progress, you will have the ability to stop and start it again, providing you with more flexibility and control.

As we go through the process of creating the timer ticker, we will pay special attention to the timer fields, managing their focus and keyboard control at certain intervals. For example, the device keyboard will pop up when entering the time values. We will also set the field type to be only numbers since those are the kind of values it requires. Additionally, you will learn how to manage the keyboard so that it only displays when there is a focus on the field.

Building this project will provide you with a detailed understanding of how to use the Jetpack Compose framework to create a countdown timer application, from the basics of creating a timer and displaying the remaining time on the screen to advanced techniques for creating reusable elements and handling state changes. The final UI will look like Figure 10.1,

DOI: 10.1201/9781032622538-10

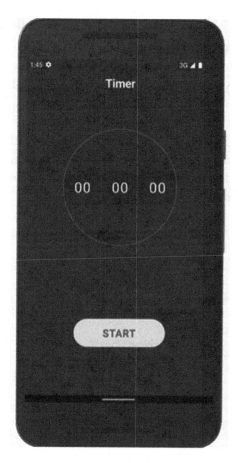

FIGURE 10.1  The final countdown timer UI result.

which will be a clean and easy-to-use countdown timer that you can customize and use in your own Android applications. With the knowledge gained from this chapter, you will be able to implement a countdown timer that meets the specific needs of your application, making it more user-friendly and efficient.

From Figure 10.1, you will notice the timer's surroundings and that it has a circular border. You will see how such a UI can be achieved using the Box border property while also using some other composables like Surface and Space for the first time.

## 10.2 CREATING THE USER INTERFACE OF THE APP

To begin creating the user interface (UI) of the countdown timer application, you will start by creating a new Empty Compose Activity project. This will provide you with a basic project structure and will allow you to focus on building the UI of the application.

Once you have created the project, the next step is to modify the Greeting function to become the CountDownTimer. This involves removing the string parameter and the Text composable from the function, as these are not needed for the countdown timer. You will then replace all calls to the Greeting composable with calls to the CountDownTimer composable. This will ensure that the UI of the application is focused on the countdown timer, rather than a greeting message.

```kotlin
class MainActivity : ComponentActivity() {
    override fun onCreate(savedInstanceState:
    Bundle?) {
        super.onCreate(savedInstanceState)
        setContent {
            CountdowntimerTheme {
                Surface(
                    modifier = Modifier.
                    fillMaxSize(),
                    color = MaterialTheme.colors.
                    background
                ) {
                    CountDownTimer()}}}}

@Composable
fun CountDownTimer() {}

@Preview(showBackground = true)
@Composable
fun DefaultPreview() {
    CountdowntimerTheme {
        CountDownTimer()
}}
```

In the CountDownTimer composable, we will first add the Column composable as the parent element. This will provide a vertical layout structure for the timer and will allow us to add additional composables as children. Following the Column, we will add a Text composable for displaying the title of the timer. This will help users to understand what the timer is counting down to.

The code to achieve this can be written as follows and Figure 10.2 shows the preview result.

```
@Composable
fun CountDownTimer() {
    Column(modifier = Modifier
        .fillMaxSize()
        .background(color = colorResource(id = R .
        color . maroon)),
    verticalArrangement = Arrangement.Center,
    horizontalAlignment = Alignment.
    CenterHorizontally) {
        Text(
            text = "Timer",
            color = Color.White,
            fontSize = 25.sp,
            textAlign = TextAlign.Center,
            fontWeight = FontWeight.Bold)}}
```

FIGURE 10.2  The preview result of the column and timer text.

## 10.2.1 Preparing the Reusable Timer Field

The timer field has a box-like border surrounded by a circle shape. There are three fields, one for the hour value, the second for the minute value, and the third for the second value. They all look the same and will therefore require a custom composable that can be reused for them rather than having an unnecessary repetition of codes. For this, we will create a reusable compose function that will have the common properties as parameters. The first parameter will be used for the field value, the second will be used for the onChanged function, and the third will be used to enable or disable the field which depends on whether the timer is in the running state or not.

In addition to the three parameters, the custom TextField will have a placeholder with a letter-spacing property, a keyboard option attribute that shows only the number keyboard, and a text style with a font size of 30sp, text align to the center, text color set to white, and letter spacing with a value of 2sp. Below is what the compose function looks like. Although you can have this in the MainActivity file, it is a common practice you create a separate file for it and additionally have it in a package that can name components where you can also create other custom composable functions.

```
@Composable
fun ReusableTextField(modifier: Modifier =
Modifier,
                        text: String, onChange:
                        (String) -> Unit,
                        enabled: Boolean) {
    TextField(
        value = text,
        placeholder = {
            Text(
                text = "00",
                fontSize = 30.sp,
                textAlign = TextAlign.Center,
                color = Color.White,
                letterSpacing = 2.sp

            )
        },
        keyboardOptions = KeyboardOptions
        (keyboardType = KeyboardType.Number),
```

```
        onValueChange = { value ->
            onChange.invoke(value)
        },
        textStyle = TextStyle(
            fontSize = 30.sp,
            textAlign = TextAlign.Center,
            color = Color.White,
            letterSpacing = 2.sp
        ),
        enabled = enabled,
        modifier = modifier
            .width(80.dp)
            .background(color = Color.
            Transparent))
    }
```

In the MainActivity file, below the Timer title, you can place the ReusableTextField three times within a Row to represent the hours, minutes, and seconds fields. For each value argument, we will provide a unique remember String value and for the onChange function, we will temporarily assign the result from its lambda to the value and will replace it with functions later. Below is what the Row will look like with Figure 10.3 showing the preview result.

```
Row {
            ReusableTextField(
                text = hoursTextState.value,
                onChange = { hoursTextState.value
                = it },
                enabled = true
            )
            ReusableTextField(
                text = minutesTextState.value,
                onChange = { minutesTextState.
                value = it },
                enabled = true
            )
            ReusableTextField(
                text = secondsTextState.value,
                onChange = { secondsTextState.
                value = it },
                enabled = true)
    }
```

FIGURE 10.3 The timer field preview result.

### 10.2.1.1 Adding the Borders to the Timer Field

As already mentioned, the Timer Fields has both a card-like border and a circular one that adds a little touch to the UI. We will achieve them using the Card element and a Box by applying specific properties. For the card-like edges, you will use the elevation property with a value of 8dp and set a padding of 8dp to it, and for the circular border, using a modifier you will add a padding of 40dp, a size of 300.dp, a circle-shaped clip and a border with a border stroke property of 2p and a pink color. It is also important to set a shape with a value of CircleShape and finally center the content of the border using a contentAlignment property. Below is what the update CountDownTimer code should look like with Figure 10.4 showing the preview result.

```kotlin
@Composable
fun CountDownTimer() {
    val secondsTextState = remember
    { mutableStateOf("") }
```

```
val minutesTextState = remember
 { mutableStateOf("") }
val hoursTextState = remember
 { mutableStateOf("") }
Column(modifier = Modifier
    .fillMaxSize()
    .background(color = colorResource(id =
        R.color.maroon)),
verticalArrangement = Arrangement.Center,
horizontalAlignment = Alignment.
 CenterHorizontally) {
    Text(
        text = "Timer",
        color = Color.White,
        fontSize = 25.sp,
        textAlign = TextAlign.Center,
        fontWeight = FontWeight.Bold
    )
    Box(
        Modifier
            .padding(40.dp)
            .size(300.dp)
            .clip(CircleShape)
            .border(
                BorderStroke(
                    2.dp,
                    colorResource(id =
                    R.color.pink)
                ),
                shape = CircleShape
            ),
        contentAlignment = Alignment.Center,

    ) {
        Card(elevation = 8.dp, modifier =
         Modifier.padding(8.dp)) {
            Row {
                ReusableTextField(
                    text = hoursTextState.
                     value,
                    onChange = {
                    hoursTextState.value = it
                    },
                    enabled = true
                )
```

```
ReusableTextField(
    text = minutesTextState.
    value,
    onChange =
    { minutesTextState.value
    = it },
    enabled = true
)
ReusableTextField(
    text = secondsTextState.
    value,
    onChange = {
        secondsTextState.value =
        it },
    enabled = true
) } }}}}
```

FIGURE 10.4   A preview of the resulting border.

## 10.2.2 Creating the Start and Stop Button

We will be using one button to start and stop the timer. It will be created as a custom composable which will have two important parameters. The isRunning and isEnabled where both are Boolean values. isRunning will be used to determine when to change the button to either a start or stop. Before the timer is started, the button will be a start one with a start text written on it and after the timer is started, the button will be used as a stop one with a stop text written on it.

Another parameter is isEnabled, which will be used to determine when to make the button clickable and when not to, reducing unnecessary clicks and crashes if the timer fields are empty. Below is how the Start and Stop composables should look like and they will be located within the component package as a new file.

```
@Composable
fun StartAndStopButton(
    isButtonDisabled: Boolean,
    isRunning: Boolean,
    onClick: () -> Unit
) {
    Button(
        onClick = {
            onClick()
        },
        modifier =
        Modifier
            .height(60.dp)
            .width(200.dp),
        shape = RoundedCornerShape(30.dp),
        colors = ButtonDefaults.buttonColors(
            backgroundColor =  if
            (isButtonDisabled)
            colorResource(id = R.color.white)
            else colorResource(id = R.color.
            pink),
            contentColor = colorResource(id =
            R.color.white),
        ),
        enabled = isButtonDisabled
    ) {
        val status = if (!isRunning) {
            "START"
        } else {
```

```
            "STOP"
        }

        Text(
            status,
            fontSize = 22.sp,
            color = if (isButtonDisabled)
              colorResource(id = R.color.white)
              else colorResource(id = R.color.
              pink),
            fontWeight = FontWeight.Bold
        ) }}
```

To change the button's color attribute, you can use the ButtonDefaults property to modify both the background color and content color. We have used the if condition to set the background of the button to white when in the disabled state and the text to pink. When in the enabled state, the background will be pink with the text set to white.

### 10.2.2.1 Testing the App

You should make sure to run the app at this stage and ensure you have the expected result with the timer fields functioning. Figure 10.5 shows the running app with the complete elements. In the following section, we will be modifying the temporary values like the timer fields value and onChanged function to achieve the expected behaviors of the timer.

## 10.3 CREATING THE APPLICATION STATE

Now that we have the UI ready, the next step is to prepare the main function that handles the timer state. First, the Android API has an inbuilt countdown timer class that provides attributes and functions that makes it easier for you to schedule a countdown. These attributes include the following.

- **Start method:** This can be used to start a timer

- **Cancel method:** This can be used to stop a timer

- **Finish method:** This is a callback that is called when the time is finished

- **onTick:** This is a callback that is called at regular intervals.

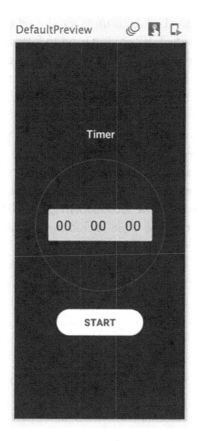

FIGURE 10.5   UI preview for the start/stop button.

The CountDownTimer class has two important parameters: a millisInFuture, which is a long value that can be used to keep track of the number of milliseconds in the future, and a countDownInterval also a long value that receives the onTick value.

### 10.3.1  Implementing the Countdown Timer Class

Various states are required to manipulate the timer fields adequately, connect them to the start and stop buttons, and ensure that the hour, minute, and second work together. We have previously mentioned the hoursText-State, minuteTextState, and secondTextState, which will each represent the three input timer fields. There is also the isRunning state, a Boolean value that will be used to track when the timer is in the start state, finished state, and canceled state. This means that when the start method from the countdown timer class is called, isRunning can be set to true, when the onFinished method is called, isRunning can be set to false and when the onCancel method is called, isRunning is set to false as well.

With the isRunning variable tracking the countdown state, it will be used to decide when to enable or disable the start and stop states. At the same time, it will be used to decide when to start the countdown or cancel it. Other essential parts of this class are three methods that are used to set the length of each time countdown that is, the hour, minute, and seconds. For each scenario, we use the coerceIn method to ensure that they lie between a specified range. The method takes in two values, the start value and the end value. For example, the hour will take in 0 and 23, the minute will take in 0 and 60 while the seconds will take in 0 and 60. Below is the CountDownTimer complete code including the initialization method. This method will be responsible for remembering and creating the instance of the state class and getting it ready for the UI. Following is the different part of CountdownTimerState class and the initializer beginning with variables holding the timer states.

```kotlin
class CountDownTimerState{
    private var countDownTimer: CountDownTimer? =
    null
/*This creates and initialize the running
variable.  It then keeps track of it and
indicates whether the timer is currently running
or not.
*/
    val isRunning: MutableState<Boolean>
        get() = _isRunning
    private val _isRunning = mutableStateOf(false)

/*_seconds holds the current seconds value of the
timer and seconds provides a value that can be
used to access it.
*/
    private val _seconds = mutableStateOf("00")
    val seconds: MutableState<String>
        get() = _seconds

/* _minutes holds the current minute value of the
timer while minutes is used to access it.
*/
    private val _minutes = mutableStateOf("00")
    val minutes: MutableState<String>
        get() = _minutes
```

```
/* hours holds the current hour value of the timer
while hours is used to access it.
 */
```

```
        private var _hours = mutableStateOf("00")
        val hours: MutableState<String>
            get() = _hours



        private val _progress = mutableStateOf(1f)
        val progress: MutableState<Float>
            get() = _progress

        var totalTime = 0L        //this holds the
          totalTime of the timer
```

```
    }
```

Within this class, we will create the function startCountDown() that will be used to start the timer. We will calculate the total time in milliseconds to be used with a new CountDownTimer object. The object has an onTick(millisecs: Long) function that is called on every timer tick. It converts the given milliseconds to seconds, minutes, and hours and updates the respective variables. Here is what this function looks like.

```
        fun startCountDown() {
            if (countDownTimer != null) {
                cancelTimer()
            }
```

```
/* Calculates the totaltimer in milliseconds to be
used by the countdownTimer object
 */
            totalTime = (getSeconds() * 1000).toLong()
```

```
/* The CountDownTimer object that handles the whole
   timer by calculating the number of seconds,
   minutes and hours and update the states variable.
 */
            countDownTimer = object :
            CountDownTimer(totalTime, 1000) {
                override fun onTick(millisecs: Long) {
                    val secs = (millisecs / MSECS_IN_
                    SEC % SECS_IN_MINUTES).toInt()
```

```
                    if (secs != seconds.value.toInt()) {
                        _seconds.value =
                        formatTime(secs)
                    }
                    val minutes = (millisecs / MSECS_
                     IN_SEC / SECS_IN_MINUTES % SECS_
                     IN_MINUTES).toInt()
                    if (minutes != minutes) {
                        _minutes.value =
                        formatTime(minutes)
                    }
                    val hours = (millisecs / MSECS_IN_
                     SEC / MINUTES_IN_HOUR / SECS_IN_
                     MINUTES).toInt()
                    if (hours != hours) {
                        _hours.value =
                        formatTime(hours)
                    }

                    _progress.value = millisecs.
                     toFloat() / totalTime.toFloat()
                    _seconds.value  = formatTime(secs)
                    _minutes.value =
                     formatTime(minutes)
                    _hours.value = formatTime(hours)
                }

                override fun onFinish() {
                    _progress.value = 1.0f
                    _isRunning.value = false
                }
            }
            countDownTimer?.start()
            _isRunning.value = true
        }
```

Next, we will add a method to modify the state for each of the timer value when collected from the input field for the seconds, minutes, and hour.

```
/* This method checks the second's input length from
   [0..59] and posts the value
*/
        fun modifySeconds(secondsValue: String) {
            if (secondsValue.isNotEmpty()) {
```

```
            _seconds.value = secondsValue.toInt().
             coerceIn(0, 59).toString()
        } else {
            _seconds.value  = secondsValue
        }

    }


/* This method checks the minute's input length from
   [0..59] and posts the value
*/
    fun modifyMinutes(minutesValue: String) {
        if (minutesValue.isNotEmpty()) {
            _minutes.value = minutesValue.toInt().
             coerceIn(0, 59).toString()
        } else {
            _minutes.value = minutesValue
        }

    }

/* This method checks the hour's input length from
   [0..23] and posts the value
*/
    fun modifyHours(hoursValue: String) {
        if (hoursValue.isNotEmpty()) {
            _hours.value = hoursValue.toInt().
             coerceIn(0, 23).toString()
        } else {
            _hours.value = hoursValue
        }
    }

    private fun formatTime(time: Int) =
        String.format("%02d", time)

    fun cancelTimer() {
        countDownTimer?.cancel()
        _isRunning.value = false
    }

    private fun getSeconds() =
        (hours.value.toInt() * MINUTES_IN_HOUR *
        SECS_IN_MINUTES) + (minutes.value.toInt()
        * SECS_IN_MINUTES) + seconds.value.
        toInt()
```

```
companion object {
    const val MINUTES_IN_HOUR = 60
    const val SECS_IN_MINUTES = 60
    const val MSECS_IN_SEC = 1000
}
```

## 10.4 CONNECTING THE STATES TO THE TIMER FIELD

With the state variables and methods ready, it is time to replace the temporary values assigned to the timer fields. The first step will be to get an instance of the state class and create access to the public variables like the field states and isRunning state. Next, we will create a variable for indicating the enabled state of the timer fields using the isRunning variable. This means that when isRunning is true, then the fields are disabled and when the value is false the fields are enabled to become clickable which is also only dependent on the state of the timer fields. You will also provide an empty state value for the fields which is zero by default except on focus. Below are the newly created variables and update to the existing value.

```
val appState = rememberCountDownTimerState()
val secondsTextState = remember { appState.
 seconds }
val minutesTextState = remember { appState.
 minutes }
val hoursTextState = remember { appState.hours
 }
val isRunning = remember { appState.isRunning }
val enable = !isRunning.value

val emptySecondsField = secondsTextState.value
 == "00"
val emptyMinutesField = minutesTextState.value
 == "00"
val emptyHoursField = hoursTextState.value ==
 "00"

/* Check if any of the input field is empty, then
   disable the timer button
*/
val enableButton = (secondsTextState.value !=
 "00" &&     secondsTextState.value.isNotEmpty())
 || (minutesTextState.value != "00" && minutes
 TextState.value.isNotEmpty()) ||(hoursTextState.
 value != "00" && hoursTextState.value.isNot
 Empty())
```

```
val keyboardController =
LocalSoftwareKeyboardController.current
```

The above code should be written at the topmost part of the CountDownTimer composable. You will see we have added a keyboard controller which can be used to get the immediate software keyboard and we will be using it to show or hide the keyboard for the timer fields.

With the updates to the timer fields state variable, you must connect the state methods to each onChange function to enable the input functionality for the entered values to reflect. This is achievable by replacing the value within each onChange block with a suitable modifier method from the CountDownTimerState class. The updated code to each block should look like the code below.

```
onChange = { appState.modifyHours(it) },
onChange = { appState.modifyMinutes(it) },
onChange = { appState.modifySeconds(it) },
```

You should run the app now to test each field and make sure the state is still functional after the changes you have just made. To make sure that there are no app crashes when the button is clicked, you must set the default input fields to 0, and to keep the field cleared on the first focus, you will set the value to an empty string. They are both achievable using the TextField focus changed modifier so each of the timer fields will be updated with a modifier and its respective state set to the required value. Below is what each updated field should look like.

```
Row {
            ReusableTextField(
                text = hoursTextState.
                value,
                onChange = { appState.
                modifyHours(it) },
                enabled = enable,
                modifier = Modifier.
                onFocusChanged{

                    if (it.hasFocus &&
                    emptyHoursField) {
                        hoursTextState.
                        value = ""
```

```
                                       } else if (!it.
                                        hasFocus &&
                                        hoursTextState.value
                                        == "") {
        hoursTextState.value = "00"
}} )
                              ReusableTextField(
                                  text = minutesTextState.
                                   value,
                                  onChange = { appState.
                                   modifyMinutes(it) },
                                  enabled = enable,
                                  modifier = Modifier.
                                   onFocusChanged {
                                      if (it.hasFocus &&
                                       emptyMinutesField) {
                                          minutesTextState.
                                           value = ""
                                      } else if (!it.
                                       hasFocus &&
                                       minutesTextState.
                                       value == "") {
        minutesTextState.value = "00"
}})
                              ReusableTextField(
                                  text = secondsTextState.
                                   value,
                                  onChange = { appState.
                                   modifySeconds(it) },
                                  enabled = enable,
                                  modifier = Modifier.
                                   onFocusChanged {

                                      if (it.hasFocus &&
                                       emptySecondsField) {
                                          secondsTextState.
                                           value = ""
                                      } else if (!it.
                                       hasFocus &&
                                       secondsTextState.
                                       value == "") {
        secondsTextState.value = "00"
}}))}
```

Now when you run the app and click on any of the fields, it becomes ready for values to be entered and if at least one of the fields gets a value other than zero, the other(s) will have a default value of zero to avoid crashes.

## 10.5 MAKING THE BUTTON FUNCTIONAL

To finalize the countdown functionality, we need to make the button active. As we recall, for the expected button functionality before the button can be enabled, at least one field should have a value. The isButtonEnabled property will be updated to reflect this by passing the enableButton variable to it as a value since it takes care of that check. Next, the isRunning property should take its value from the isRunning variable created above to ensure that the button switches between the two states (start and stop) as expected.

Finally, the onClick function will be implemented with three logics in mind. The first is that before the timer starts the keyboard should be removed from the screen. This is achievable using the keyboard controller to call the hide method. Next, we check if the timer is not running then clicking the button should call the startTimer method from the state class and if the timer is already running then it should call the cancelTimer instead. Below is the call to StartAndStopButton composable with the updated code.

```
StartAndStopButton(
        isRunning = isRunning.value,
        onClick = {
            //Hide the soft-keyboard when
                running the timer
            keyboardController?.hide()
            //Check if timer not running,
                start timer else stop(cancel)
                timer
            if (!isRunning.value ) {
                appState.startCountDown()
            } else {
                appState.cancelTimer()
            }
        },
        isButtonDisabled = enableButton)
```

FIGURE 10.6   The timer running state and finished state.

### 10.5.1 Testing the App

The countdown timer is complete and ready for complete testing. Enter your desired value preferably a low number and click the start button. Watch the timer and wait for it to finish, then notice the button becoming disabled again. Figure 10.6 shows the timers running state and finished state.

## 10.6 USING REMEMBERSAVEABLE TO RESTORE UI STATE

Although the compose remember object remembers the state of an object, it does not survive process recreation. This is because the configuration changes that cause the system to restart are required by the application to adapt to the new changes by reloading the application. On the basic level, rememberSaveable is an alternative to using just remember to hold the composable state. It ensures that if your application is reloaded due to configuration changes, the data states are recovered before being displayed in the UI.

One of the processes that can cause configuration changes to occur is screen rotation. Now run your app and start the timer, change the screen rotation from portrait to landscape, and keep your eye on the timer fields. You will notice that the values return to the default state which is 00. Depending on your screen size, some of the UI might fall off the screen when in Landscape mode. To enable the scrolling feature, you can call the verticalScroll() property on the Column modifier and pass in remember-ScrollState() as an argument. This way you can scroll up to see the other parts of the screen that are not immediately visible. Below is what the Column update will look like.

```
Column(
        modifier = Modifier
            .fillMaxSize()
            .background(color = colorResource(id =
            R.color.maroon))
            .verticalScroll(
                rememberScrollState()
            ),
        verticalArrangement = Arrangement.Center,
        horizontalAlignment = Alignment.
        CenterHorizontally)
```

You can start the timer in the landscape mode and change rotation back to portrait. The values will also go back to the default state again. Let's fix this by changing the remember states to rememberSaveable instead. Below are the code samples with updates to the state holders will look like.

```
fun CountDownTimer() {
    val appState = rememberCountDownTimerState()
    val secondsTextState = rememberSaveable {
    appState.seconds }
    val minutesTextState = rememberSaveable {
    appState.minutes }
    val hoursTextState = rememberSaveable {
    appState.hours }
    val isRunning = rememberSaveable { appState.
    isRunning }
}
```

Run the app again and perform the configuration tests once more. This time you will see that in the change from one orientation to another, the timer value remains the same and continues from the last counter. Having looked at using mutable states with remember and rememberSaveable for managing compose states, we will see how this is also possible using ViewModel and LiveData in the coming chapters.

## 10.7 SUMMARY

- A Composable can be customized and made reusable functions to reduce code repetition.

- A Keyboard controller gives access to the immediate keyboard to allow manipulation as required.

- With the Modifier, you can access the TextField focus to listen to even changes.

- Android API provides the CountDownTimer object to help implement countdown features.

- You can make a compose UI scrollable using either the horizontalScroll or vertical Scroll.

- With rememberSaveable, an application's data can remain in its previous state when changes can cause a restart to occur.

# CHAPTER 11

# Room Database with Jetpack Compose

## 11.1 THE WISH LIST APP OVERVIEW

The project you will build in this chapter is an interactive and functional wish list application. This application will allow users to save their wishes by simply entering the title and description of the wish. The application will also allow users to edit each wish when selected and swipe left to delete or right to undo the delete. The wish will be saved on the device using the Room database library. This will provide a solid foundation for understanding how to use the Room database in Jetpack Compose applications.

The application will be divided into several parts: an input screen for creating a new wish, a LazyColumn displaying all the saved wishes, and an edit screen for updating an existing wish. The input screen will have a simple layout with an input field for the title and a text area for the description. The LazyColumn will display all the saved wishes in a scrollable list format. Users will also be able to select a wish from the list to view it in more detail and make any necessary updates.

The edit screen will allow users to change the title and description of the selected wish. Users can also delete a wish by swiping left or undo a delete by swiping right. The Room database library will handle all the data storage and retrieval, making it easy for users to make changes and view their wishes anytime. Figure 11.1 shows the different parts of the application's screen that will help you to understand the overall functionality of the application.

DOI: 10.1201/9781032622538-11

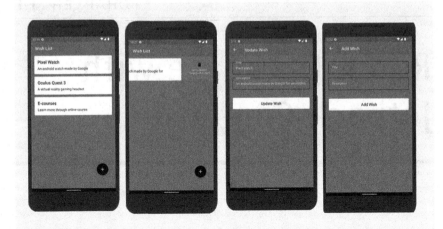

FIGURE 11.1    The wish list applications screen.

## 11.1.1 Understanding the UI of the Application

In this chapter, you can test your Jetpack Compose skills by creating most of the user interfaces for the wish list application. Some of the composable elements used in this project, such as buttons, text, and images, have already been discussed in previous chapters, so you will have a solid foundation upon which to build. However, this chapter will focus on implementing the Room database, navigation, and Lazy Column in the application.

A starter folder for this project's repository has been provided to make things easier for you, which already has the basic UI screens created. This will allow you to focus on the discussion topics and better understand how to implement the Room database, navigation, and Lazy Column in Jetpack Compose applications. This starter folder can be downloaded from the repository, and you can use it as a reference or a starting point for your project. It will help you understand the overall structure of the application and make it easier for you to start working on implementing the different features.

### 11.1.1.1 A Walk-Through of the Starter Folder

The starter folder contains the ADDEDITVIEW file with a composable function comprising the OutlinedTextField and a Button. This function is named AddEditDetailView() and builds up a single UI that will be used to add a new wish to the list, view a wish from the list, and edit a wish. Figure 11.2 shows what the preview of the UI should look like.

FIGURE 11.2   The AddEditPreview user interface.

For the other parts of the UI, including the WishList screen, let's list what Composables will be needed to complete its UI.

### 11.1.1.2 Introducing the NEW Composables

We will start a breakdown from the first screen to quickly grasp the Composables required to complete each screen. It contains a LazyColumn, TopBar, and a Floating action button (FAB) where the LazyColumn will display the list, the TopBar will display the title of the screen, and the FAB will be clicked on to open the Add Wish screen. We will discuss each element in a bit. The Add Wish screen will also contain a title bar which will help differentiate the immediate action being performed since it will be used for three different actions. The TopBar and the FAB are part of an element, the Scaffold. Let's learn what it is and how it is used.

## 11.2 THE SCAFFOLD LAYOUT

The Scaffold is a composable typically used as the root container for an app's UI. It is a container that provides a visual structure for an app's UI.

```
@Composable
fun Scaffold(
    modifier: Modifier = Modifier,
    scaffoldState: ScaffoldState = rememberScaffoldState(),
    topBar: @Composable () -> Unit = {},
    bottomBar: @Composable () -> Unit = {},
    snackbarHost: @Composable (SnackbarHostState) -> Unit = { SnackbarHost(it) },
    floatingActionButton: @Composable () -> Unit = {},
    floatingActionButtonPosition: FabPosition = FabPosition.End,
    isFloatingActionButtonDocked: Boolean = false,
    drawerContent: @Composable (ColumnScope.() -> Unit)? = null,
    drawerGesturesEnabled: Boolean = true,
    drawerShape: Shape = MaterialTheme.shapes.large,
    drawerElevation: Dp = DrawerDefaults.Elevation,
    drawerBackgroundColor: Color = MaterialTheme.colors.surface,
    drawerContentColor: Color = contentColorFor(drawerBackgroundColor),
    drawerScrimColor: Color = DrawerDefaults.scrimColor,
    backgroundColor: Color = MaterialTheme.colors.background,
    contentColor: Color = contentColorFor(backgroundColor),
    content: @Composable (PaddingValues) -> Unit
) {...}
```

FIGURE 11.3   The scaffold with the MDC components and content composable.

It consists of many material design components (MDC) that help developers build uniform, beautiful, reliable, and functional Android apps. These components include the top app bar, a floating action button, a bottom app bar, a snackbar, and a drawer. Aside from the mentioned menu components, there is also a content slot to implement the rest of the user interface. Figure 11.3 shows the crucial part of the Scaffold.

Now that we have an idea about the Scaffold, we will add the TopAppBar and the FAB to the app using the Scaffold. The FAB is created to float on the screen on top of every other element in the same layout, while the TopBar stays at the top-level part of the screen. Before we can add a Scaffold to the home screen, we will create a reusable compose function to be used by both screens' title bars. The function will contain the TopAppBar composable with a String as a parameter for the title text. The WishList and ADDEDIT screens will use the same top bar but with title changes to denote the current screen and action.

The TopAppBar will have a NavigationIcon, which in our use case, is only needed on the ADDEDIT screen for moving back to the home screen when clicked. Therefore, a condition is set to show a navigation icon only when the home screen is in view.

Below is what the function should look like.

```kotlin
@Composable
fun AppBarView(
    title: String
) {

    val navigationIcon: (@Composable () -> Unit)? =
        if (title.contains("Wish List")) {
            {
                /* Check if title is [Wish List]
                   hide icon else show icon
                */
                IconButton(onClick = { }) {
                    Icon(
                        imageVector = Icons.
                          Filled.ArrowBack,
                        tint = Color.White,
                        contentDescription = null
                    )
                }

            }
        } else {
            null
        }
    TopAppBar(
        title = {
            Text(
                text = title,
                color = colorResource(id =
                  R.color.white),
                modifier = Modifier
                    .padding(start = 4.dp)
                    .heightIn(max = 24.dp)
            )
        },
        elevation = 3.dp,
        backgroundColor = colorResource(id =
          R.color.app_bar_color),
        navigationIcon = navigationIcon
    )
}
```

Now we can add a scaffold to the HomeView and, in the scaffold, provide a TopAppBar and the FAB button. This FAB, when clicked, will open the screen to add a new wish but will be implemented later. Below is what the code should look like with Figure 11.4 showing the UI result when you run the app.

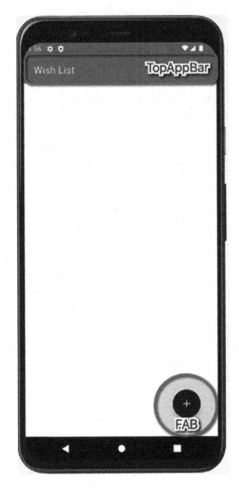

FIGURE 11.4   The WishList app with a TopAppBar and FAB.

```kotlin
@Composable
fun HomeView() {
    Scaffold(topBar = { AppBarView(title =
        stringResource(id = R.string.app_name))},
        floatingActionButton = {
            FloatingActionButton(
                modifier = Modifier.padding(all =
                    20.dp),
                onClick = {

                },
                contentColor = colorResource(id =
                    R.color.white),
```

```
backgroundColor = colorResource(id
   = R.color.black),
) {
Icon(
     imageVector = Icons.Default.
     Add,
     contentDescription = null
) }}) { }}
```

When you run the app, you should see the following UI.

The Scaffold is a layout and has a slot for UI content. We will add the Lazy column as its content for displaying the WishList items but first, let's learn about this widget and how it is used in compose.

## 11.3  DISPLAYING A LIST OF ITEMS USING LAZYCOLUMN

In Chapter 7, we learned about RecyclerView and how it displays a list of items when using XML to create your Android user interface. With Jetpack Compose, there are Lazy Layouts that you can use for this purpose. These include LazyColumn for displaying items vertically on the screen, LazyRow for displaying items horizontally on the screen, and Lazy grids for displaying a list of items in the form of a grid view.

When you have a large data set, the lazy layouts will help you render a scrollable list of items as they become visible on the screen. Having experienced the RecyclerView and seen the many codes and classes, you must write to display lists. With Jetpack Compose lazy layouts, it has become significantly easier and faster to achieve the same result as with way lesser codes. From the UI of the WishList app, the LazyColumn is the layout we need to display its list vertically on the screen. The lazy layouts have a LazyListScope parameter used to receive an item or item for its layout. This scope is an interface with different methods that you can call depending on the use case your app requires. The common property is items() which require two important arguments, the items list and the item composable template.

The wish list item requires two Text composable to display a title and description. To make the UI look card-like, we will use a card composable as the Parent layout and then a Column as the direct layout to the two Text Composables. Below is what the item composable should look like.

```
@Composable
fun WishItem(wish: Wish) {
    Card(
```

```
modifier = Modifier
    .fillMaxWidth()
    .padding(
        top = 8.dp,
        start = 16.dp,
        end = 16.dp,
    )
    .clickable { },
    elevation = 10.dp,
    backgroundColor = Color.White
){
    Column(modifier = Modifier
        .padding(16.dp)) {
        Text(text = wish.title, fontWeight =
            FontWeight.ExtraBold)
        Text(text = wish.description)
    }
}
}
}
```

The WishItem composable has a parameter of type Wish object that references the wish title and description. Also, notice the call to the clickable function. This will make the card clickable and enable an action to be added at the click of a wish item. The implementation will be added in the Navigation section. Every composable without the onClick has access to the clickable function to add the click action. In the LazyColumn, which should be the body of the Scaffold, you will pass in the WishItem as a content value to the items object and then a list of items to be displayed.

A hard-coded list of items has been created to be displayed on the LazyColumn. The list has four wishes and will serve as temporary content until we learn how to use the Room Database. Below is the list of items with the data class model.

```
data class Wish(val id:Long = (0L..100L).shuffled().
    last(),
                val title:String,
                val description:String)

object DummyWish{
    val wishList = listOf(Wish(title = "Google
        Watch", description = "An android watch" +
            "made by Google for tracking health
                fitness"),
```

```
Wish(title = "Oculus Quest 2", description
    = "A VR headset for " + "playing
    games"),
Wish(title = "A Sci-fi, Book", description
    = "A science friction book" +
        "from any best seller"),
Wish(title = "Bean bag", description = "A
    comfy bean bag to substitute" +
        "for a chair")
    )
}
```

Then in the Scaffold content, add the LazyColumn.

```
LazyColumn(modifier = Modifier.fillMaxSize()) {
/* The items function emits each item from the list,
    thereby providing us with a Wish object
*/
            items(DummyWish.wishList) { wish->
                WishItem(wish)
            }
        }
```

A preview of the HomeView composable, including the LazyColumn should look like Figure 11.5.

With the WishList screen's UI in place, the next step is to look at compose navigation and implement it into the app.

## 11.4 NAVIGATING BETWEEN COMPOSABLES

Moving from one screen to another is an essential part of an application. We have learned about navigation between activities and the Fragment, but the implementation is different when navigating between Composables while the concept remains the same. The NavHost and NavHostController are key components during the navigation process. The first is used to provide a place for navigation to occur, while the latter is used to handle navigation. Like all composable elements, the NavHostController has a remember variant that ensures each compose screen is remembered after it's recreated during recomposition. We will implement navigation for the WishList app to see the technical difference between compose Navigation and XML Navigation.

### 11.4.1 Adding Navigation to the WishList App

Implementing navigation in compose requires a dependency to be added to the build.gradle file. After adding and syncing the dependency, you

FIGURE 11.5 The lazy column displaying hard-coded list.

will create a sealed class called Screen with a string property called route in its constructor. This class can then be used to create subclasses for any number of screens you will need during navigation. In this case, we have two screens, the home and add edit screen. Each subclass will provide a value for its route name to be used when a screen route is required. Below is the dependency for navigation to be added within the dependency block.

```
def nav _ version = "2.5.3"
    implementation("androidx.
        navigation:navigation-compose:$nav_version")
```

Here are also the Screen class and the subclasses.

```
sealed class Screen(val route:String) {
    object HomeScreen : Screen("home_screen")
    object AddScreen : Screen("add_screen")
}
```

The next step is preparing the NavHost. A NavHost requires a start destination of type String that indicates the first screen to be displayed when the application is launched. In this case, it is the home screen, and its route name will be passed as the start destination value to the NavHost. Another requirement for setting up the NavHost is providing the compose screens to the NavGraphBuilder to build each destination and to the NavHost. This requires calling the composable function, passing in the route for each screen, and providing the Screen composable name. We will create a file for all navigation-related implementations, and the code looks like as shown below.

```
@Composable
fun Navigation(){
    val navController = rememberNavController()
    NavHost(navController = navController,
        startDestination=Screen.HomeScreen.route){
        composable(Screen.HomeScreen.route){
            HomeView(navController)
        }

        composable(Screen.AddScreen.route){
            AddEditDetailView()

}}}
```

This is the common way to implement navigation that only requires moving from one screen to another. For the WishList app, there are two scenarios. The first is to open the ADDEDIT screen at the click of the FAB button, while the other is to open the details of an item from the screen. While the same screen is opened for the different processes, there are instances to differentiate both. When an item from the list is clicked, the top bar title and the button text will read Update Wish, and when the FAB is clicked, both will read Add Wish. This can be achieved by checking if an id value is passed during navigation which only happens when opening an item. If the id is not 0, an existing item is being opened for a possible update or to view the detail. Otherwise, it is a new screen to create a wish. We will now look at the steps required for passing data between composables during navigation.

### 11.4.1.1 Passing Data Between Composables

To pass data from one composable to another, first you need to create the key and declare the item types within the compose function of the receiver screen. Second, the required value or object will be retrieved through the backstackEntry of the receiving screen and passed in as an argument to the composable function. Let's update the code to reflect changes with the passing of the data.

```kotlin
fun Navigation() {
    val navController = rememberNavController()
    NavHost(
        navController = navController,
        startDestination = Screen.HomeScreen.
            route
    ) {
        composable(Screen.HomeScreen.route) {
            HomeView(navController)
        }
        composable(route = Screen.AddScreen.route
        +"/{id}/{title}/{desc}",
            arguments = listOf(
                navArgument("id") {
                    type = NavType.LongType
                    defaultValue = 0L
                    nullable = false
                },
                navArgument("title") {
                    type =NavType.StringType
                    defaultValue = ""
                    nullable = true
                },
                navArgument("desc") {
                    type = NavType.StringType
                    defaultValue = ""
                    nullable = true
                }
        )) { entry->
        val id  = entry.arguments?.
            getLong("id")
```

```
            val title = entry.arguments?.
              getString("title")
            val desc = entry.arguments?.
              getString("desc")
            id?.let { Wish(id = it,title = title.
              toString(), description = desc.
              toString()) }
                ?.let { AddEditDetailView(it) }
        }
    }
}
```

The AddEditDetailView compose function also requires a modification. A Wish object where its TextField component will read its values will be added as a parameter and, in turn, passed to remember variables to ensure recomposition occurs when needed. Below is the said implementation.

```
@Composable
fun AddEditDetailView(wish:Wish) {
    var title by remember {
        mutableStateOf( wish.title)
    }
    var desc by remember {
        mutableStateOf( wish.description)
    }
    var id by remember {
        mutableStateOf(wish.id)
    }}
```

These variables will then be used to keep track of the value changes by setting the onValueChanged result. Additionally, we will add the scaffold to this screen and update the title and the button to reflect the current action. This is done using the if statement to check the id value and set the right text. Here is the code update for the components of the ADDEDIT-DETAILVIEW with changes as mentioned.

```
Scaffold(topBar = {
        AppBarView(
            title = if (id != 0L)
              stringResource(id = R.string.update_
              wish) else stringResource(
                id = R.string.add_wish
            ))}) {
```

```kotlin
Column(
    modifier = Modifier
        .wrapContentSize()
        .padding(16.dp),
    horizontalAlignment = Alignment.
        CenterHorizontally,
    verticalArrangement = Arrangement.
        Center
) {
    Spacer(modifier = Modifier.height(10.
        dp))

    WishTextField(
        label = stringResource(id =
            R.string.title),
        value = title,
        onValueChanged = {
            title = it})
    Spacer(modifier = Modifier.height(10.
        dp))
    WishTextField(
        label = stringResource(id =
            R.string.description),
        value = desc,
        onValueChanged = {
            desc = it})
Spacer(modifier = Modifier.height(40.dp))
        Button(
            onClick = {

            },
            enabled = true,
            modifier = Modifier
                .fillMaxWidth()
                .size(55.dp),
            shape = MaterialTheme.shapes.
                small,
            colors = ButtonDefaults.
                buttonColors(
                backgroundColor =
                    colorResource(id = R.color.
                    white),
                contentColor =
                    colorResource(id = R.color.
                    black),
```

```
        )
    ) {
        Text (
            text = if (id != 0L)
                stringResource (id =
                R.string.update_wish) else
                stringResource (
                    id = R.string.add_wish
                ),
            style = TextStyle (
                fontSize = 18.sp
        ) ) } } }
```

We will now add the implementations for the click navigations. Using the navigate method from the NavController, we will navigate to the AddEditDetailView. For both processes, within the HomeView composable, values for the arguments will be passed where in the case of the FAB onClick, the default values are used. For the selected WishItem, the values are assigned respectively. The codes are as follows.

FAB onclick:

```
navController.navigate(Screen.AddScreen.route
    +"/0L"+"/ "+"/ ")
```

WishItem onCLick:

```
        val id   = wish.id
        val title = wish.title
        val desc = wish.description
        navController.navigate(Screen.AddScreen.route
            +"/$id/$title/$desc")
```

It's time to run the app and test the navigation process. Important points to ensure are that the WishList screen has no navigation icon and that when the FAB is clicked, the ADDEDIT screen is opened. On this screen, the navigation icon should be on the TopAppBar, and when clicked and depending on the immediate action will show the required text. This can be either the Add Wish or Update Wish, which will be the same as the Button text. Figure 11.6 shows the UI display for the said features.

With the Navigation completed, we will learn how to use Room database to store these wish items on the device and make the list dynamic.

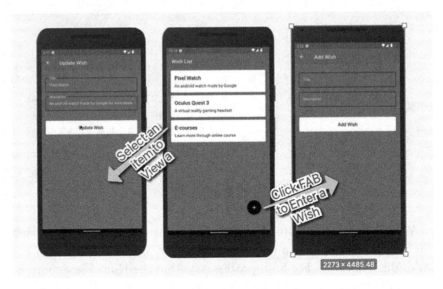

FIGURE 11.6  Navigating to the AddEditDetail screen in two different processes.

## 11.5  SAVING DATA LOCALLY ON ANDROID

Saving data locally on Android stores data on the device itself, such as in a file or database. This can help improve performance and reduce the need to access external data sources. Additionally, it can help make an application more secure by preventing sensitive data from being exposed over the internet. There are several ways to save data locally on an Android device. Below are the listed options and their explanation:

- **Shared Preferences:** Shared Preferences is a simple key-value storage system that allows you to save small amounts of primitive data (such as Strings, Int, and Booleans) in a file on the device. You can use Shared Preferences to store user preferences, application settings, or any other small pieces of data you need to persist.

- **Internal Storage:** Internal storage is a file system specific to your app and accessible only by your app. You can use internal storage to save private files to your app, which should not be accessible to other apps or to the user.

- **External Storage:** External storage refers to storage that is not internal to the device, such as an SD card or USB storage. You can use external storage to save files intended to be shared with other apps or users.

- **SQLite and Room:** These are options you can use to save structured data with a chance for manipulation. We will be learning about them in detail shortly.

Which option you choose will depend on the specific needs of your app. For example, if you need to store small amounts of data that do not require a structured database, you may use Shared Preferences. On the other hand, if you need to store structured data and perform complex queries, you may choose to use SQLite or Room.

### 11.5.1 Introduction to Room Database

SQLite is a lightweight, embedded SQL database engine that is well-suited for storing and retrieving data in Android apps. You can use SQLite to store structured data in a database and perform queries on the data. Over time it was found to be complex requiring long lines of code for its actualization. Room was created to reduce this complexity. It is an Android library that makes it easier to work with SQLite data-bases. It provides an abstract layer over SQLite, allowing you to interact with the database using the Data Access Objects (DAO) so you can focus on building the app's features. Room introduced some key features that facilitate the integration of local database into your application. They are listed below.

- **Entity class:** An Entity class is often a data class representing a table in the SQLite database. You can annotate an Entity class with Room annotations to define the tables' names and the columns' names. This class must have a primary key for differentiating between each data entry. This is also identified using a primary key annotation. Below is what an entity class in Room

```
@Entity(tableName = "person-table")
data class Person(
    @PrimaryKey(autoGenerate = true)
    val id: Long = 0L,
    @ColumnInfo(name = "l_name") var lastName:
      String = "")
```

In the Person class above, the @Entity annotation has an option param-eter where the table name can be provided. It is optional because Room by default will use the name of the class as its table name. The class has an id property with the `@Primary` key annotation. It also has an optional parameter where you can enable `autoGenerate` feature by setting it to true if the type is of a number with no value from the data entry. Third, there is the `@ColumnInfo` annotation, which can be used to provide an alternative column name or Room will use the property name by default to create that column.

- **DAO (Data Access Object):** A DAO is an interface that defines methods for accessing the database. These methods can be used to perform the CRUD operations, which are the delete, update, and query processes. You can use four basic annotations on these methods to signify the operation performed in the database. There is the insert annotation for creating an entry, the query annotation for fetching specific information, and the update and delete annotations for updating and deleting an existing entry respectively. Below is an example of a DAO class.

```
@Dao
abstract class PersonDao {

    @Insert(onConflict = OnConflictStrategy.
      REPLACE)
    abstract suspend fun addAUser(person: Person)

    @Query("Select * from `person-table`")
    abstract fun getAllUsers(): Flow<List<Person>>

    @Update
    abstract suspend fun updateAUser(person:
      Person)

    @Delete
    abstract suspend fun deleteAUser(person:
      Person)

    @Query("Select * from `person-table` where
      id=:id")
    abstract fun getAUserById(id:Long):
      Flow<Person>

}
```

- **Database:** A Database is an abstract class that represents the database itself. You can use it to get a DAO or to run a transaction. This class extends the RoomDatabase class and is annotated with the database keyword with the Entity provided as a value to tell it what table or tables to use. Below is an example class.

```
@Database(
    entities = [Person::class],
    version = 1,
    exportSchema = false
)
abstract class PeopleDatabase : RoomDatabase() {
    abstract fun personDao(): PersonDao
}
```

- **DatabaseBuilder:** The DatabaseBuilder class is used to create a RoomDatabase instance. You can use it to specify a database name and the type of migration you want for it. Next, we will implement the Room features of the WishList app using all the elements we have talked about.

### 11.5.1.1 Adding Room Database to your project

To work with the Room database, we need to add the libraries dependencies to the app level build.gradle file. First, at the top we should enable the kapt plugin by adding the following.

```
plugins {
    id 'kotlin-kapt'
}
```

The kapt plugin will work with its dependency to generate the code for the annotations used for the Room implementations. Below are the required Room dependencies.

```
def room = "2.4.3"
        implementation "androidx.room:room-runtime:
           $room"
implementation "androidx.room:room-ktx:$room"
kapt "androidx.room:room-compiler:$room"
```

Sync the project and we are ready to begin the Room code implementations.

## 11.6 PERFORMING CRUD OPERATIONS IN ROOM

With the dependencies completely setup, the next step is preparing the Entity class. We already have a wish class that we can update to become the database table. This can be done by using the @Entity on the class, making the id its primary key and specifying a column name using the @ColumnInfo. Below is the updated Wish class.

```
@Entity(tableName = "wish-table")
data class Wish(
    @PrimaryKey(autoGenerate = true)
    val id:Long=0L,
    @ColumnInfo(name = "wish-title")val
      title:String="",
    @ColumnInfo(name = "wish-desc")val
      description:String="")
```

### 11.6.1 Defining the DAOs

The Entity class will be used to create the DAO class providing the methods need for the CRUD operations. Within the app we will perform the following.

- Insert a Wish using the @Insert method

- Fetch all Wish using the @Query method

- Update a Wish using the @Update method

- Delete a Wish using the @Delete method.

- Fetch a single wish by id using the @Query method.

The insert, update, and delete methods are all suspend functions. This is because they can be a long-running operation and need to be performed outside of the main thread. By default, all Room operations are not allowed to run on the main thread and if you try to do so you will get the following error.

For the query operations, they use the Flow reactive stream which is like LiveData. It is part of the Kotlin coroutines library and is designed to provide a simple and efficient way to handle asynchronous data streams in a reactive way. It works well with Room to fetch and emit updates during data manipulation. Below are the DAO class and the method definitions.

```
@Dao
abstract class WishDao {
    @Insert(onConflict = OnConflictStrategy.
      IGNORE)
    abstract suspend fun addAWish(wishEntity:
      Wish)

    @Query("Select * from `wish-table`")
    abstract fun getAllWishes(): Flow<List<Wish>>

    @Update
    abstract suspend fun updateAWish(wishEntity:
      Wish)

    @Delete
    abstract suspend fun deleteAWish(wishEntity:
      Wish)

    @Query("Select * from `wish-table` where
      id=:id")
    abstract fun getAWishById(id:Long): Flow<Wish>
}
```

The @Query annotations require a raw SQL (Structured Query language) statement to perform more custom queries. An SQL is a programming language used to manipulate data within a database structure. Some of these statements are what embedded by default within the DAO annotations. But with the Query, we need to provide one for it depending on the process you want to perform. There are two @Query methods in the code above. The getAllWishes selects all the wishes in the database table while the getAWishById selects one wish using an ID.

With the Entity and DAO class, we will create the intended database.

## 11.6.2 Creating the Room Database

We will create a database class. This must be an abstract class, extend the RoomDatabase, and be annotated with the Database keyword. Here we will also define the table, the DAOs, and database versions. Here is what the code should look like.

```
@Database(
    entities = [Wish::class],
    version = 1,
    exportSchema = false
```

```
)
abstract class WishDatabase : RoomDatabase() {
    abstract fun wishDao(): WishDao
}
```

Before we can complete the database creation, let's create a repository class so that we can keep the DAO class away from the presentation layers and only access its methods through the repository. Below is what the Repository class looks like.

```
class WishRepository(private val wishDao: WishDao) {
    suspend fun addAWish(wish: Wish) {
        wishDao.addAWish(wish)
    }

    fun getWishes() : Flow<List<Wish>> = wishDao.
      getAllWishes()

    fun getAWishById(id:Long) {
        wishDao.getAWishById(id)
    }

    suspend fun updateAWish(wish: Wish) {
        wishDao.updateAWish(wish)
    }

    suspend fun deleteAWish(wish: Wish) {
        wishDao.deleteAWish(wish)
    }
}
```

### 11.6.2.1 Initializing the Database Using the DatabaseBuilder

Now we will have to initialize it using the database builder and provide a database name. We briefly talked about dependency injection in an earlier chapter, we are not using any of the libraries in this book, but we will create a class to provide the necessary dependencies at once. This class will be called a Graph just like how the injection libraries see their objects. Below is what the class looks like.

```
object Graph {
    private lateinit var database: WishDatabase

    val wishRepository by lazy {
```

```
    WishRepository(wishDao = database.
      wishDao())
  }

  fun provide(context: Context) {
      database = Room.databaseBuilder(context,
        WishDatabase::class.java, "wishlist.db")
          .build()
  }
}
```

### 11.6.2.2 The Application Class

Finally, the database initializer needs to be called from a global context that will trigger its creation at the launch of the application. In Android, we have the Application class that is useful for initializing any global state that needs to be available throughout the app. This class is instantiated before any other class when the process of an application is created. To use the Application class, you are required to subclass it by creating a new class and extending it. Below is what our application class should look like.

```
class WishListApp : Application() {
    override fun onCreate() {
        super.onCreate()
        Graph.provide(this)
    }
}
```

To ensure the project is aware of the Application class, it must be registered within the Android manifest using the android:name attribute. This must be done within the application tag to avoid a crash form happening when the app tries creating its database creation is attempted. Figure 11.7 shows its place in the Manifest file.

The presentation layer is the next step where we will create the View-Model class and connect the methods with the respective UI components.

## 11.7 MANAGING COMPOSE STATE USING VIEWMODEL

We have looked at the ViewModel class in Chapter 8, where we learnt about the importance of using it to architect an Android project. This is the same when using the compose element—a change in how the state is managed, including reading and writing data. For each Room operation,

```
<?xml version="1.0" encoding="utf-8"?>
<manifest xmlns:android="http://schemas.android.com/apk/res/android"
    xmlns:tools="http://schemas.android.com/tools"
    package="eu.tutorials.wishlistapp">

    <application
        android:name=".WishListApp"
        android:allowBackup="true"
        android:dataExtractionRules="@xml/data_extraction_rules"
        android:fullBackupContent="@xml/backup_rules"
        android:icon="@mipmap/ic_launcher"
        android:label="WishList"
        android:roundIcon="@mipmap/ic_launcher_round"
        android:supportsRtl="true"
        android:theme="@style/Theme.WishListApp"
        tools:targetApi="31">
```

FIGURE 11.7  Where to add the application class in the manifest file.

we run them using a coroutines viewmodelscope because they are suspend functions.

Room is designed to work with Android's threading model, ensuring database operations are executed asynchronously in the background. Attempting to execute database operations on the main thread can lead to a poor user experience, as it can slow down the responsiveness of your app and cause the UI to freeze.

It's recommended to use asynchronous database operations which is why we have used the coroutine class for each operation. Using background operations can keep the main thread free to respond to user inputs and keep your app responsive and fast. Additionally, performing database operations in the background can help avoid ANR (Application Not Responding) errors, which can occur when a long-running task blocks the main thread.

We also need to modify the existing projects to accommodate the ViewModel class. First, the field state holders will be gotten directly from the ViewModel class rather than been in the AddEditView composable. This includes both the read value and onValueChanged properties. The repository class will be provided to the ViewModel class to give access to all DAO objects for performing the CRUD operations. Below is the WishViewModel class and its content.

Below is the ViewModel class

```
class WishViewModel(
    private val wishRepository: WishRepository
    = Graph.wishRepository
) : ViewModel() {

    var wishTitleState by mutableStateOf("")
    var wishDescriptionState by mutableStateOf("")


    fun onWishTitleChanged(newString: String) {
        wishTitleState = newString
    }

    fun onWishDescriptionChanged(newString:
      String) {
        wishDescriptionState = newString
    }

    lateinit var getAllWishes: Flow<List<Wish>>

    init {
        viewModelScope.launch {
            getAllWishes = wishRepository.
              getWishes()
        }
    }

    fun addWish(wish: Wish) {
        viewModelScope.launch(Dispatchers.IO) {
            wishRepository.addAWish(wish = wish)
        }}

    fun getAWishById(id:Long):Flow<Wish> {
            return wishRepository.getAWishById(id)
    }

    fun updateWish(wish: Wish) {
        viewModelScope.launch(Dispatchers.IO) {
            wishRepository.updateAWish(wish =
              wish)
        } }
```

```
fun deleteWish(wish: Wish) {
    viewModelScope.launch(Dispatchers.IO) {
        wishRepository.deleteAWish(wish =
            wish)
}}}
```

Starting with the HomeView, we will connect the getAllWishes method to the composable, observe the list from the database, and replace the dummy list.

## 11.7.1 Observing the Data Items from Room

Aside from replacing the dummy list with the items from the database, the two navigation actions into the AddEditView will be modified. This is because we will only need to pass the item id during navigation rather than all wish object properties. Since we have a Room method to fetch a wish by its ID, this method will use the id of the selected item to process the required wish directly within the AddEditView screen, thereby eliminating the keys for the other properties from the navigation action and its declaration in the Navigation file. Below are all the code changes to both files.

```
@Composable
fun Navigation(viewModel: WishViewModel =
    viewModel(),
navController: NavHostController =
    rememberNavController()) {
    val navController = rememberNavController()
    NavHost(
        navController = navController,
        startDestination = Screen.HomeScreen.route
    ) {
        composable(Screen.HomeScreen.route) {
            HomeView(navController, viewModel)
        }
        composable(route = Screen.AddScreen.route
            +"/{id}",
            arguments = listOf(
                navArgument("id") {
                    type = NavType.LongType
                    defaultValue = 0L
                    nullable = false
                }
```

```
)) { entry->
val id = if(entry.arguments != null)
  entry.arguments!!.getLong("id") else
  0L
AddEditDetailView(id,viewModel,navCon
  troller)
  }
  }
}
```

The HomeView component with the navigation action passing only the ID.

```
@Composable
fun HomeView(navController: NavController,
viewModel: WishViewModel) {
    Scaffold(topBar = { AppBarView(title =
      stringResource(id = R.string.app_name)) },
        floatingActionButton = {
            FloatingActionButton(
                modifier = Modifier.padding(all =
                  20.dp),
                onClick = {
                   navController.navigate(Screen.
                     AddScreen.route +"/0L")
                },
                contentColor = colorResource(id =
                  R.color.white),
                backgroundColor = colorResource(id
                  = R.color.black),

                ) {
                Icon(
                    imageVector = Icons.Default.
                      Add,
                    contentDescription = null
                )
            }
        },
        backgroundColor = colorResource(id =
          R.color.app_bar_color)) {
        val wishList = viewModel.getAllWishes.
          collectAsState(initial = listOf())
```

```
LazyColumn(modifier = Modifier.
    fillMaxSize()) {
        items(wishList.value) { wish->
            WishItem(wish) {
                val id  = wish.id
                navController.navigate(Screen.
                    AddScreen.route +"/$id")
        } } } }}
```

## 11.7.2  Inserting and Updating a Wish

In the AddEditView composable, several changes have to be made to reflect a reasonable user experience when inserting or updating a wish. This includes checking that the entry is not empty before calling any of the methods to complete the operation. A second modification is adding a SnackBar message to notify the user of any ongoing or completed process, like when the Wish has been inserted or updated successfully and if the entries you tried to add to the database is an empty.

Also, the AppBarView component will be updated to include optional onClick action, allowing the navigation back into the WishList screen to be implemented. Figure 11.8 shows the required update to achieve the click action. Then the main action is inserting or updating a Wish. Each field state will be replaced with the variable from the ViewModel class. And the onValueChange value will also be observed using the methods created in the said class. Within the onClick block of the screen button, we will check when the id is not 0L and call the update method while we call the insert method if otherwise.

```
@Composable
fun AppBarView(
    title: String,
    onBackNavClicked:() ->Unit = {}) {

    val navigationIcon: (@Composable () -> Unit)? =
        if (!title.contains( other: "WishList")) {
            {
                IconButton(onClick = {onBackNavClicked()}) {
                    Icon(
                        imageVector = Icons.Filled.ArrowBack,
                        tint = Color.White,
                        contentDescription = null
                    )
```

FIGURE 11.8   Updating the AppBarView component to include onClick action.

Below are the updated components with the code changes.

```
@Composable
fun AddEditDetailView(
    id: Long,
    viewModel: WishViewModel,
    navController: NavController
) {
    var snackMessage = remember {
        mutableStateOf("")
    }
    val scope = rememberCoroutineScope()

    val scaffoldState = rememberScaffoldState()
    if (id != 0L) {
        val wish = viewModel.getAWishById(id).
          collectAsState(initial = Wish(0L, "",
          ""))
        viewModel.wishTitleState = wish.value.
          title
        viewModel.wishDescriptionState = wish.
          value.description
    }else{
        viewModel.wishTitleState = ""
        viewModel.wishDescriptionState = ""

    }
    Scaffold(topBar = {
        AppBarView(
            title = if (id != 0L)
              stringResource(id = R.string.update_
              wish) else stringResource(
                id = R.string.add_wish
            )
        ){navController.navigateUp()}
    },scaffoldState = scaffoldState) {
        Column(
            modifier = Modifier
                .wrapContentSize()
                .padding(16.dp),
            horizontalAlignment = Alignment.
              CenterHorizontally,
            verticalArrangement = Arrangement.
              Center
        ) {
```

```
Spacer(modifier = Modifier.height(10.
  dp))

WishTextField(
    label = stringResource(id =
      R.string.title),
    value = viewModel.wishTitleState,
    onValueChanged = {
        viewModel.
          onWishTitleChanged(it)
    }
)

Spacer(modifier = Modifier.height(10.
  dp))
WishTextField(
    label = stringResource(id =
      R.string.description),
    value = viewModel.
      wishDescriptionState,
    onValueChanged = {
        viewModel.
          onWishDescriptionChanged(it)
    }
)

Spacer(modifier = Modifier.height(40.dp))
Button(
    onClick = {
        if (viewModel.wishTitleState.
          isNotEmpty() && viewModel.
          wishDescriptionState.
          isNotEmpty()) {
          if (id != 0L) {
              viewModel.updateWish(
                Wish(
                    id = id,
                    title =
                      viewModel.
                      wishTitle
                      State.
                      trim(),
                    description =
                      viewModel.
                      wish
```

```
                        Description
                        State.trim()
                    )
                )
            snackMessage.value
                = "Wish has been
                updated"
        } else {
            viewModel.addWish(
                Wish(
    title = viewModel.wishTitleState.
      trim(),
    description = viewModel.
      wishDescriptionState.trim()
                    ))
            snackMessage.value
                = "Wish has been
                created"
        }
    }else{
snackMessage.value = "Enter all
  required fields"
    }
        scope.launch {
            scaffoldState.
                snackbarHostState.
                showSnackbar
                (snackMessage.value)
            navController.navigateUp()
        }
    },
    enabled = true,
    modifier = Modifier
        .fillMaxWidth()
        .size(55.dp),
    shape = MaterialTheme.shapes.
      small,
    colors = ButtonDefaults.
      buttonColors(
        backgroundColor =
            colorResource(id = R.color.
            white),
        contentColor =
            colorResource(id = R.color.
            black),) ) {
    Text(
```

```
text = if (id != 0L)
  stringResource(id =
  R.string.update_wish) else
  stringResource(
    id = R.string.add_wish
  ),
  style = TextStyle(
    fontSize = 18.sp)) }}}}
```

Before we can test the changes we just made, let's learn about state hoisting, a concept we have used while making the changes.

### 11.7.3 State Hoisting vs. Single Source of Truth

In Jetpack Compose, "state hoisting" refers to moving the state used to render a part of the UI out of the composable function that defines that part of the UI and into a separate, standalone state object. This can make it easier to manage the state as it is not tied directly to the UI and can be modified and observed independently. There are different ways of accomplishing this, which include using the ViewModel as a single source of truth and hoisting your data state within it. Therefore, we moved the state for the Wish properties into it so we can call any state independently when needed.

Talking about the single source of truth, the different Composables have often needed a reference to important values like the navigation controller, ViewModel, and the id of a wish. Rather than creating a separate object every time they are needed, we move it up to the lowest common ancestor to create the object one and provide it down to other composable that need it. Therefore, we have only declared a reference in the compose function as a parameter and initialized it at the Navigation function's topmost level.

Run the app and test the four existing features of our app. Adding a wish, viewing the wish list from the WishList screen, selecting an item, and making changes to update. Also, ensure that the SnackBar is displayed after each action is completed.

### 11.7.4 The Database Inspector

While the app is running and you are manipulating each data, you can also view them through the App inspector by clicking on the menu at the bottom of the IDE, select your device > Database inspector> table name as shown in Figure 11.9.

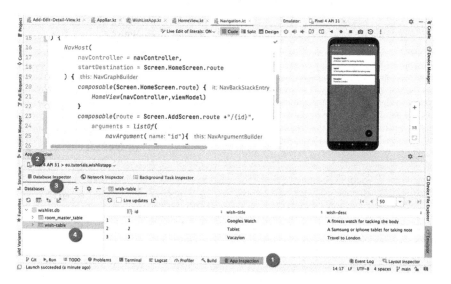

FIGURE 11.9   Viewing the database through the app inspector.

### 11.7.5 Swipe to Delete a Wish From the List

We are at the last section of the application feature where we can swipe to delete an item. Swipe to dismiss is a feature in the LazyColumn composable in Android that allows users to swipe horizontally on an element in the column to remove it from the column. This is typically used for deleting items from a list or for dismissing notifications. To implement swipe to dismiss in the LazyColumn composable, you will need to wrap the items in the column with the SwipeToDismiss function and specify the behavior for what should happen when the user swipes on an element. This could include triggering an animation to slide the element out of the column or calling a function to delete the element from the data source.

Now we will update the LazyColumn within the HomeView so a user can swipe left to delete an item. The WishItem will be wrapped with the SwipeToDismiss function and a dismiss state will be assigned. This state will define when to delete the item and any other actions that follows like showing the SnackBar. Below is an updated items object for the Lazycolumn.

```
items(wishList.value) { wish->
            val dismissState =
              rememberDismissState(
                confirmStateChange = {
                    if(it == DismissValue.
                      DismissedToEnd ||
```

```
                    it == DismissValue.
                    DismissedToStart){
                        viewModel.
                           deleteWish(wish)
                    scope.launch {
                        scaffoldState.
                        snackbar
                        HostState.
                        showSnackbar(
                          "${wish.title}
                            has been
                            deleted"
                        )
                }}
            true})

        SwipeToDismiss(
            state = dismissState,
            modifier = Modifier
                .padding(vertical =
                    Dp(1f)),
            directions = setOf(
                DismissDirection.
                    EndToStart
            ),
            dismissThresholds = {
              direction ->
                FractionalThreshold(if
                    (direction ==
                    DismissDirection.
                    EndToStart) 0.1f else
                    0.05f)
            },
            background = {
                val color by
                    animateColorAsState(
                      when (dismissState.
                        targetValue) {
                          DismissValue.
                            Default
                            -> Color.
                            Transparent
                          else -> Color.Red
                    }
                )
                val alignment = Alignment.
                CenterEnd
```

```
        val icon = Icons.Default.
          Delete

        val scale by
          animateFloatAsState(
            if (dismissState.
              targetValue ==
              DismissValue.
              Default) 0.75f else
              1f
        )

        Box(
            Modifier
                .fillMaxSize()
                .background(color)
                .padding
                    (horizontal =
                        Dp(16f)),
            contentAlignment =
              alignment
        ) {
            Column(
                vertical
                    Arrangement =
                    Arrangement.
                    Center,
                horizontal
                    Alignment =
                    Alignment.Center
                    Horizontally
            ) {
                Icon(
                    icon,
                    content
                        Description
                        = "Delete
                        Icon",
                    modifier =
                        Modifier.
                        scale(scale)
                )}}}){
WishItem(wish) {
    val id = wish.id
    navController.navigate(Screen.
        AddScreen.route +"/$id")
} }}
```

```
@OptIn(ExperimentalMaterialApi::class)
@Composable
fun HomeView(navController: NavController,
viewModel: WishViewModel) {
    val scope = rememberCoroutineScope()
    val scaffoldState = rememberScaffoldState()
    Scaffold(topBar = { AppBarView(title = stringResource(id = "WishList"))
        floatingActionButton = {
            FloatingActionButton(
                modifier = Modifier.padding(all = 20.dp),
```

FIGURE 11.10  Optin to use the experimental features of SwipeToDismiss.

Note that most properties of this feature are still in the experimental stage and will require you to opt into using it by annotating the function like in Figure 11.10.

The SwipeToDismiss feature is a common experience found in many Android applications. This chapter has taught you how to integrate it into your app, display a list using a LazyColumn, navigate between Composables, and save structured data using the Room Database. In Chapter 12, we will learn more about other navigations that will teach us how to integrate the common menu types found in many applications to provide a familiar user experience.

## 11.8 SUMMARY

- LazyColumn composable can be used to display dynamic lists with quick integration to swipe to dismiss behavior.

- Scaffold is a layout that can include menu components like the TopAppBar and the BottomNavigation Bar to provide consistent layout structure for an application.

- The NavHost, NavController, and composable destinations are important parts of Compose navigation.

- Room Library is an abstract layer over Android SQLite that makes it easier to integrate offline database to an application.

- There are four features to using the Room Database, the Entity, DAO, Database class, and the database builder.

- @Insert, @Update, @Query, and @Delete are useful annotations available within the Room library.

- The @Query annotation requires an SQL statement to process its methods request.

- With the Flow state holder, you can efficiently fetch data from Room database and display on a composable UI.

- The ViewModel class can be used to hoist state for composable with independent access to the data.

- To display short messages to a user, you can use the SnackBar composable.

- With the database inspector on your Android Studio, you can observe or see the changes and structures of your applications database.

# CHAPTER 12

# Menus and Navigation in Jetpack Compose

## 12.1 AN OVERVIEW OF THE MUSIC ANDROID APP

The project we will create in this chapter is a music app that utilizes different types of menu navigation options to provide a seamless user experience. The menu options include a bottom bar located at the bottom of the screen that consists of three options: home, library, and browse. These sections will allow the user to easily navigate to different parts of the app.

Additionally, the app will feature a TopAppBar at the top of the screen that displays the app's title or current screen. This bar will also include an icon for the more button, which when clicked will reveal a bottom sheet with options for help, settings, and logout. On the TopAppBar, there will also be an icon for a user avatar, which when clicked, opens the Navigation Drawer. This drawer will consist of options such as About, Subscriptions, and Add the account, which allow the user to manage their account details. When the Add Account option is clicked, an Alert Dialog will be displayed, showing an input field where the user can add details for a new account.

The app will consist of the following screens:

1. Home screen, which displays the main feed of the app.

2. Library screen, which allows the user to access their saved music.

3. Browse screen, where the user can search for specific songs or artists.

 DOI: 10.1201/9781032622538-12

FIGURE 12.1   The application's screens.

4. Help, Settings screen, and Share available on the Bottom Sheet.

5. About screen, which provides information about the app.

6. Subscriptions screen, where the user can manage their subscription options.

7. Add account screen, where the user can add a new account. Below is what the user interface looks like.

Figure 12.1 shows the different screens within the app. Now, we will proceed to Section 12.2 where we will gain an understanding of the standard menu options commonly used in the app.

## 12.2 INTRODUCTION TO MENUS AND DIALOGS

Jetpack Compose allows you to easily handle navigation within your app using composable functions. These composable functions provide a flexible and customizable way to create and modify the layout and behavior of navigation elements such as menus and dialogs. They are integrated as components of the Scaffold layout, which acts as the foundation for your app's user interface.

As previously discussed, the Scaffold layout provides a structure for your app's UI. It includes designated areas, or slots, for various navigation elements such as menus, dialogs, and more. By using these slots, you can easily add and customize the navigation elements in your app. We will delve deeper into these slots and the functions required to set up the menus in the next section of this chapter.

In addition, Jetpack Compose provides a set of composable functions that allows you to easily create navigation elements like, BottomNavigation,

Drawer, TopAppBar, and more. These composable functions are easy to use and allow you to create a consistent and user-friendly navigation experience across your app. Let's begin with the navigation drawer to gain an understanding of the structure and template for each menu.

## 12.2.1 The Navigation Drawer

The Navigation drawer is typically located in the left edge of the screen and can be opened and closed by swiping or clicking on a button. It can contain items such as links to different parts of the app. To create a navigation drawer, you can utilize the drawerContent slot within the Scaffold layout. This slot provides a composable function that is scoped within a Column by default, meaning that elements added to it will be arranged in a vertical order. Here is an example of how it can be implemented in your code:

```
Scaffold( drawerContent = {
    //The content of the drawer goes in here
},)
```

To display items within the Navigation Drawer, you must add them to the drawerContent slot. However, an action is required to open the drawer and view those items. To accomplish this, three states are necessary: the drawerState, the scaffoldState, and the coroutineScope.

The drawerState holds the current state of the drawer, whether open or closed. This state can be used to toggle the drawer open and close in response to user interactions. The scaffoldState is used to store the state of the Scaffold, and the coroutineScope is used to handle the execution of coroutines because the open and close methods are both suspend functions. The above code assumes an onClick function for any composable element clicked to open a drawer. The scope variable and the scaffoldState are both remember variables declared at the topmost part of the compose function.

```
onClick={
    scope.launch{
        scaffoldState.drawerState.open()
    }
}
```

## 12.2.2 How to Add a Bottom Bar

A Bottom bar is a UI component typically located at the bottom of the screen. It can be added to a Compose UI using the BottomNavigation composable. This composable is a child of the Scaffold composable and is passed as a value to the bottomBar slot. The BottomNavigation function takes a list of BottomNavigationItem as its children with essential properties like selected and onClick to set the selected item and the click action, respectively. Below is the code template.

```
Scaffold(bottomBar = {
        BottomNavigation() {
            screensInBottom.forEach { item ->

                BottomNavigationItem(selected =
                false, onClick = {

                },
                    icon = {

                }, label = {

                })
            }}
        }) {}
```

### 12.2.3 Using Actions for the TopAppBar

In Chapter 11, we saw that the TopAppBar also has a slot in the Scaffold, but we only had a feel of setting a title and a NavigationIcon to it. The actions property can also be used to add custom options positioned on the right side. Below is a sample template for adding these actions.

```
actions = {
        IconButton(onClick = {}) {
          Icon(imageVector = Icons.Default.
          MoreVert, contentDescription =
          "More")}}
```

The above code has only one IconButton. It's worth noting that the actions function provides a RowScope which allows multiple items to be added horizontally. You can also use other composable elements such as Text, Image, Chip, or any other custom composable element.

## 12.3 UNDERSTANDING THE OPTIONS DIALOG

In Compose, dialogs display important information or prompt the user for an action. The AlertDialog composable is one of the dialogs used in Compose, and it is used to interrupt users with urgent information, details, or actions. You can display an alert dialog box at the middle of the screen with a title, message, and a set of buttons.

There is also the BottomSheet which is an alternative to the AlertDialog. It presents a set of choices providing room for more content, icons, and actions. It slides in from the bottom, blocking interactions with the rest of the screen. Let's look at how to add them to your apps.

## 12.3.1 Alert Dialog

To add an alert dialog to your compose screen, you must call the AlertDialog composable and values of the required properties. These properties include the onDismissRequest, triggered when the user tries to dismiss the dialog by clicking outside or pressing the back button.

Below is the template for each UI, starting with the Alert Dialog. There is the confirmButton that is meant to complete the action that triggered the dialog. This is where you should add an implementation to complete the intended process. Another property is the dismissButton which is meant to dismiss the dialog when clicked. We have a title that specifies the purpose of the dialog. Finally, the text property presents the detail of the dialog. You can customize this property by adding more content using the layout of your choice. Below is what the code template looks like.

```
@Composable
fun showAlertDialog() {
    AlertDialog(
        onDismissRequest = {

},
        confirmButton = {
            TextButton(onClick = {

}) {
                Text(text = "Confirm")
            }
        },
        dismissButton = {
            TextButton(onClick = {

}) {
                Text(text = "Dismiss")
            }},
```

```
title = { Text(" Dialog Title") },
text = {
    Column {

},)}
```

### 12.3.2 BottomSheet

Adding the BottomSheet requires its layout, which has a sheetContent property for providing the content of the bottom sheet. This layout also provides a default content property for providing the content for the rest of the UI. There are other properties like the sheetState monitoring its state and the sheetShape for describing its shape. Below is the code for the BottomSheet.

```
ModalBottomSheetLayout(
    sheetState = modalSheetState,
    sheetShape = RoundedCornerShape(
        topStart = roundedCornerRadius,
        topEnd = roundedCornerRadius
    ),
    sheetContent = {MoreBottomSheet(modifier =
    modifier)
}){}
```

Now that we understand the use of these menu options, we will go ahead to implement them in the Musical Android app.

## 12.4 BUILDING THE APP

To fully utilize and follow along with the app for this chapter, it is important to be familiar with certain existing codes. As we will primarily be focusing on the menu and navigation elements of the app, the starter code for the remaining portions of the project will be made available for download. This starter code includes the various screens used for composing messages within the different destinations of the app. To access the project code, you can use the provided link: https://github.com/tutorialseu/Tiny-Kotlin-Projects/tree/main/Chapter%2012. It is important to note that having a solid understanding of the existing codebase will be crucial for effectively working with and building upon the app in this chapter.

## 12.4.1 Setting Up the App's Navigation Graph

The navigation graph for our app is a comprehensive collection of all the intended destinations that the user can navigate to. To create this, we will be defining all the screens that exist within our app, including the Home, Browse, Library, Accounts, and Subscription screens. To accomplish this, we will begin by creating a sealed class for the screens, which will be utilized to specify the different destinations within the app.

As our app features two distinct menus—the BottomBar menu and the Drawer menu—there will be a parent Screen class, as well as two subclasses specifically designated for each of these menus. Each screen has three distinct properties, which include a title, a route, and a drawable icon. The following code snippet illustrates the implementation of this class:

```
sealed class Screen(val title: String, val route:
 String) {

    sealed class BottomScreens(
       val bTitle: String, val bRoute: String,
       @DrawableRes val icon: Int
    ) : Screen(bTitle, bRoute) {
       object Home : BottomScreens(
          "Home", "home",
          R.drawable.ic_music_player_green
       )

       object Library : BottomScreens(
          "Library", "library",
          R.drawable.ic_baseline_video_library_24
       )

       object Browse : BottomScreens(
          "Browse", "browse",
          R.drawable.ic_browse_green
       )
    }


    sealed class DrawerScreen(val dTitle: String,
       val dRoute: String,
                               @DrawableRes val
                                 icon: Int) :
       Screen(dTitle, dRoute) {
```

```
object Account : DrawerScreen(
    "Account",
    "account",
    R.drawable.ic_account
)

object Subscription : DrawerScreen(
    "Subscription",
    "subscribe",
    R.drawable.ic_subscribe
)
object AddAccount : DrawerScreen(
    "Add Account",
    "add_account",
    R.drawable.c_baseline_person_add_
        alt_1_24
)}}
```

Using the sealed class, the list of screens will be created at the bottom of the same class to be used later by the required menus. Here is how the list looks.

```
val screensInBottom = listOf(
    Screen.BottomScreens.Home,
    Screen.BottomScreens.Browse, Screen.
     BottomScreens.Library
)

val screensInDrawer = listOf(
    Screen.DrawerScreen.Account,
    Screen.DrawerScreen.Subscription,
    Screen.DrawerScreen.AddAccount
)
```

We will now create a NavHost in the MainView file to hold each destination by passing them to their respective route while declaring Home as the start destination. Below is the code for this.

```
@Composable
fun Navigation(
    navController: NavController,
    viewModel: MainViewModel, pd: PaddingValues
) {
```

```
NavHost (
    navController = navController as
    NavHostController, startDestination =
    Screen.BottomScreens.Home.bRoute, modifier
    = Modifier.padding(pd)
) {
    composable(Screen.BottomScreens.Home.
    bRoute) {
        Home()
    }
    composable(Screen.BottomScreens.Browse.
    bRoute) {
        Browse()
    }

    composable(Screen.BottomScreens.Library.
    bRoute) {
        Library()
    }
    composable(Screen.DrawerScreen.Account.
    dRoute) {
        AccountView()
    }
    composable(Screen.DrawerScreen.
    Subscription.dRoute) {
        Subscription()
    }}}
```

The navigation graph for our app includes an additional destination, specifically for the "Add Account" feature. This destination will be implemented as an Alert Dialog, allowing users to easily add additional accounts to the app. It's important to note that dialogs such as this cannot be directly integrated into the navigation graph as they have a unique integration process. We will address the integration of this destination as an Alert Dialog in later sections of this chapter.

With the creation of the navigation graph and its associated destinations complete, the next step is to connect each destination to its corresponding menu within the MainView. This process involves creating the necessary connections between the different screens within the navigation graph and the menu items within the MainView. This will ensure that when a user selects a specific menu item, the app will navigate to the corresponding destination within the navigation graph.

*12.4.1.1 Integrating the Drawer Menu*

To begin, we will create composable functions for the Drawer and Bottom menus, respectively, so that we can easily reference them at the point in the code where they are needed. We will start by creating a composable function for the Drawer Menu, which will include the creation of a Row with two elements—an icon and text—to represent each item in the drawer. In addition, we will create a function to handle the click event of each item in the drawer.

Using the DrawerItem composable function, we will then add the list of screensInDrawer that we created earlier as the content within the Scaffold. This will ensure that the drawer menu displays the correct list of items, and that the user can easily navigate to the different destinations within the app.

Here is an example of what the DrawerItem composable function might look like in code:

```
@Composable
fun DrawerItem(
    item: Screen.DrawerScreen,
    onDrawerItemClicked: () -> Unit
) {
    Row(
        Modifier
            .padding(horizontal = 8.dp, vertical =
            16.dp)
            .clickable {
                onDrawerItemClicked()
            }) {
        Icon(
            painter = painterResource(id = item.
            icon),
            contentDescription = item.dTitle,
            Modifier.padding(end = 8.dp, top =
            4.dp)
        )
        Text(
            text = item.dTitle,
            style = MaterialTheme.typography.h5,
        )}}
```

Within the drawerContent property of the Scaffold, we use a LazyColumn to display them by adding the following code.

```
drawerContent = {
            LazyColumn(Modifier.padding(start
            = 16.dp, end = 16.dp, top =
            32.dp)) {
                items(screensInDrawer) { item
                    ->
                    DrawerItem(item = item) {
                        scope.launch {
                            scaffoldState.
                            drawerState.
                            close()
                        }
                        if (item.dRoute ==
                        "add_account") {

                            dialogOpen.value =
                            true
                        } else {
                            controller.
                            navigate(item.
                            dRoute)
                            title.value =
                            item.dTitle
}}}}}
```

Having created the initializers for different scopes and states required for the menus and navigation at the topmost section of the MainView function, in the code above, we implemented the drawer item click action to close the drawer and open the destination of the clicked item if any of them is clicked aside from the Add Account. Now to open this drawer we need an icon at the left side of the screen usually where the navigation icon is placed. The TopAppBar of the Scaffold has a slot for the Navigation Icon which is suitable for this use case. Instead of a back arrow, we will add a user icon button which will be shown at this spot. Within its onClick block, the Scaffold state will then be used to open a dialog. Below is the code for the TopAppBar which can be added to its slot on the scaffold.

```
Scaffold(topBar = {
            TopAppBar(title = {
                Text(title.value)
            }, navigationIcon = {
                IconButton(
                    onClick = {
```

```
                        scope.launch {
                            scaffoldState.
                              drawerState.open()
                        }
                },
            ) {
                Icon(imageVector = Icons.
                Default.AccountCircle,
                contentDescription = "Drawer
                Menu")
            }
    })
```

Now you should run the app and click on the user icon to open the drawer menu. Figure 12.2 shows the state of the open drawer menu.

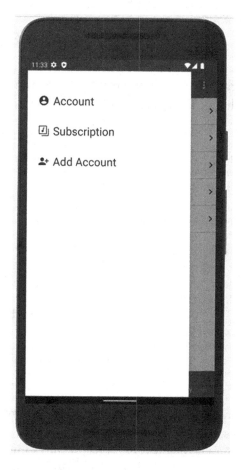

FIGURE 12.2   The drawer navigation in an open state.

Next, we will add a functionality to identify the selected item when any drawer content is clicked.

### 12.4.1.2 Identifying the Selected Destination

For each selected destination, we need to mark it as the currently selected item for the user. To do this, we will make changes by first getting the current route through the navigation graph. Using the navBackStackEntry, we can get the route of the destination and compare it to the items route. Then, we check if both are the same, identify that destination as the selected item, and change the colors of the menu item. First, we will get the current route and make it visible to all the members of the MainView component.

```
val navBackStackEntry by controller.
currentBackStackEntryAsState()
    val currentRoute = navBackStackEntry?.
    destination?.route
```

Then in the DrawerItem, we can create a Boolean value as a parament and use this to change the background color of the Row item using the code below.

```
@Composable
fun DrawerItem(
    selected:Boolean,
    item: Screen.DrawerScreen,
    onDrawerItemClicked: () -> Unit
) {
    val background = if (selected) Color.DarkGray
     else Color.White
    Row(
        Modifier .fillMaxWidth()
            .padding(horizontal = 8.dp, vertical =
16.dp).background(background)
            .clickable {
                onDrawerItemClicked()
            })
```

Update the DrawerItem within the Scaffold to contain the selected argument, with its value determined by comparing the route of the destination to the item route. Below is the code for the example.

DrawerItem(item = item, selected = currentRoute == item.dRoute )

FIGURE 12.3  The drawer menu with an item selected.

Rerun the app to test again. Now open the drawer and select an item. You will see a black background on any selected option. The image result is shown in Figure 12.3.

### 12.4.1.3 Adding the Bottom Menu

Earlier it was mentioned that to add a Bottom menu, there are two crucial compose functions, BottomNavigation and BottomNavigationItem. We will create a compose function and, with the help of the two mentioned functions, prepare the bottom menu contents. A condition will be set to ensure the menu always shows, including when both Drawer destinations are open. Below is what the code looks like.

```
val bottomBar: @Composable () -> Unit = {
        if (currentScreen is Screen.DrawerScreen
        || currentScreen == Screen.BottomScreens.
        Home) {
            BottomNavigation(Modifier.
            wrapContentSize()) {
                screensInBottom.forEach { item ->

                    BottomNavigationItem(selected
                    = false, onClick = {
                        controller.navigate(item.
                        bRoute)
                        title.value = item.bTitle
                    },
                        icon = {
                            Icon(
                                painter =
                                painterResource(id
                                = item.icon),
                                contentDescription
                                = item.bTitle
                            )
                        }, label = {
                            Text(text = item.
                            bTitle)
                    })}}}}
```

This function will be called within the bottomBar block of the Scaffold like in the code bellow.

```
bottomBar = {
        bottomBar()
    }
```

Run the app to see the bottom navigation

### 12.4.1.4 Identifying the Selected Item
As we did for the Drawer item, we need to set the selected item for the bottom bar. Using the exact condition of checking if the current route and the item route are both the same and identify that destination as the selected item, then change the colors of the menu item. Below is the code to achieve this. Run the app and see what the bottom menu looks like as seen in Figure 12.4.

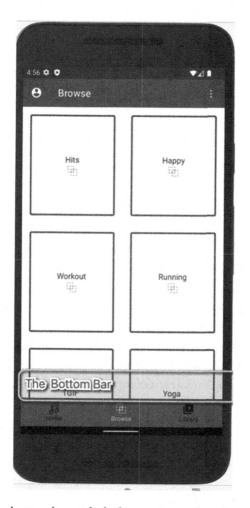

FIGURE 12.4   The bottom bar with the browse item selected.

```
BottomNavigation(Modifier.wrapContentSize()) {
            screensInBottom.forEach { item ->

    BottomNavigationItem(selected = currentRoute
       == item.bRoute,
         onClick = {
                    controller.navigate(item.
                      bRoute)
                    title.value = item.bTitle
               },
                 icon = {
                     Icon(
```

```
                              painter = painter
                                 Resource(id =
                                 item.icon),
                              contentDescription
                                 = item.bTitle
                              )
                  }, label = {
                         Text(text = item.
                              bTitle)
              }, selectedContentColor = Color.
                 DarkGray, unselectedContentColor
                 = Color.White)
              }}
```

## 12.5  IMPLEMENTING THE MENU DIALOGS

We are considering two dialogs: the Alert dialog and the Bottom sheet. When the AddAccount is clicked, an alert dialog is displayed in the middle of the screen with two TextFields for entering new account information. Then there is the Dismiss button, which can be used to close the dialog, and Confirm button, which can be used to complete the intended purpose of the dialog. Below is a compose function that creates the Dialog contents.

```
@Composable
fun AccountDialog(dialogOpen:
  MutableState<Boolean>) {

    if (dialogOpen.value) {
        AlertDialog(
            onDismissRequest = {
                dialogOpen.value = false
            },
            confirmButton = {
                TextButton(onClick = {
                    // perform the confirm action
                    dialogOpen.value = false
                }) {
                    Text(text = "Confirm")
                }
            },
            dismissButton = {
```

```
        TextButton(onClick = {
            dialogOpen.value = false
        }) {
            Text(text = "Dismiss")
        }
    },
    title = {
        Text(text = "Add account")
    },
    text = {
        Column(
            modifier = Modifier
                .wrapContentHeight()
                .padding(top = 16.dp),
            verticalArrangement =
            Arrangement.Center
        ) {
            TextField(value = "",
            onValueChange = {

            }, modifier = Modifier.
            padding(top = 16.dp),
                label = { Text(text =
                "Email") }
            )
            TextField(value = "",
            onValueChange = {

            },
                modifier = Modifier.
                padding(top = 8.dp),
                label = { Text(text =
                "Password") })
        }},
modifier = Modifier // Set the width
 and padding
    .fillMaxWidth()
    .padding(8.dp),
shape = RoundedCornerShape(5.dp),
backgroundColor = Color.White,
properties = DialogProperties(
    dismissOnBackPress = true,
    dismissOnClickOutside = true
))}}
```

In the MainView composable where the DrawerItem action is, we will update the implementation to check if the route is for the add account and then the alert dialog will be opened. Here is what the code looks like.

```
if (item.dRoute == "add_account") {

                            dialogOpen.value =
                                true
                        } else {
                            controller.
                                navigate(item.
                                dRoute)
                            title.value =
                                item.dTitle

                        }
```

Next, we have the BottomSheet that slides up from the bottom of the screen when the more action button is clicked. The sheet contains a Column with three Row items showing a Text and an icon. Below is a compose function for the sheet content.

```
@Composable
fun MoreBottomSheet(modifier: Modifier) {
    Box(
        Modifier
            .fillMaxWidth()
            .height(300.dp)
            .background(MaterialTheme.colors.
                primarySurface)
    ) {
        Column(
            modifier = modifier.padding(16.dp),
            verticalArrangement = Arrangement.
                SpaceBetween
        ) {
            Row(modifier = modifier.padding(16.
                dp)) {
                Icon(
                    modifier = Modifier.
                        padding(end = 8.dp),
                    painter = painterResource(id
                        = R.drawable.
                        ic_baseline_settings_24),
```

```
                contentDescription =
                "Settings"
            )

        Text(text = "Settings", fontSize =
            20.sp, color = Color.White)
    }
    Row(modifier = modifier.padding(16.
    dp)) {
        Icon(
            modifier = Modifier.padding(
            end = 8.dp),
            painter = painterResource(id
            = R.drawable.
            ic_baseline_share_24),
            contentDescription = "Share"
        )

        Text(text = "Share", fontSize =
            20.sp, color = Color.White)
    }
    Row(modifier = modifier.padding(16.
    dp)) {
        Icon(
            modifier = Modifier.
            padding(end = 8.dp),
            painter = painterResource(id =
            R.drawable.ic_help_green),
            contentDescription = "Help"
        )
        Text(text = "Help", fontSize =
            20.sp, color = Color.White)
}}}}
```

Now in the MainView composable, we will use the ModalBottom-SheetLayout to add the above items to the screen. It has a sheetContent and a content slot where the former accepts a bottom sheet element and the latter accepts the other contents of the UI, which is the already existing Scaffold. MoreBottomSheet created above will be shown at the click of a button.

On the TopAppBar, we will add this button as an action element, and within the onClick block, use the modalsheetState to show the bottom sheet. Below is the code with the ModalBottomSheeLayout added as the parent of the Scaffold layout.

```
ModalBottomSheetLayout(
        sheetState = modalSheetState,
        sheetShape = RoundedCornerShape(
            topStart = roundedCornerRadius,
            topEnd = roundedCornerRadius
        ),
        sheetContent = {
            MoreBottomSheet(modifier = modifier)
        }) #A{
        Scaffold(topBar = {
            TopAppBar(title = {
                Text(title.value)
            }, navigationIcon = {
                IconButton(
                    onClick = {
                        scope.launch {
                            scaffoldState.
                                drawerState.open()
                        }
                    },
                ) {
                    Icon(imageVector = Icons.
                    Default.AccountCircle,
                    contentDescription = "Menu")
                }
            }, actions = {
                IconButton(onClick = {
                    scope.launch {
                        if (modalSheetState.
                            isVisible)
                            modalSheetState.
                                hide().
                        else
                            modalSheetState.
                            animateTo(ModalBottom-
                            SheetValue.Expanded)
                    }
                }) {
                    Icon(imageVector = Icons.
                    Default.MoreVert,
                    contentDescription = "More")

                }
            })
        }, scaffoldState = scaffoldState,
```

```
drawerContent = {
    LazyColumn(Modifier.padding(start
    = 16.dp, end = 16.dp, top =
    32.dp)) {
        items(screensInDrawer) { item
        ->
            DrawerItem(item = item,
            selected = currentRoute
            == item.dRoute ) {
                scope.launch {
                    scaffoldState.
                    drawerState.
                    close()
                }
                if (item.dRoute ==
                "add_account") {

                    dialogOpen.value =
                    true
                } else {
                    controller.
                    navigate(item.
                    dRoute)
                    title.value =
                    item.dTitle
                }
            }
        }
    }
}, bottomBar = {
    bottomBar()
},
) { innerPadding ->

    Navigation(
        navController = controller,
        viewModel = viewModel, pd =
innerPadding
    )

    AccountDialog(dialogOpen = dialogOpen)
}}
```

Run the app now, click the more icon to see the Bottom Sheet. Figure 12.5 shows the open Bottom Sheet..

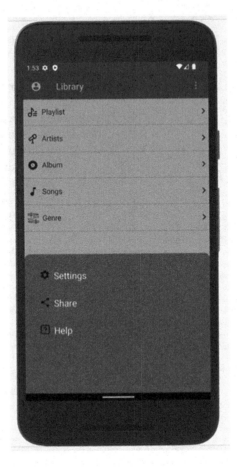

FIGURE 12.5   Opening the bottom sheet at the click of the more icon.

## 12.6 SUMMARY

- Menu Options allow users to navigate to different destinations on the app without leaving the main screen.

- The Navigation Drawer is a component that provides a way to organize navigation options for your app at the left edge of the screen and can be opened and closed by swiping or clicking on a button.

- The BottomNavigation menu is located at the bottom of the screen, providing easy access to different sections of an app using a set of icons and labels.

- An Alert Dialog displays a message or prompts the user for input. It can be used to display important information, ask for confirmation of an action, or provide the user with a choice.

- A Bottom Sheet is a component that slides up from the bottom of the screen to reveal additional content or options. It can present a secondary layout or set of options while still allowing the user to interact with the main layout of the screen.

# Appendix

## SYSTEM REQUIREMENTS FOR ANDROID STUDIO

Android Studio is a heavy software as it comes with a lot of features and tools. Additionally, if you plan to test your app with a virtual emulator, you need to consider some specifics when choosing your computer.

The recommended specifications for running Android Studio include the following.

- A 64-bit Windows 8/10 operating system with at least 8GB of ram, 8GB available disk space, second-generation CPU, and support for Windows Hypervisor.

- A Mac OS 10. 14 or higher with ARM-based chips, second-generation Intel core or newer with support for Hypervisor framework, and at least 8GB of RAM and 8GB available disk space.

- A 64-bit Linux distribution that supports Gnome, KDE, or Unity DE, GNCU library 3.1 or higher with second-generation Intel core or newer or AMD processor with support for AMD virtualization and SSSE3 and at least 8GB RAM or higher with 8GB available disk space.

Anything lesser than mentioned above will be a struggle and slow development but could still work.

## DOWNLOAD AND INSTALLATION

To download Android Studio, visit the following website https://developer. android.com/studio and you will find the latest version for your operating system. Usually, your operating system is detected and automatically displayed for you.

Click on the download button and accept the terms and conditions for the download to begin.

After a successful download, you can follow the instruction for your operating system type from this link https://developer.android.com/studio/install to perform the full installation.

## INSTALLATION ON MAC

After downloads, the following screen will appear.

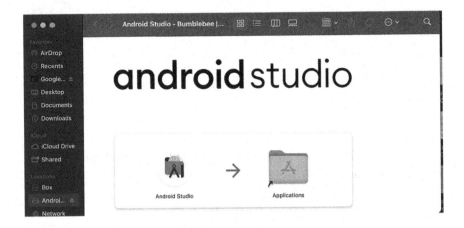

Drag and drop Android Studio in Applications, and installation will begin. When completed, you will find the icon in Applications with other apps. Click to open and see what the welcome screen looks like.

## THE ANDROID SDK

After the installation, you should run the Android Studio to open the IDE. This is the time to add an SDK that will support your development because it is not done automatically during installation. Different versions are available, but you should always have the most recent one installed. To add this to your IDE, click on customize and All Settings on the welcome screen.

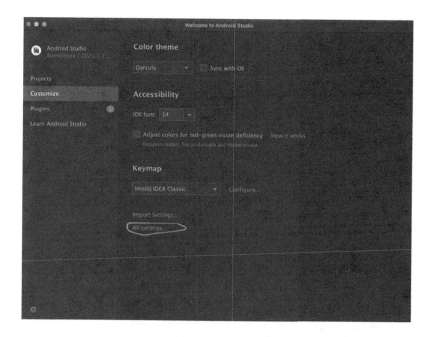

Select API 32 and any other version you are interested in, click apply, and then ok.

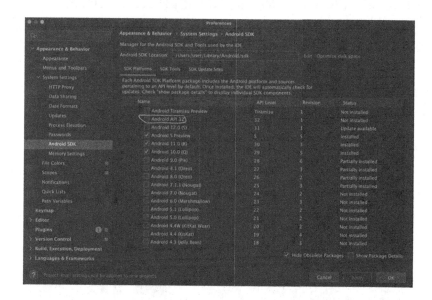

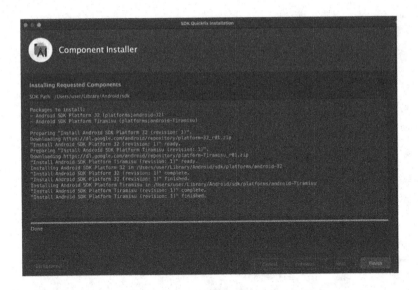

While at it, ensure you have a strong internet connection to avoid encountering errors.

After the installation completes, click finish and close the Preference screen. Now you are ready to create your first project.

## CREATING A NEW PROJECT AND SETTING UP THE TEST DEVICES

To create a new project, select New Project from the Projects section.

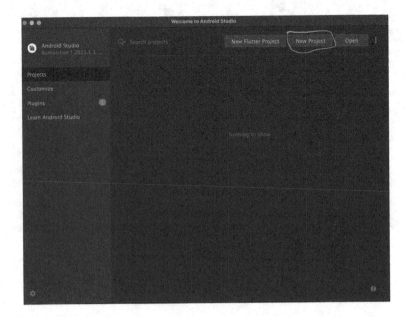

The screen that appears contains different templates for different devices. They include phones and tablets, Wear OS, Android TV, and Automotive, providing you with visual user interfaces and startup code to begin development. With phone and tablet selected, we will choose the Empty Activity template from the list provided and click Next.

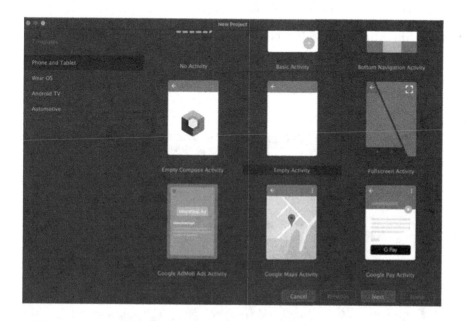

The next screen requires some information about the app which includes the following,

- The Name is where you enter the name of the app. This shows by default when the app is installed but can be changed later in the project

- The Package name provides the app with a unique identification which is most important when releasing the app to the public. The format is usually a sort of domain name in reverse and should be specific to the app plus the name of the app but for now, you can name it anything or use exactly what we have here.

- Save location tells Android Studio where to save the app. You can choose any location you want on your computer by clicking the folder icon to the right.

- Language is the programming language you want to use for your application and has the option of Java or Kotlin. We will be using Kotlin throughout this book.

- The Minimum SDK sets the minimum version of the Android app you would like to support. Depending on the version you select, you will support a certain percentage of Android devices. With API 21, you will support 98%.

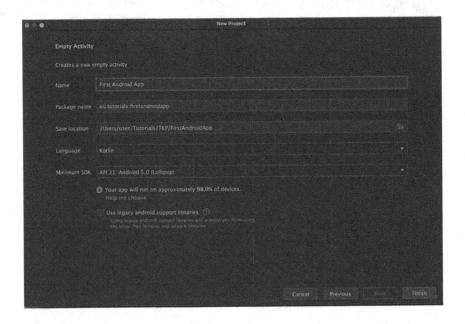

Now click the Finish button. It will take some time to complete the process depending on your internet connection. When the process is complete, you will see the below screen.

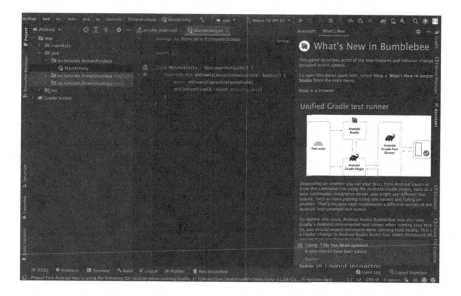

With the first project created, let's look at the main window of the IDE and what it encompasses.

## GETTING FAMILIAR WITH THE ANDROID STUDIO MAIN WINDOW

The main window is displayed when you create a new project or open an existing one. If a new project was created, you'll see the `MainActivity` class and its layout file open. The last viewed file, tool, or panel is displayed for existing projects. This window typically consists of a project tool window, menu bar, toolbar, navigation bar, status bar, and editor bar, as shown in the figure below.

The menu bar is the most important element in the main window, providing various options that allow you to perform various operations. These options include File, Edit, View, Navigate, Code, Refactor, Build, Run, Tools, VCS, Windows, and Help menus. The second element is the Toolbar, which provides shortcuts to the most used actions such as the Run button, Device Manager, Debugging Apps, SDK Manager, etc. The navigation bar is the third element that provides convenient access to open files and folders. By default, when the display space is occupied, a dropdown menu will

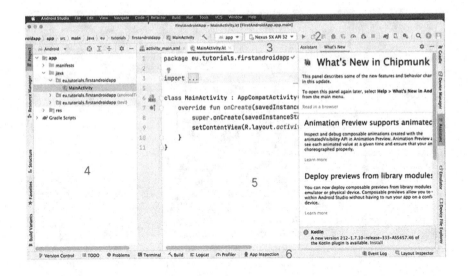

appear with a list of files to choose from. The Project tool window provides a hierarchical view of your project file structure. The project files and structure can be navigated in the Android View and the Project View. Android View is the default view you see when you open a project, but the project view can be changed from the dropdown in the toolbar if required, especially if you need to access other unusual files. A fifth element, the editor window, allows you to view the current working file. This can be activity code, a layout file, or another supported Android resource. The sixth element is the status bar, which allows you to monitor your application during different stages of project execution. The bar has various items to interactively display informational messages about your project.

## TESTING DEVICES FOR YOUR ANDROID APPLICATION

A device, either an emulator or a physical device, is required to run the application. An emulator environment provides an Android Virtual Device (AVD) for testing your application but must first be created and configured to conform to the specifications of your device model. You can create an AVD by clicking Device Manager on the toolbar.

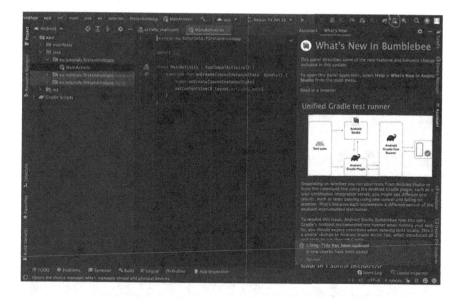

The Device Manager section appears with an option to create a device.

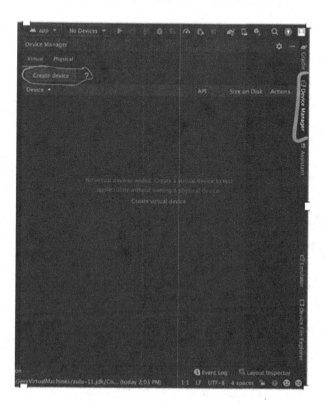

With Phone selected, choose any device with a Play Store icon.

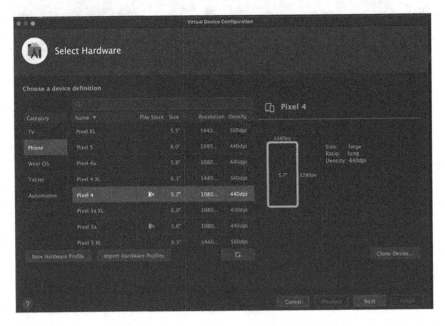

Click Next to see a list of Android versions available, Select API 32, and download its image.

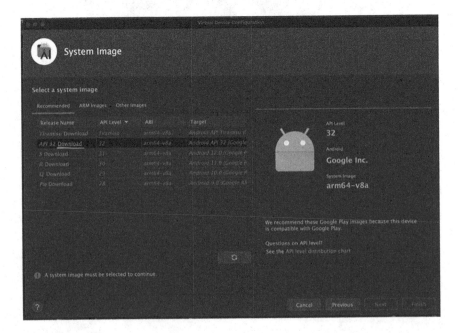

Make sure you have a strong internet connection and plenty of free space on your computer while downloading. This may take some time, depending on your internet speed. An installation window appears with the component being downloaded in progress.

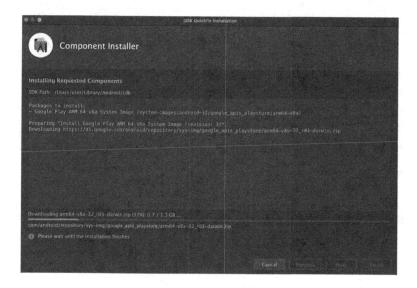

Click Finish when it's done.

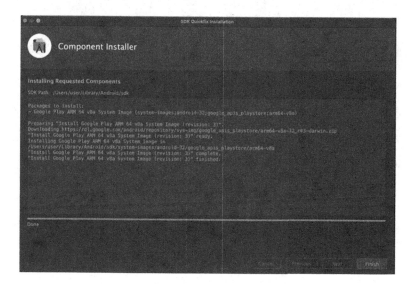

With the downloaded image selected, click Next to continue.

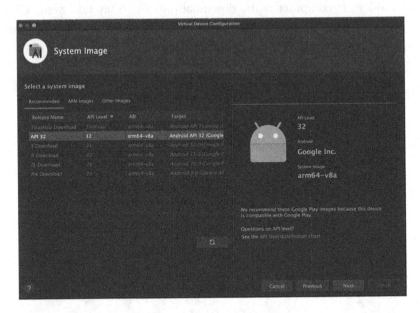

You can name the virtual device or keep the default name.

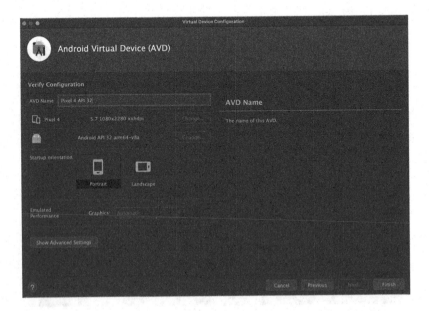

Now click Finish.

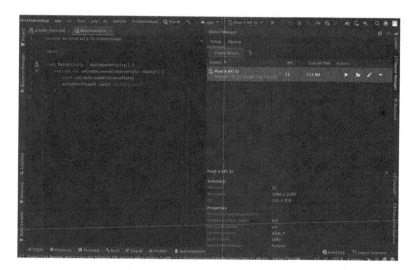

You will see it added to your list of devices.

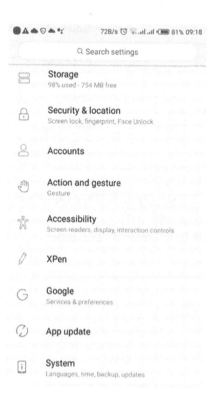

## SETTING UP A PHYSICAL DEVICE FOR TESTING

Alternatively, you can use your real device to run Android Studio applications. To get your device ready, Open the Settings app on your device.

For some phones, you will find the About phone immediately and for some, you will have to click osystemem before you will find About phone, click on it.

On the About screen, scroll and find the Build number, keep tapping on the build number and it will go from "You are now four steps away from being a developer" to "You are now a developer".

Now go back to the Settings page, and you will see a new item, Developer Options

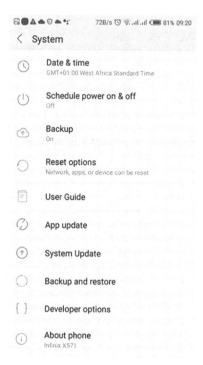

Tap on Developer options and scroll to find USB debugging.

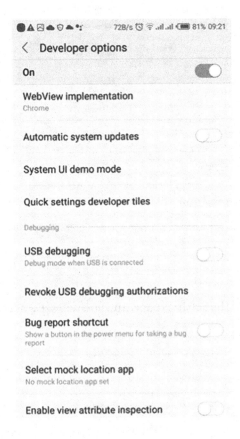

Toggle on USB Debugging, a popup will appear, click OK.

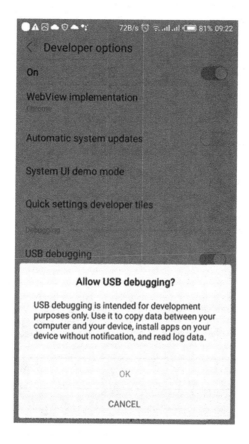

Now connect your device using USB to your computer, and a popup will appear asking to authorize the RSA fingerprint.

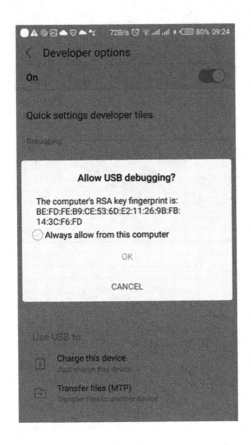

Click ok, and with USB debugging turned on and allowed on your computer, you can run your app from Android Studio through USB. You will see your device showing as an option for running the project.

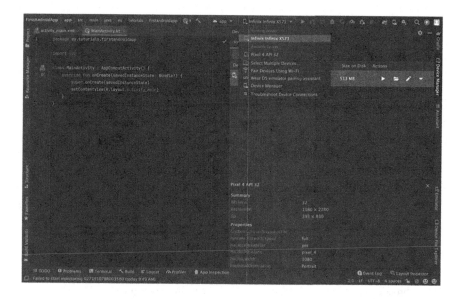

With a device selected you can click on the green run button beside the device selector to run the application.

# Index

Pages in *italics* refer to figures.

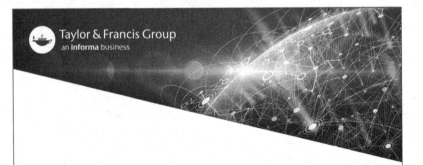

Printed in the United States
by Baker & Taylor Publisher Services